SO, WHO DO YOU THINK *You* ARE

(The Real You)

By Farrell Ellis

McClure Publishing, Inc.

Copyright © 2012

Farrell Ellis for McClure Publishing, Inc.

All rights reserved. Printed and bound in the United States of America. According to the 1976 United States Copyright Act, no part of this book may be reproduced or utilized in any form or by any means, electronic or mechanical, including photocopying, recording, or by any information storage or retrieval system, except by a reviewer who may quote brief passages in a review to be printed in a magazine or newspaper, without permission in writing from the Publisher: Inquiries should be addressed to McClure Publishing, Inc. Permissions Department, 358 West Army Trail Road, #205, Bloomingdale, Illinois 60108. First Printing: December 12, 2012.

Scripture taken from the King James Version of the Bible are marked KJV in quotations.

Scripture taken from Contemporary English Version (New Testament) Text: Copyright © 1995, American Bible Society Printed in the United States of America Eng. N. T. CEV 250-106335 ABS-5/98-50,000-50,000-W1

Scripture taken from THE MESSAGE. Copyright © 1993, 1994, 1995, 1996, 2000, 2001, 2002. Used by permission of NavPress Publishing Group.

Scripture taken from the HOLY BIBLE, NEW INTERNATIONAL VERSION ®NIV®. Copyright © 1973, 1978, 1984 by International Bible Society®. Used by permission of International Bible Society.

"Scripture taken from THE AMPLIFIED BIBLE, Old Testament copyright © 1965, 1987 by the Zondervan Corporation. The Amplified New Testament copyright © 1958, 1987 by The Lockman Foundation. Used by permission."

The author and publisher have made every effort to ensure the accuracy and completeness of information contained in this book. We assume no responsibility for errors, inaccuracies, omissions, or any inconsistency therein. Any slights of people, places, belief systems or organizations are unintentional. Any resemblance to anyone living, dead or somewhere in between is truly coincidental.

ISBN-13: 978-0-9833697-6-9

ISBN-10: 0-9833697-6-3

LCCN: 2013930266

Cover Art by Kala and Kaleaha Ayers

To order additional copies, please contact:
McClure Publishing, Inc.
www.mcclurepublishing.com
800.659.4908
mcclurepublishing@msn.com

We have a High Priest!

For we have not an high priest which cannot be touched with the feeling of our infirmities, but was in all points tempted like us as we are, yet without sin.
    Hebrews 4:15 (KJV Bible)

For we do not have a high priest who is unable to sympathize with our weaknesses, but we have one who has been tempted in every way, just as we are—yet without sin.
    Hebrews 4:15 (Women's Devotional NIV Bible)

For we do not have a High Priest Who is unable to understand and sympathize and have a shared feeling with our weaknesses and infirmities and liability to the assaults of temptations, but one who has been tempted in every respect as we are, yet without sinning.
    Hebrews 4:15 (The Amp Bible)

Acknowledgement

I give God all the glory, the honor, and praise for the inspiration to write another book. I'm truly grateful for such a gift that continues to fuel my belief that all things *truly* are possible with God!

The vision for the cover design was expressed through two young sisters, Kala and Kaleaha Ayers. Together they labored and collaborated together on this drawing. It was obvious to me when Kala and Kaleaha successfully completed the art work and presented it to me, this drawing was done with spirits of excellence. I also want to mention that Kala and Kaleaha are also Honor Roll Students. In 2010, Kala was recognized for her school academics, along with three of her peers. She received the President's Award for Academic Excellence and Achievement from President Obama.

I'm very glad I used this opportunity to sow into the young lives—perhaps the dreams of these two talented and gifted young girls. Kaleaha and Kala are already demonstrating they indeed know who they are as children of God, thereby exercising their faith to receive the desires of their hearts!

Kaleaha and Kala Ayers, I believe you are destined for greatness! Allow hope to be the wings beneath your feet, able to transport you beyond limitation. Permit faith to be the driving force inside your heart to lead you to your appointed, God-ordained destiny! Kala and Kaleaha, I pray both of you will indeed, *go beyond your dreams!* My thanks to both of you for giving life to the vision for this cover design!

In loving Memory
of
Levoular Ellis-Smith

My second book is being dedicated to my mother. She taught me early on that I could accomplish anything I focused my mind to do. My mother was right. I am forever grateful for the morals and values she poured into me as a young girl.

Although my mother is no longer with me, there's a special place in my heart that is reserved especially for her. I miss her everyday. Yet, because of the support and encouragement she provided over the years, I'm able to continue pursuing my dreams.

Thanks mommy! I love you!

Contents

Chapter One 13
    Identity Theft

Chapter Two 39
    The Power of Our Thoughts

Chapter Three 69
    Who Is That In Your Mirror?

Chapter Four 97
    Value The Value In You

Chapter Five 125
    You Must Choose To Be Happy

Chapter Six 151
    Female Acquaintances
    (Friendships & Relationships)

Chapter Seven 173
    The Things We Do For Love
    (Male Relationships)

Chapter Eight 223
    Snared By The Words of Our Mouth

Chapter Nine 237
    Count It All Joy

Chapter Ten 251
    Only You Can Be The Best
    At Being Who You Are

Chapter Eleven 269
    Embrace Your Life

Chapter Twelve 283
    You Can't Pour New Wine
    Into Old Wineskin

Introduction

First, let me start off by thanking every woman who sowed into my debut book, *Go Beyond Your Dreams! (Live Them!)*. Your response was overwhelmingly humbling. During the final stages of collaborating with my publisher to tie up any loose ends before the book was actually ready for final print, I prayed page after page of *Go Beyond Your Dreams* would inspire the women who read it. I sincerely hoped they would be encouraged to get up off the couch and follow their visions and dreams! More importantly, I prayed every reader would learn to *really* trust God at His infallible Word!

I'm learning in my Christian walk that a determined attitude realigned with the spirit, mind and heart has the potential to propel us closer to our God-ordained destiny. This is a great time to be alive! I truly believe that God is moving in a mighty powerful way on behalf of His chosen female vessels. Everything He promised in His spoken and written Word is available to us, and for us, if only we can believe. Girlfriend, be encouraged to trust God (by faith) unlike you ever have before! Whatsoever you desire to see change within yourself or your life, believe it will come to pass! Having said that, I have six words for you, know who you are in God!

Yes, I'm still the same down-to-earth, unpretentious woman I was in the first book. So you know what that means. That's right! You guessed it!

This book will be easy for you to understand, light-hearted and honest. May I ask you a question? *"Girlfriend, so, who do you think you are?"* We're going to focus on that very question throughout this book. Now, I certainly can't speak for another female, and I wouldn't dare try. But I've been in situations where the mere tone of certain words literally causes my toes to curl inside my four inch heels!

What we hear can immobilize us with silent fears starting from the time we're old enough to understand the words coming out of the mouths of our mothers, as well as anyone else we come in contact with. During our developmental years words can have more of an effect on us than is realized. Sadly, once many of us reach adulthood pretty much of what we heard spoken over us, to us, and around us is the person we think we ought to be. Meanwhile, the real female living on the inside of us is screaming to the top of her lungs to be heard. *"I'm the real you! Let me out!"* For years we ignore her cries because she isn't who people think we're supposed to be. Out of fear or whatever, we repress our true self.

When I speak of fear in this sense, I'm not referring to the obvious scary kind of fear that's easily recognizable. There are all types of fears. Little do we know over a period of time as subtle fears go undetected, they begin to shape the female God hadn't intended for us to become. Often when I think of the word fear, I think of it as the enemy's cowardly act of twisting faith. For example: If I'm more comfortable watching TV night after night instead of applying my time and energy toward a dream, TV watching has conveniently become an excuse for not doing what I know I need to be doing. In actuality I have taken on a fear. I'm afraid to pursue the thing that I claim to have a desire to see manifest in my life. It's a subtle fear that I'm unaware is residing on the inside of me.

Fear is an emotional attempt used by the enemy to make us knowingly, or unknowingly sabotage ourselves. We can easily hinder ourselves by what we feel, how we feel, and what we see. That's why it's imperative for females to focus (spiritually) on becoming the women God says we are. I seriously doubt most women, whether she's a Christian or not, understand how effortless it is to try to conquer anything if she lacks the know-how. Let me assure you. Fear isn't prejudice. It rests itself upon every skin color, nationality, shape, and shoe size. Fear isn't just a female emotion. Fear goes much deeper than being afraid. Fear is an ugly spirit that has the ability of taking on many appearances. Fear will often blend itself with other emotions, commonly associated with being a female. Fear will quietly make itself comfortable while unnoticeably wreaking havoc in us spiritually and mentally. We need to discern when we've come under the attack of fear, and stop blaming others for holding us back. Only then will inner change be possible.

People don't prevent us from moving forward. We do. If we don't know that fear, is keeping us from putting one scared foot in front of the other, it will hinder us from becoming the abundantly blessed and fulfilled female God has created us to be. The next time you hear yourself say, *"Why is this happening to me?"* I'd be willing to bet fear has a lot to do with your situation." We've got to learn to stop blaming other people for situations that occur in our lives. The truth is. We've been misinformed. No one can hold us back from experiencing God's best, except us! You and I have been designed to soar to new levels spiritually, and regularly. However, it's vital that we grasp this simple truth! We are capable of becoming so much more than the woman we see staring back at us from the bathroom mirror. Each of us is a valuable individual to God. You were born with a specific plan and purpose for existing on this planet—God's perfect will, plan and purpose.

I will always be appreciative for the kind of parent my mother was. I'm very proud to say she did a great job raising my siblings and me to be confident and comfortable in our own skin. She also taught us that our lives meant something in this big ole' world, and shouldn't be taken lightly. While she may have been an unwed mother at age eighteen, my birth had not been a mistake. I was born with purpose. My mother never let me forget that. So you see. We really are products of our environments and our upbringing. I thank God for blessing me with such a wise mother. She left behind countless fond memories of the times she and I shared together. For that I'm forever thankful.

I miss mommy terribly. That's how this book came to be written. It was inspired out of a broken heart. Within weeks of my mother's home-going service, I forgot who I was as a child of God. I felt alone, and worth little without my mother. I forgot who I was according to the Word of God. It was in one of my quiet moments, the Holy Spirit reminded me how the devil will pervert the Word of God, and use it against us, especially when we're most vulnerable, racked with feelings of pain and hurting. But no more lies! It's time for you and me to reclaim our true identities! We are daughters of the Most High (El-Elyon), Almighty God (El-Shaddai), no matter what may happen in our lives!

Hopefully, while reading this book, your level of self-awareness and self-acceptance will climb to new heights. God says you are His precious delight. He created you with purpose. I believe God's Will is for all of His daughters to emphatically be aware of whom they were created to be. Girlfriend, the bottom line is this. It doesn't matter what mommy, daddy, sister, brother, auntie, uncle, or anyone else may think, or say. God says you are beautiful and His peculiar treasure. He sees you as special—unique—different from every other female. You were created to stand out from me. I was created to stand out from you. As individuals, we can be comfortable in being ourselves, all the while loving who we are. So girlfriend, buckle up your platform shoes! Get ready to take back the blessed heritage that the enemy has stolen from one female generation after another.

I pray the following pages will enlighten, inspire and encourage you to embrace (accept) the female you were created to be!

Chapter One

Identity Theft

So God created man in his *own* image, in the image of God created he him; male and female created he them.

Genesis 1:27 (KJV)

I guess you could say I wrote this book as much for myself as I did for you. If I was going to survive the sudden death of my mother, I had to act on what I knew to do. As I was drafting this chapter, my thoughts kept returning to two words: *identity theft*. The best way to explain writing this chapter is to be candid—to be transparent. When my mother went home to be with the Lord in 2008, her death resulted in both a spiritual and mental struggle.

Let me share. It was a beautiful June day. I'd gone out to lunch with a couple of girlfriends. I returned to work an hour later, but I don't recall what I was doing when the phone rang at my desk. I remember quickly glancing at the time on my desk phone. It was just a little past 3:00 that afternoon. As I listened to the compassionate urgency in the voice of the woman on the other end of the phone, her words stung me. For a few minutes I literally couldn't move. Then I heard myself respond. *"I'll be right there!"* My legs temporarily lost their strength. Within a matter of what seemed like seconds the phone rang again. I was sitting at my desk numb trying to digest what I'd heard. My brother Avery spoke in quick panicky breaths. He'd gotten a call at his job to come to the hospital right away.

Hearing his voice jolted me back to reality as I jumped to my feet. With tears streaming down my face questions began flooding my mind. What did she say about my mother? What happened? Why God, why? When my phone rang that afternoon at work, I never could have imagined my life was about to change forever.

Following my divorce I had gone through a lot of changes, but what I was about to experience would be of no comparison. I can still recall how beautiful it was that afternoon. It was a beautiful day that would shock, devastate, and bring disbelief for my younger siblings and me. To speed things along, my mother had been discovered slumped over the steering wheel of her car. She was unconscious. She'd slipped into a coma. Naturally there were other complications which led up to it, but in spite of the facts, God performed a miracle, which I'll talk about shortly. For fourteen days mommy was sustained by life support.

My dearest friend Jeannette didn't hesitate to put her life on hold from the moment I made the initial call about mommy's condition. Once I phoned her of mommy's death, within a couple of days Jeannette was at my side, where she remained for the following three weeks. I couldn't ask for a more devoted friend. Jeannette is my sister in so many ways. I thank God for her. I make it a conscientious point to always tell Jeannette how much I love, and appreciate her.

Before Jeannette left for Atlanta a few days after mommy's funeral, we discussed the future. I had reached a decision to move out of the condo mommy and I had shared for three years. Suddenly there were decisions I was being forced into making. The months of June and July of 2008 were the biggest tests of my life. Jeannette agreed that moving was probably the best thing I could do for myself and to keep her posted in the days ahead.

SO, WHO DO YOU THINK YOU ARE

During the time when mommy was hospitalized, I barely knew one day from the other. In my state of mind, with so much that had to be taken care of, the days seem to blend together. I would stay up late at night unable to sleep thinking about my mother. I wanted her to be in the bedroom next to mine. I'd get up in the morning physically tired and spiritually drained. Other than occasional meowing from my cat, the condo was much too quiet. I pretty much knew I wouldn't remain living at the condo without mommy. Moving there had been the one place I found a sense of peace. With my mother now gone, I didn't think I could ever be happy living there alone. The laughter was gone. I'd never hear mommy singing along with her favorite gospel CD's in the kitchen while she was cooking. Her voice had been silenced. Had I not moved out of the condo, I know her absence would've taken a toll on me. In the meantime, July had passed. The month of August arrived while I continued going forward without mommy. This year I would omit celebrating my birthday. The thought of not having her with me to celebrate was too much to bear. I thought it was best to concentrate on vacating the condo instead. Everywhere I looked sat empty cardboard boxes waiting to be filled.

One evening in between sipping cold iced tea and packing one box after another I felt an urge to stop for a minute. I wandered over to my computer and sat down, but I wasn't motivated to type a single word. I stared at the monitor like I expected a sentence to magically begin writing itself. While I was sitting there, my mind carried me back to one evening when I came in from having dinner with another good friend of mine, Monica. She too put her life on hold to be at my side from the moment I phoned that mommy had been rushed to the hospital. Within what seemed like one minute, she arrived at the hospital. You know someone is truly a friend (to be treasured) when they offer to forfeit their family vacation. Of course I couldn't let Monica do that. However, once I promised to talk to her everyday while she was vacationing in Florida with a progress report of mommy's condition, she seemed at ease to leave my side.

I bid Monica good evening before parting company as I returned home. I rode the elevator to the third floor. I stood outside the condo door somewhat hesitant slowly unlocking the door. I stepped inside taking a long look around the living room engulfed in silence—a deafening silence. Even though the condo was quiet, I wandered down the hall to mommy's bedroom. I poked my head inside like I'd done so many times before. I wanted to believe this had all been a bad dream and I'd find mommy in her room watching TV. *"Mommy, I'm home."* But she wasn't in her room. Her bed had been stripped down to the mattress and box spring. My eyes watered as I scanned the large bedroom. I couldn't ask mommy how her day had gone. I felt so lost without her! Truth be told, I wasn't sure at that particular moment as I stood in the doorway to her bedroom crying, if I'd ever recover from losing mommy so suddenly. A big part of me had died with her. How would I be able to go on living without my best friend? Here I was standing there, a 50-something year old woman feeling more like an abandoned, frightened little girl. My mind was in turmoil. *"Mommy, what am I going to do! I need you!"* I heard my voice cry out of a broken heart. This had been her personal domain—her space—her bedroom. Now it was an empty shell of a room deprived of life.

In the days following mommy's funeral I had the daunting task of sorting through her belongings. It wasn't all bad because I learned a few things about this woman I called mommy for over 50 years. I discovered if my mother liked a certain item of clothing or a pair of shoes, she bought them in various colors. Upon making this discovery it became important that whoever I offered to give her clothing and shoes to would have to be a woman who would appreciate them as much as she had. I also found that mommy had an attraction to butterflies. Some of the trinket boxes she had with butterflies on them I kept for myself. As much as I thought I knew mommy, I realized while packing away her things you can live with someone and still not know them—completely. I sure do miss my best friend!

The first Monday in August I returned to work. In the evenings when I came home the living room was cluttered with cardboard boxes filled and sealed to their capacity. Everything had been arranged. I spoke with my landlord a few weeks earlier to inform her I was moving at month's end. By Labor Day my move was completed. I fell asleep in my new home the first night knowing it had been the right decision to move. That night was the first time in two months I actually slept until morning without waking up crying or longing for mommy. When I awoke I felt refreshed! I was excited! This was the new start to a new adventure in my life. Yet, I was afraid to be alone. For a second I realized I was moving on without mommy. Suddenly the excitement left and guilt set in. Feeling guilty for being happy made me uncomfortable, but I couldn't shake it off. Was this part of the grieving process? I tried to remember how I felt when my brother died. Although I missed him, I was able to move pass my hurt and find joy in my life. As I changed out of my work clothes it became clear to me that this hurt was going to be different.

Well, let me get back to the point of this chapter. I sat down to my computer, but I couldn't type one word. Like in times past I decided to postpone trying to write. I went to the kitchen to resume packing. As it turns out not forcing myself to write was a good thing. The next day something happened. It wasn't anything earth shattering, but nonetheless it got my attention. I was riding the bus headed home. Normally, I pay little attention to the people getting on, or off the bus. However, I observed a young woman stepping on. Just slightly in front of her was a toddler who looked to be about two years old. The young woman attentively shifted a small baby in her arms, struggled with a folded stroller, and feverously was digging in her back pants pocket for money to pay her fare. Needless to say never having had any children of my own to juggle from one side of my hip to the other, while supervising another small child standing at my knees whining, I was definitely impressed with her. Not wanting to appear to be gawking I turned looking out of the window. Out of the corner of my eye I noticed the young woman searching for an empty seat. From the frustrated, drawn look on her face, it was easy to see she was tired. Capturing her expression caused me to wonder. Did she know with God's Word, she possessed the power to turn her life around?

Usually the bus wasn't crowded during rush hour, but on this day it was. It was also very hot with barely any air conditioning coming through the vents. I sat staring straight ahead. Surely one of the men would give up his seat for this young mother. She stood trying to steady her footing and balance her toddler against the sudden stops and starting of the bus. WRONG! Not one of them offered to let her sit down with those babies! Quickly my mind computed...*pitiful excuses for men*! I thought to myself what kind of life had this young woman experienced before becoming the mother of two small children. She didn't look to be a day over eighteen, at the most.

It was obvious to me there weren't any gentlemen riding the bus. I returned my gaze to the window. My thoughts floated back to the days of my own youth. At age 15, I ignorantly found myself pregnant. I use the word ignorant because that's exactly what I was at that age. Dumb to fall for a boy's lies of flattery. I was ignorant about the changes taking place within my body. Ignorant about the consequences of letting a boy go too far—ignorant! I nearly died out of my ignorance because I couldn't answer mommy when she asked, "how far along are you?" I couldn't answer, because I didn't know. I'm talking clueless—ignorant! At that age I had no knowledge that the devil was using ignorance as a means to kill me. (Ephesians 4:18) To make a long story short, I had a miscarriage. But in the process I nearly hemorrhaged to death. Turns out I was close to six months pregnant. But God is a merciful God! For as long as I live, I will never forget what He did for a naïve teenage girl.

It was a sunny and warm spring afternoon. My mother peeked in on me before going outside to hang clothes on the line. I laid flat on my back in the bedroom I shared with my sister Renee. I laid there floating in and out of life when I thought I saw someone. At first I thought I was imagining this shadowy figure, but it was real alright. In my dazed state of mind, I saw standing positioned outside of the bedroom doorway a tall image. Even though I was kind of out of it, I sensed the shadow was the figure of a man. Silently, he beckoned me to get up from the bed to follow him. Now mind you, I was extremely weak from the loss of so much blood. As I attempted to raise my limp body from off the bed, I managed to stand to my feet. Within seconds my dying body crashed to the floor. The next thing I knew mommy was rocking me in her arms sobbing. "I called an ambulance!" mom exclaimed.

God saved me from premature death that spring in the afternoon. I haven't shared this story with a lot of people because not everyone believes in angels. Nor does everyone believe angels walk among us. But I do believe because they're written about in the Bible. Till this day, I will always believe my assigned guardian angel was dispatched to my bedroom. I say this because the day after I was rushed to the hospital mommy told me one of the attending physicians in emergency informed her had she not gotten me to the hospital when she did, I would've been dead 45 minutes to an hour later. Glory to God! If I hadn't gotten up from that death bed, I wouldn't be here today! God had a plan for my life and it wasn't to die at age 15! Thank you, Lord!

Let me get back to the young woman on the bus. Where was I? Oh! Now I remember. As I sat staring out the window feeling agitated not one man had given up his seat, I silently questioned what might the future hold for this young woman and her two children. Did she have a positive role model, someone she could look to for wisdom and guidance? Was there an older woman in her life to inspire her—to encourage her? Would she be another single unwed mother statistic raising two children alone? Had she completed high school? Did she envision going off to college? Did she have dreams before she became a mother? Did she have any goals she desired to see accomplished? All sorts of questions filled my head. I turned once more facing the dirty window as the bus passed by front porches of houses along the tree lined street. People were out in full force busily going about their business. I thought about a Scripture in Ephesians. God's Word says we were created before the very foundation of this world.

Ephesians 1:4 reads:

"Even as [in His love] he chose us [actually picked us out for Himself as His own] in Christ before the foundation of the world, that we should be holy (consecrated and set apart for Him) and blameless in His sight, *even* above reproach, before Him in love." (AMP)

At God's appointed time you and I were conceived. It was at His precise timing we entered this world. You see, God already had you and me on His mind long before our parents did. (Jeremiah 1:5) It's what happens after we come into this corrupt world that shakes things up a bit. May I ask you a few personal questions? Who do you most look like? Your mother? Your father? A combination of both? Are you short? Tall? Somewhere in between? Are you slender? Full figured? Maybe somewhere in the middle? Do you have imperfect vision? Perfect vision? Is your hair short? Is it curly? Is your hair long? Do you have a large nose? Is it small? Flat? Pointed? What about your feet? Do you wear a size five shoe? Do you have a slightly larger foot?

I asked all of these probing questions because I'm trying to convey a point. It has nothing to do with being nosey—okay? Girlfriend, it's not by accident or any coincidence that our facial features and body frames mirror that of other family members, regardless whether it's daddy, mommy, a sister or brother. Our physical makeup has a lot to do with genetics, DNA, and bloodlines. Perhaps you're the only one in your immediate family with the exact shade of green eyes as your grandfather. Even still, how we come into existence goes far beyond generational transference of genes and chromo-zones. Before we are embryos nestled in our mother's wombs, we are created in the spirit realm. We're created to worship and glorify God in *all* that we do.

Isaiah 43:7 reads:

"*Even* everyone that is called by my name; for I (have created him for my glory, I have formed him, yea I have made him." (KJV)

SO, WHO DO YOU THINK YOU ARE

Isn't that something? We aren't born a second too soon. Nor a minute too late! God signaled each one of us the exact moment He wanted us to enter this world! God has a well-defined plan and purpose in the earth for us—our destiny. (Psalms 104:30) You are as they say in the fashion industry, a *Designer's Original*! There will never, ever be a duplicate (physically or spiritually) of you. Even if you are an identical twin, you are not a spiritual duplicate. There are people who may try to imitate your style, but they will only be a knockoff copy. Our God creates one-of-a-kind beings. He's so awesome! God made you, me, and the entire universe to possess something only He has the ability to provide—individuality! Unfortunately, when we begin this journey on earth as baby beings, it isn't long before we become products of our environment. Growing up shaped by what we've learned and heard spoken over us throughout our developmental years is usually who we become as we approach our teens.

I'm assuming most of us (if not all), are familiar with news reports concerning identity theft. Consumers are constantly being advised to proceed with caution when using plastic as a means of payment. We're often warned if we make purchases with our credit card, use our bank debit card, buy gas with our credit card, or shop online supplying credit information, we do so at our own risk. We've been forewarned how easily it is to become sitting ducks for just *anyolebody* to steal personal data. Now isn't that just like the devil? It's obvious to me the people who commit these criminal acts of stealing someone else's identity don't have one of their own. If they did, what would they want with yours? Thanks to the constant persuasion of advertising by large companies to lure consumers into using plastic more frequently than cash money, thieves have practically been given the green light with access for theft.

While thinking about the subject matter for this chapter, I began to consider perhaps identity theft went beyond illegal theft of personal information. I thought perhaps identity theft was starting to take root within the mind, heart, spirit, and soul of the female population.

Now stay with me girlfriend. I'm going somewhere with this. I think spiritual identity theft can be just as lethal as personal data theft. The Bible says the enemy roams about seeing who he can devour—destroy. (I Peter 5:8) Whenever we permit others to define who we are, or judge us by our physical appearance, a bell should ring loudly in our ears. **WARNING! WARNING!** You're in danger of taking on the personality of someone you're not!

The more we digest perceptions expressed by another, unconsciously we risk transforming ourselves to fit into the mold of their preconceived ideas. How we measure our self-worth and self-value is prevalent both spiritually and mentally for our overall well being.

Proverbs 18:14 reads:

"The spirit of a man sustains him in bodily pain *or* trouble, but a weak *and* broken spirit who can raise up or bear?" (AMP)

God says you're beautiful! He says you're gifted and well equipped with everything He already knew you'd need. God says you've been wonderfully and fearfully made. (Psalms 139:14) There are so many qualities and abilities that God took the time to lovingly place on the inside of each of us. Yet seldom do we take advantage of these great attributes. Every positive thing God says we are, whether knowingly or unknowingly, will always try to be tarnished at the hands of others. Why is it that nearly every time the word of man is spoken, it's so readily accepted over the Word of God?

Do you realize whenever we practice using verbal control of manipulation we're trying to change another individual? Well, can I let you in on something? God said subdue and take dominion over the earth. (Genesis 1:26) I have yet to find in His written Word where He said to take dominion over another human being. If someone doesn't think like we do, we try to change their way of thinking over to ours. If someone doesn't do things exactly the way we think they should, we try persuading them our way is much better. If someone doesn't look like we do, we try suggesting they change their style of dressing, their hairstyle, and so on. Are you aware the use of certain words toward another will produce either a constructive character, or a destructive character? More times than not, we're taught early on to perceive others simply based on their outward appearance. But I ask you, how unfair is that to plant a seed of judgment into the minds and hearts of our innocent young children? We do so because it's usually what we do ourselves. We quickly assume how someone else is or isn't based upon what we can see with the physical eye. Quite frankly, no one has the right to speak against anybody else when they have so much junk going on within themselves!

Do you know when you gossip about someone else that is slander? Your mouth commits a character assassination against another. We've all done it, and that includes me too!

Now, I want to switch gears for a second. The door to identity theft is opened the second one human being takes it upon themselves to strip away the self-worth of another. Think about this. A thief trespasses onto the property of another with the intent to take what doesn't belong to them. If they succeed, they quickly move on to the next unsuspecting victim.

It's been documented that victims of identity theft suffer emotionally and become mentally depleted. The criminal has that person right where he wants them, feeling helpless and hopeless of recovering what was stolen. While it's been widely reported that identity theft is one of the most active crimes in America, there are no proven statistics available in relation to spiritual identity theft. However, all we need to do is look around. There's definitely something in the air. Spiritual identity theft has even managed to deceive its way into the minds and hearts of Christians.

I personally think identity thieves are repeat offenders. I don't think they do it one time, get away with it and decide not to do it again. On the contrary, I think once they see that they have gotten away with it, they continue until they're caught in the act. It's my guess over time these offenders will have a profound effect on the future of fellow Christians. Spiritual thieves control the tongues of people by using them to spew negative words, which ultimately produces unhealthy emotional constraints against another. There should be a thin line drawn in separating ourselves from people who do not edify our spirit in a positive way—a productive way. If you're always within close proximity of communication driven by negativity, you need to distance yourself. A thief is clever enough to know how to disguise their real intentions. That's why we need to know the Word of God by educating ourselves in how to unmask this fraudulent spirit. Reading the Word of God serves as clear and concise insight to discern deception.

Sadly, too many females (me included), have come in contact with spiritual identity theft. But guess what! This crime is generally committed by those we love and trust most. How so? This kind of fraud is subtle. Spiritual identity theft gains entry through methods not easily detected. All throughout our upbringing, parents, siblings, grand parents, aunties, uncles, cousins, friends, and friends of our families are free to voice their opinions. They offer ideas. They give us advice. They openly express who they think we ought to be, or how they think we ought to behave. The thing is. More times than not, family members are allowed to get away with saying things that are contrary to God's Word.

Luke 6:45 reads:

"A good man out of the good treasure of his heart bringeth forth that which is good; an evil man out of the evil treasure of his heart bringeth forth that which is evil; for out of the abundance of the heart his mouth speaketh." (KJV)

Girlfriend if you want a child who can't think or do for him/herself, keep telling that child how useless and dumb they are. What you are doing is robbing that child of an opportunity to mature into the kind of man or woman God has created them to become. Years later when they have difficulty functioning on their own in the big ole' world, don't forget who constantly reminded them how dumb they were! Spiritual identity theft begins with negative choices of words. Understanding who we are in the eyes of God, and what we stand to inherit in the Kingdom as His daughters, frightens the enemy. This is why so many females constantly come under attack.

In the Book of Genesis following Eve's deception by the serpent (the devil), God decreed He'd put enmity between the woman and the devil. (Genesis 3:15) I wanted to grasp the full meaning of the word *enmity*. The interpretation in the Webster's Dictionary is defined as a strong feeling of hatred, hostility, animosity, antagonism, the bitter attitude or feelings of an enemy or of mutual enemies. There it was in black-n-white. **THE DEVIL HATES US!** He will use those closest to us to undermine and pervert the very Word of God! But it's like I always say, "*the devil is a liar!*"

Females come in all shapes, sizes, and skin tones. We're all created to be different. For instance: Some females dress provocative. Some behave a certain way, out of a need for acceptance and sociability. For other women it's all about their physical appearance. They allow themselves to become a plastic surgeon's favorite patient. But regardless of the kind of identity crisis we might suffer from, there isn't anything we can't overcome! God's love is unconditional. He accepts our shortcomings, our faults, and physical flaws. As daughters of the Almighty God, each one of us is beautiful in His eyes. We have been created to be empowered, fearless, victorious, and wise. It's time to stop taking everything the word of man says as bible. You must start believing in the person God has created you to be—a godly, virtuous female!

I like to think I'm observant, especially when I'm in a room filled with more than two females. I often notice we can be discussing the same topic, yet each individual's character will define every woman inside that room the moment she opens her mouth. In other words, while we may all be on the same page, by the time the conversation and/or discussion has ended, that page will contain variations of each woman's input. No two voices will be the same. God is so awesome! He imparted special gifts, talents, visions, ideas and dreams on the inside of each of His daughters. God on purpose made me to be me. And, He on purpose made you to be you. How much plainer can that be said? Ugh? Still, there are far too many females who go through life wanting—wishing they were more like someone else. And why is it that suddenly it appears women across the country wanna make physical changes to themselves? Girlfriend, don't you know cosmetic alterations have nothing to do with who you were created to be? God didn't make a mistake when He made you! Please note. If a physical change to your nose, your cheeks, your breasts, or your buttocks wasn't something you wanted to do for yourself, why would you alter your appearance at the suggestion of somebody else? It's one thing to have your eyebrows plucked. It's a whole other thing when we start fixing what we perceive to be wrong, or ugly about our bodies. Believe this. Our body is exactly the way God created it. Now grant you, there's every possibility you may have added a few pounds to the body frame, but nevertheless, it's still the body God gave you. Love it! Your face, your body frame, the color of your eyes, the color of your hair, and the color of your skin is God's very own personal masterpiece. You are His signature stamp.

When I was a child I encountered a number of hurtful comments from other girls my age. My voice has always been heavy. On occasion these little girls would poke fun at me. "You sound like a boy!" It would be years later before I could appreciate the sound of my voice. I wasn't born with long, flowing wavy black hair. No, on the contrary, my hair grows slow and it's always been on the kinky side. During my teen years I wore my hair cut short for this very reason. Although I was part of the Afro-style era, it didn't protect me from being teased about my short hair. The harsh words I received from other girls were deliberate and they attacked my self-esteem. As my body transitioned in preparation for womanhood, my body frame remained unchanged. The girls with more meat on their bones called me skinny and sometimes boney.

I recall as a child having to defend my mother to other children. "Why is your name Ellis? Why is your mom's last name Smith?" My mother gave birth to me at age eighteen. She was a single parent. Naturally her last name was passed on to me (which I'm very proud of), but I didn't feel like I had to explain that to a bunch of knuckleheaded kids! Later, three other children were born. These children would have my mother's married name, Smith. However, I never felt loved any less because my step-father wasn't my biological father. I thank God for sending that man into my mother's life. He loved my mother so much he willingly accepted the responsibility of caring for another man's child. He raised me as his own. He had my love and respect. My step-father played a significant role in my upbringing. Thanks daddy!

For my single girlfriends with children who are reading this book, take note. If the man in your life doesn't want to accept your children as part of the package, he ain't the one! It's obvious you're investing time and energy into the wrong man. He doesn't really love you, because if he did, he'd want to be a male figure in their lives as well. But that's a whole other subject. Sorry. I'll try to reframe from jumping from one thought to another while I'm writing, but I carry on some conversations the same way. I'll be talking about one thing and skip over to something else. Isn't that right, Renee? Do it all the time, don't I, Jeannette? I'm telling the truth, aren't I, Monica?

So let me get back on track. I have to give my mother credit where credit is due. She raised my sister Renee and I to think for ourselves, as well as grow up to be self-sufficient women. I thank God for deciding to use this chosen vessel to birth me into existence. Mommy impressed teachings upon my siblings and I that were handed down to her. The legacy of childrearing from generations before her left quite a mark on my mother. The Ellis women (mommy and her sisters), passed on what they learned and what they experienced to their children. The Ellis family bloodline was woven together by trial and error, situations and circumstances, faith and fears like so many families are.

Routinely we've seen similarities within families spill over from one generation into the next. Whenever that happens, there's always the possibility of an innocent daughter repeatedly hearing her mother make certain references to another family member. "You're just like your Auntie! She hated school too, and you see how she turned out! Three kids by two different boys before she was nineteen! Now she's working two jobs to feed them kids! If you don't start getting better grades in school and stop running around with them girls you think are your friends, you gonna end up pregnant and be a high school dropout too! Then what'cha plan to do?"

Whoa! Ever been compared to a relative, especially the one considered to be the black sheep of the family? What about a neighbor's kid? How about one of your siblings? Whether those words are spoken intentionally or not, my guess is all of us have probably heard negative, derogative statements spoken to us and over us from a loved one at one time or another. Ironically, people making those charges usually try to justify what they say to make themselves feel better for saying the very thing they knew wasn't right. My point being, WORDS take flight. You can best believe words will bring back what you've said. Children are easily influenced. They listen more closely than we may give them credit for. If you and I constantly refer to our children as stupid or dumb, then guess what? They probably won't amount to much of anything productive later in life. If you and I make a habit of comparing our child to another child, guess what? That child grows up uncertain if he or she will ever be good enough to please us.

Girlfriend, do you see where I'm going with this? Identity theft lurks right within the walls of our homes. From infancy, our little brains begin computing the tones and sounds of different voices as a means of communication. I believe babies absorb blunt force traumas as a result of an untamed tongue. The enemy uses family, friends and whoever else he can find to help pull off his schemes of destruction. What is the enemy's primary goal? Glad you asked. He wants the next generation of daughters and grand-daughters to walk around deflated in their spirit and stumble through life confused. The truth is. Females should understand who they *really* are in Christ, and in the eyes of God. Then they could send a strong message to the opposition. The devil is more afraid of you than you need be of him! Serve notice! Let the enemy know he can no longer deceive you by distorting your identity! From this day forward when you look upon your reflection in the bathroom mirror, take in God's creation staring back at you—a female of power—a female of victory—a female of beauty!

For as far back as I can remember, mommy uttered phrases like: "Ladies don't do this. Ladies don't do that. Ladies don't talk like that." And the infamous line of all lines. "Have some pride in yourself!" Mommy was constantly pouring into my sister Renee and me how to behave...*like a lady*! Well, now that she's gone, I'm so very grateful for everything that mommy taught me. Sure, I got tired of hearing it over and over again when I was a kid, but I'm so glad mommy didn't let up. What she told me and taught me from a young girl I grew to appreciate as a woman. Make no mistake. It wasn't always easy. Mommy and I butted heads on a number of occasions, especially when I was a teenager. Mommy had a mind of her own, and I had no problem showing her I had a mind of my own too! My introduction to a leather belt came at an early age. I can laugh now, but it wasn't so funny back then!

I'm sharing some of these childhood memories because today's young females should be taught how special they are. Not only are they special in our eyes, but they're most special in the eyes of God. Little girls (age two and up), imitate what they see. Girl children are led by the influence of words spoken to them as well as the words spoken over them. I wasn't fortunate to have any children, even though I always wanted to have a daughter. Mommy also wanted me to have a daughter so I could experience undisciplined and rebellious moments like the ones I took her through while growing up. That being said, I view mothering instincts and skills as extraordinary gifts. That's partly why I feel so strongly about single mothers understanding who they are. Life can be tough enough, but knowing we have a divine connection to the one person who can turn our lives around for the greater good can make living less stressful.

Little girls won't know how special they are if you and I aren't willing to invest the time to teach them how to love, value and appreciate life. The Bible says we are wonderfully and fearfully made. (Psalm 139:14) That means what God has created, no female has the right to abuse, neglect, mistreat, or tear down a precious child from God. The female body is an instrument which God designed to help populate this world for increasing His kingdom family. When you think about it, females are human incubators, carefully designed to reproduce after the image of God.

May I clarify something? Children are on loan. They actually belong to God, just as we too belong to God. Sure, females labor and birth children into the world, but they are still God's property. Men and women are the vessels He uses, thereby referencing us as mothers and fathers. But everybody knows carrying a baby nine months, and giving birth does not make a female a mother. Neither does sperm make a man a father. I must be getting older because I find myself cringing whenever I hear a teenage mother calling her children out of their name. I do a double take when I see pre-teens dressed provocatively. I can't say what they're putting in our food these days, but this millennium generation of teenage girls are developing sooner, and filling out with body frames of twenty year old women! I often wonder when I see them looking and behaving too grown, "*where is your mother?*"

What's going on? Is it just me? Don't mothers bother to discipline their daughters anymore? Why aren't they monitoring what their eleven and thirteen year olds leave out of the house wearing? Do they have any idea perhaps it's what they aren't saying that is speaking louder than anything they might be saying? It's almost as though kids today are being left to raise themselves. I've heard more young children telling their parent what he or she isn't going to do—in the house their parents are paying the rent and/or mortgage! When I was young, you didn't talk back to your parent(s) if you wanted to keep living. Now, I'll be honest. I did speak my mind once, twice, three or four times to my mother. I also got my behind tore up too! In our house mommy was law! But I'll admit, as a kid, I didn't have much sense. I had to learn the hard way to keep what I was thinking to myself.

After a number of times when that leather strap went upside my backside, it finally occurred to me to shut-up! But there again, I had to learn to keep my lips zipped. Mommy couldn't beat me for what I may have been thinking, but she could if I was dumb enough to give voice to my thoughts! So I learned to shut-up and go along with the program, especially if I ever wanted to leave the house again. My uncontrollable tongue kept me on punishment. I even think my mother got a thrill out of telling me. "You're not to receive any phone calls, and no TV. Tell Jeannette, you'll talk to her in two weeks. You go to school and come straight home!" In fact, I know she did. Whenever she said it, mommy would get this gleam in her dark brown eyes, followed by a big smile across her face.

But let me get back to discussing today's female generation. In this day and critical age, it's imperative that young girls understand how valuable they are. What they're being exposed to will ultimately shape their adult years. What they learn will remain a part of them. Meanwhile, they're being robbed of their true identities. Any female's lack of self-worth will openly intensify over time. Unless, our young females change from the way they look at themselves and think about themselves, they're headed for big trouble later on. As adults these same young females will be walking around with not a clue of who God intended for them to be.

I really think God is holding older, mature Christian females accountable for representing women of virtue. And why should we be held accountable for our actions? Because God equipped us with God-given skills and the intellectual ability to be women of character, and integrity. While I'm speaking about this, I'd also like to say I'm not addressing Christian women exclusively. I'm talking to every woman who is reading this book. I believe it is God's Will for all of His daughters to blossom into women of wisdom, distinction, knowledge and virtue. But the truth is. Before any of us can start imparting to another female, we must first know who we are. Probably when each of us looks into a mirror, we only see a small fragment of who God says we are. Far too many females have allowed their true identities to become blurred during the developmental years. By the time she reaches early adulthood, her mindset has settled into being who she thinks others think she should be. Sometimes not being our true self comes as a result of what we've heard spoken over us, or mimicking a person we admire, thinking we'd like to be like them instead of simply being ourselves. Well, here's a newsflash! It's time to take back everything the enemy has stolen from us, starting with our God-given identities! It's time to rise up and step into the women God has called us to be!

Do you realize for every one of God's creations there is purpose? You are not in the earth by chance. God has a specific reason and divine order that He commands be carried out. Every female (and those yet to be born), are created in His image—a beautiful image. While however true that may be, too many females (young or old) don't *see* themselves as physically or spiritually beautiful. To develop an image of ourselves the way God sees us begins by reading His Word. The Word of God will eliminate standards set up by the wayward thinking of mankind. God's Word will unmask a lie by revealing the truth. Many of us have been programmed to see our physical selves through the eyes of someone else's perception. Girlfriend, we've been deceived. How we see ourselves, or feel about ourselves does impact how far we advance in life. You can't walk around believing you're incapable of becoming all that God says you can be. It will take the God-kind of wisdom to over come negative thoughts that continuously bombard your mind.

Proverbs 1:5 reads

"A wise man will hear and will increase learning; a man of understanding shall attain unto wise counsels." (KJV)

Let me ask you something. How do you value life? When you were a girl were you repeatedly told by family members you'd never amount to much of anything? Has somebody quenched a burning desire to pursue a dream by making you think you will fail? Do you frequently agree with unproductive advice from others instead of listening to the voice within your heart? Does something a parent once spoke over you still ring fresh like it was yesterday when they said it?

Are you aware eventually the amount of self-value we place upon ourselves will openly display itself? Just think about that. When we feel good inside, it shows. If we're feeling not-so-good, that shows too. Negative self images can also be detected just by opening our mouths. (Matthew 12:35) A person's self image, whether it's negative or positive is like a mental photograph etched upon the canvas of their heart. The very idea that females suffer from bouts of low self-esteem is nothing more than a lie from the devil to set them up for failure. This subtle, miserable useless emotion has the capability to cripple us spiritually. As mentioned in my first book. We are spirit beings first—natural beings second. Overtime when a spirit has been bruised, I don't care how much makeup a woman puts on her face to cover up the sadness, her state of mind will still expose her when she opens her mouth. But there's hope. Thank God for hope! Girlfriend, can I get an Amen? God's Word will heal a broken spirit. If I didn't know this for myself, I certainly couldn't say it. But I've come to learn the Word of God is the most powerful medicine on the face of the earth! Proverbs 4:22 says, "For they (God's Word) are life to those who find them and health to all our flesh." That's worth shouting about! Hallelujah!

Another thing should be noted with regard to self images. While we're preoccupied concentrating on what we think is wrong with us, the enemy is snickering behind our back! He's gleefully happy whenever females believe the worse about themselves. If the enemy is unsuccessful in keeping our mind on lock-down, there's every possibility that our real identity will surface. The devil is counting on us forfeiting God's plans and purpose. That's why he's constantly stroking our low self-esteem. But he's a liar!

Unbeknownst to most females (I only recently discovered this myself), one of the key elements necessary to achieving happiness, peace, joy and success in life comes by possessing self-knowledge. Spiritual identity theft is deliberately meant to hold us back from discovering and understanding our true character, qualities, skills, gifts, talents, and abilities. If the spiritual sight of our self image somehow grows dim, how then can we speak or behave any differently? Girlfriend, we won't put forth any effort to do one thing to change unhealthy thinking towards ourselves. But Jesus said. ***"All things are possible to them who believe."*** (Mark 9:23) The enemy doesn't want any of God's daughters to know or believe this! God's Word is powerful enough to strip away a negative self image. Your Creator can give you a new heart that will beat with rhythm in perfect sync with a mind being restored in the truth. The more you read the Word, the more your thoughts begin developing a new photograph—an image of the beautiful woman God says you are.

I think achieving a healthy self image is vital to our spirit as well as to our future. God has a prosperous and successful plan for our lives. This is what the enemy is afraid we'll find out by reading God's Word. He doesn't want us comprehending how valuable we are to God. He doesn't want us to find joy being completely happy with our true self. You know why? Because once we wake up to the realization that a whole spiritual self image goes further than physical beauty (which wears down), he won't be able to continue manipulating us into believing his lies! After digesting that piece of information, the enemy will have a much harder time deceiving us. Girlfriend, there is real freedom in knowing that a clear mind releases positive action. Women who see themselves as worthy and valuable in the eyes of God, lead spiritually fulfilled lives. **THEY KNOW WHO THEY ARE! THEY KNOW TO WHOM THEY BELONG!** These women without any doubt know God loves them! Our Heavenly Father created us to possess healthy (spiritual and mental) positive self images. He desires that each of us sees exactly what He sees when He gazes upon His workmanship.

SO, WHO DO YOU THINK YOU ARE

Ephesians 2:10 reads:

"For we are God's [own] handiwork (His workmanship), recreated in Christ Jesus, [born anew] that we may do those good works which God predestined (planned beforehand) for us [taking paths which he prepared ahead of time], that we should walk in them [living the good life which He rearranged and made ready for us to live]." (AMP)

If we allow him, God will provide restoration to our mind and heart. He watches over His daughters. He thinks of us more than we can imagine. Females were created to be strong, courageous, successful creatures. I believe with God's help we can overcome anything the devil tries to throw our way. The enemy doesn't have any authority over us! The only authority the enemy has is what we give him. Girlfriend, you were uniquely designed. God believes in you more than you probably believe in yourself! You have the power to change a negative image. Trust God to do His part. He's waiting for a commitment from you in changing your mindset. Serve notice on the enemy by letting him know that you know who you are in God! Change is inevitable once you start agreeing with God, and His Word. He says you're beautiful. Believe it! Look in the bathroom mirror each morning and tell that woman you love her! With God's help the photographic image in your mind will be spiritually air brushed and made to look like new!

We mustn't let our self image become distorted, nor defined by others. We can't let circumstances interfere with our self image. We must learn to reject that which is contrary to the Word of God. We have to become acutely aware when we're slipping back to an old way of thinking. Situations and circumstances can become road blocks. People we associate ourselves with play a huge part in how we think and feel. The wrong people have the ability to cheat you out of greatness. The right people have the ability to propel you into greatness. Please, always remember. The enemy uses anybody he can to help carry out his plan to prevent you from knowing your value and your true identity.

Women plagued by a poor image (low self-esteem) usually feel insignificant. They don't see themselves worthy of receiving God's forgiveness or His love. Well girlfriend, that's a lie straight from the pit! God loves you very, very, very much! He sent His only Begotten Son, Jesus Christ to save you! Jesus was crucified out of the love He has for you! If that isn't love, I don't know what is! The enemy observes a female's demeanor. If you struggle with low self-esteem, he knows he can toy with you because you won't believe inner change is possible. The improper way we feel and think about ourselves keeps us from exercising God-given gifts and talents that exist on the inside of us. Low self-esteem (identity theft), deems us powerless, thereby unable to enforce the spiritual power and authority we have over the enemy. Low self-esteem will rob us of joy, happiness, peace and abundant living. Our lives project little meaning when dominated or controlled by low self-esteem.

This isn't what God intended for any of His daughters. He wants to see the mass female population progressing in every area of their lives. It's not God's Will that any of us should perish for a lack of knowledge. (Hosea 4:6) Gaining a clear understanding of who we are as the children of God is the first step to spiritual recovery in overcoming every obstacle the enemy tries, or places in our way. He'll do anything to keep us from learning the truth.

Psalm 111:10 reads:

"The reverent fear *and* worship of the Lord is the beginning of Wisdom *and* skill [the receding and the first essential, the prerequisite and the alphabet]: a good understanding, wisdom *and* meaning have all those who do [the will of the Lord]. Their praise of Him endures forever." (AMP)

Until we make a quality decision that we're going to possess everything The Bible says is available, many of us will blindly continue letting our identities be stolen right out from under us. I want to ask this. How can we tell our daughters, grand-daughters, nieces and other young females how beautiful and special they are in the eyes of God, if we don't believe that to be the Gospel truth for ourselves? But you want to hear good news? It's never too late to start over with God! So, what do you say? Will you join me and boldly take a stand? As females in the body of Christ, our time is now! It's time to reclaim our true identities. The time has come to take back our covenant birthright!

Our True Identity in Christ

Romans 3:24
We are justified (declared "not guilty" of sin)

Romans 8:1
No condemnation awaits us

Romans 8:2
We are set free from the law of sin and death

I Corinthians 1:2
We are sanctified and made acceptable in Jesus Christ

I Corinthians 1:30
We are righteous and holy in Christ

I Corinthians 15:22
We will be made alive at the resurrection

II Corinthians 5:17
We are a new creation

II Corinthians 5:21
We receive God's righteousness

Galatians 3:28
We are one in Christ with all other believers

Ephesians 1:3
We are blessed with every spiritual blessing in Christ

Ephesians 1:4
We are holy, blameless and covered with God's love

Farrell Ellis

Ephesians 1:7
Our sins are taken away and we are forgiven

Ephesians 1:10
We will be brought under Christ's headship

Ephesians 1:13
We are marked as belonging to God by the Holy Spirit

Ephesians 2:6
We have been raised up to sit with Christ in glory

Ephesians 2:10
We are God's work of art ("His workmanship")

Ephesians 2:13
We have been brought near to God

Ephesians 3:6
We share in the promise of God

Ephesians 3:12
We can come with freedom and confidence into God's presence

Ephesians 5:29
We are members of Christ's body, the church

Colossians 2:10
We are complete in Christ

Colossians 2:11
We are set free from our sinful nature

II Timothy 2:10
We will have eternal glory

SO, WHO DO YOU THINK YOU ARE

Chapter Two

The Power of Our Thoughts

For as he thinks in his heart, so is he.

Proverbs 23:7 (AMP)

As little girls, we grow up exposed to all kinds of situations and circumstances that take place within our family structures. Even though we may have been too young to have any input in the decisions our parents made, ultimately their decisions affected our lives in one way, or another. Within our homes if we observed our parents openly displaying acts of affection toward each other, more than likely being an affectionate person became a part of our character as well as demonstrating affection outside the boundaries of home. During childrearing we're taught how to respond to another person by how we feel, and what we think towards them. Did you catch that? I said we'*re taught.*

When babies are born, they enter this world solely dependent upon someone else to feed them, change their soiled diapers, bathe them, and dress them. While a baby's brain may be small, it isn't long before they discover they possess other dependencies that need to be fulfilled at a particular time that fits a particular need. Upon making this discovery, their wants and needs develop throughout the growth process and carry over into adulthood. Much, if not everything we are taught from children remains with us.

Farrell Ellis

I was raised in the type of family structure that provided stability. The need for stability spilled over into my adult life. I have this need to feel grounded—solid in my relationships. Over the years, the older I get, the quicker time seems to pass. Feeling stable is the utmost importance for me. I've made it a point to keep drama as far from me as possible, which tends to unearth instability. Now, you may think I'm taking things a bit too far when I say this, but with all these new technological distractions going on, I cannot help but wonder is it somehow giving leverage to the enemy? After all, the more we're dazzled and charmed by new techno-gizmos, the more they distract us, and the enemy can then quietly invade homes and churches, committing one spiritual assault after another. Every time the devil finishes scrambling the brains of one family, he moves on to the house next door and scrambles their brains too.

Sadly, it's nothing new. This has gone on for years. And, why has it taken a millennium to notice there are a lot of households being sustained by one parent—the female. Yet, in spite of men missing from these homes what we really seem not to notice is how much the children are being affected because of the absence of a male figure. The youth today are hurting! This chapter is written from personal experiences as the eldest child of two female children growing up with two younger brothers in a two parent home.

My step-father went home to be with the Lord when I was fifteen. Pretty much at that age between the rearing of both parents, my personality had been molded into the person I am today. Still, there were things in my youth I would have to learn on my own, no matter how much my parents tried to shield me from enduring hardships along the way. That's just life. I could be wrong, but I don't believe any parent can protect their child from *everything*. There are some things we need to learn in order to help transition us into adulthood. I'm sure if any parent could keep their child under house arrest until they turned 30 they wouldn't have any mistakes to speak of, but that's unrealistic. Besides, what would any of us have to base our lives upon if we lacked having experienced a few trials and errors along the way?

SO, WHO DO YOU THINK YOU ARE

Falling down, scraping our knees on occasion can be a good thing. Falling down and getting back up teaches determination. It adds to a person's character. As we grow in our faith, we learn how to keep from constantly falling once we understand how to balance ourselves spiritually/daily in The Word, learning to walk by our faith.

In my previous book, I placed emphasis on establishing our hearts in faith. I honestly believe faith provides the power to overturn any and every circumstance. Jesus said, *"With men it is impossible, but with God all things are possible."* (Mark 10:27) Jesus is the living Word. Therefore, I believe Him. God's written Word is the Gospel—the truth. I choose to believe God's truth over man's so-called truth. In other words, if Jesus says everything is possible, then that tells me there is every opportunity available to me whenever I set my heart (by faith) to accomplish something. I've learned change involves evaluating and looking intently at oneself. We mustn't be afraid to tear down negative, hindering mindsets. We must choose to loose ourselves from the bondage of strongholds followed by negative behavior patterns. Ugly thinking doesn't produce thoughts of beauty. Thinking you're unworthy only stifles true value. The ways in which we were taught to think, to talk, to react, to approach, to discard, and to receive during our early years has everything to do with where we are right now. However, having a lack of faith will prohibit us from believing in God's Word. But know this. He is a man who cannot lie. God says I am His peculiar treasure. That's exactly what I believe! I'm a very special child in God's eyes because He says so!

Exodus 19:5 reads:

"Now therefore, if ye will obey my voice indeed, and keep my covenant, then ye shall be a peculiar treasure unto me above all people; for all the earth *is* mine." (KJV)

I think of God valuing me like an art collector takes pride in his rare, most expensive paintings. I realize you may think it's silly of me talking this way, but when you've overcome a troubling, confusing time in life when feelings of loving oneself were practically non-existent, you might better understand. If you've always loved and liked yourself, it's probably somewhat harder for you to grasp what I'm saying. Each of us must grow (spiritually) to a place of believing what we say has the ability to change how we feel about ourselves. Personal success requires changing a mindset, while working to change the heart too. The mind and the heart must assist each other in this process. They have to be on one accord in complete agreement with each other.

Girlfriend, it will take discipline, consistency, and a boat load of faith if you're serious about making character changes. It's also going to take time. We can't undo years of nonproductive thinking patterns and negative behavior over night. I remember the first time I really looked at myself directly in the eye standing in front of the bathroom mirror. *"I love you."* Truth be told, what I heard myself say was about as believable to my ears as believing cats could fly. I have a cat. I'm telling you firsthand. He's old, spoiled, eats and sleeps a lot. He talks back in cat language whenever I won't let him have his way. But let me assure you, my cat does not fly.

I didn't believe what I was saying to my reflection in the mirror, but I kept repeating it. That's why it's imperative to consistently speak a truth over and over until what you're saying becomes real for you. Regardless whether all you ever heard were words that crushed your spirit, there's no need to go on professing you're a victim of circumstance. With the appropriate faith driven words you can quickly become the victor! After all these years the enemy probably thinks he's won because not once has he heard you dispute any of his condescending lies. The enemy uses people to hurt you. But if God be for you, who can stand against you?

Psalms 124:2-3 reads:

"If *it had* not *been* the Lord who was on our side, when men rose up against us: Then they had swallowed us up quick, when their wrath was kindled against us." (KJV)

I don't care what type of environment you were raised in—one parent or two. If the enemy has you thinking and feeling the opposite of who God says you are, there's definitely a work that needs to be done on your mind, and your heart. As adults (Christian women especially), we must learn how to take control over subtle fears that have held us back far too long. Even more importantly, we have to silence the enemy's taunting lies once and for all. Fear is a spirit! It wears many disguises. One of the biggest fears many of us have encountered is the fear of the unknown. Being uncertain of who we are as daughters of the Most High God is one of the main tricks the enemy uses against us. He knows by keeping us in the dark, fear will stand in the way of becoming everything God says we are. Fear is also a spiritual attack to undermine your ability for achieving faith. Girlfriend, despite what someone says, or how others may feel about us, we should always be comfortable (at ease) in whom we know ourselves to be on the inside. The bottom line is. Fear is the total opposite of faith.

Faith understands that if you're in the process of becoming whole (spiritually and mentally), it's only a matter of time before you'll blossom into a victorious woman, if you faint not. With faith you can overcome past failures. Whatever you do, don't allow the past to determine your future! With God, situations as you know them today are subject to change rather quickly. I've come to learn faith can be just as demanding as fear is. Both of them require a willing participant. For instance: Faith forces us to do something! Fear suggests doing nothing. Faith needs for us to trust and believe in every Word of God. Fear says what's putting trust in God going to prove. What if you still fail?

Whatsoever we desire by faith to see change, whether it takes place within ourselves or within our lives, begins by accepting the Word of God in seed form. We first must sow the Word (seed) in our mind. This is what the Bible refers to when it speaks of renewing the mind in the things of God everyday—on purpose. We must then allow the Word to take root inside our hearts where restoration and the faith to believe in the Word can begin to grow. For every problem in life there is a solution in the Word of God. I think the best way to know what God is saying, is by reading (feeding) our spirit on His Word. God's Word is nourishment for the mind, the heart, and the spirit.

Proverbs 4:5 reads:

"Get skillful *and* godly Wisdom, get understanding (discernment, comprehension, and interpretation); do not forget and do not turn back from the words of my mouth." (AMP)

Personally, I find it more fulfilling to read the Word aloud so my ears can take it in while processing my brain. It helps to digest (comprehend) the Word better. That being said, I urge each female reading this book to do yourself a big favor. Read God's Word for yourself. Don't take everything I've written for granted. Read the Bible for yourself. As you read over the Scriptures in each of the chapters throughout the Bible, you'll enhance *your level* of understanding and interpretation. I allow God to use me through writing and motivational speaking to convey His message to my fellow sisters. However, when it comes to fully understanding His infallible Word, reading it for oneself definitely serves of more importance. After all, this gift (writing) isn't really about me. It's all about God—for His glory. I didn't just wake up one morning and say to myself, *"I think I'll write a book."* No. On the contrary, even though I discovered my love for writing at eleven years old, it would be years later before the dream of being published took hold of me. I'll admit it also helped having a mother who was constantly telling my siblings and me when we were children, "cut out all that noise! Get somewhere and read a book!" Hearing those words often resulted in me going off to myself. I began walking to the neighborhood library on Saturdays. I checked books in and out so frequently the librarians started addressing me by name. At the suggestion of one of the librarians, I began to read biographies of famous people and historians. I still enjoy reading them today.

Between writing and reading, is it any wonder why I truly enjoy doing this kind of work? Before I was born this gift was graciously bestowed upon me. I do not take being able to write lightly. This isn't anything God owes me. It's a gift. I accept it, and I respect it as such. We do however owe it to ourselves to study, educate and renew our minds by taking time out of our busy schedule to read His empowering Word!

Proverbs 4:7 reads:

"The beginning of Wisdom is: get Wisdom (skillful and godly Wisdom)! [For skillful *and* godly Wisdom is the principal thing]. And with all you have gotten, get understanding (discernment, comprehension, and interpretation)." (AMP)

While it might take a while before actually noticing changes are taking place within you, don't become discouraged. Stay with the Word! The Bible is the greatest book ever written! It serves as a tool for life—a handbook to living up to our fullest—our best God-given potential. Girlfriend, there are no failures in God! There is no defeat in God! Naturally, you may slip up every now and then. You're human. But if you continue trusting God to do what only He can do (clean up the twisted perception you have of yourself), then a month from now, or perhaps a little longer, when you look into the bathroom mirror you'll honestly be able to tell that woman staring back at you, "I love you!" You'll be speaking from a changed heart, as well as an inspired spirit.

God has promised to be the supplier of our every need. (Philippians 4:19) However, I no longer think of that Scripture as referring to material things and objects. I interpret it differently now to mean *all* of our emotional needs as well. That's great news, isn't it? We don't have to be afraid to stand up against adversity. Our Heavenly Father working on our behalf will supply (provide) the emotional stamina needed for facing difficult challenges. There isn't anything impossible or too hard for God! (Genesis 18:14)

Most females in general have found themselves entangled in situations that brought discomfort. The Word of God can help reinforce the mind, and strengthen the heart during trying moments, especially if what the person is going through are extreme circumstances. Nevertheless, however grave the pain, no matter how often you might have had to endure negative words imposed upon you from another, please believe God can turn things around in your favor.

Romans 8:28 reads:

"And we know that in all things God works for the good of those who love him, who have been called according to his purpose." (NIV)

I have a question. Did you emulate your mother when you were a little girl? I sure did! I started wearing high heels at the age of four! I was always click-clacking around the house in my mother's heels. That could explain the shoe fetish! As a child, I remember thinking I had the prettiest mommy in the whole wide world! I wanted to be *just like her* when I grew up. The thing is, oddly enough, she was thinking along those same lines herself. Mommy didn't want me to be a carbon copy of her, but she wanted me to possess some of the same characteristics she did, yet remain my own person. I hadn't realized my mother and I shared so many things in common until I reached my mid-to-late 20's. She and I enjoyed doing a lot of things together. I suppose that's why it made perfect sense for her to come live with me following my divorce. Our close mother-daughter relationship often drew criticism from other females. All I had to do was look at their faces to know what they were thinking. No doubt they were wondering had the umbilical cord been cut at birth. But I didn't care. There were moments when I discerned our relationship was the butt of a few remarks made under someone's breath. I've heard women snickering when she and I entered a room. But, the bottom line is this. I was secure within myself not to let what other women thought about my relationship with my mother affect me. As a matter of fact, I'm thankful—grateful mommy and I were able to share so much time together, especially now that she's gone. As a grown woman, I appreciate mommy's tireless effort instilling morals and values in me; for teaching me not to be influenced, pressured, or intimidated by other females.

At age ten, I felt somewhat awkward because other girls my age would poke fun at me because of my short, kinky hair.

SO, WHO DO YOU THINK YOU ARE

Their words hurt. Plenty of days I came home from school crying to mommy. I even remember crying, asking her. "*Why do I have to have short nappy hair!*" Mommy glared into my teary eyes. She planted her hands upon my small shoulders giving me a shaking. "Look! You have to like yourself! Even if nobody else does, you gotta like yourself! Stop running home from school telling me how those little girls keep hurting your feelings! There's nothing wrong with you or your hair! And, don't you ever ask me about it again!" Well, needless to say, had it not been for my mother's stern words (probably the shaking too) I wouldn't have found the courage to defend myself. From that day on, I stopped coming home from school crying. I started telling those little girls just what I thought of them, but I'm a Christian now. I'll keep what I said to myself.

By the time I started attending Jr. High, I realized the length of my hair really didn't have anything to do with much of anything. I decided if any female, outside of my friendships with Renee and Jeannette, was going to be a real relationship, then it would be based on who I was as a person. Maintaining my integrity and my character was more important than the length, or texture of my hair.

I was a kid growing up in the 60's listening to the Motown sound, pretending to be Diana Ross of the Supremes. The world was a less violent place to live in back then. Girls looked up to their mothers as their role models. Most girls hung onto their mother's every word. Back then our mothers set the standards in her house. Girls had a lot of respect for their mothers. I guess you could say I was born during an era when parents didn't let their children forget who was in charge. Kids today seem to be the ones letting their parents know who's large and in charge. THEM! When riding the bus home from work, I'm always amazed at some of the conversations I overhear. I've witnessed words falling out of the mouths of babes that would make your toes curl. I'm not kidding! Normally I try to give young children the benefit of the doubt. I think to myself: Maybe this child is paying all the household expenses. That would certainly explain why this mom is allowing him/her to blatantly disrespect her! I tell myself that's got to be the only reason why a mother would permit someone who stands roughly two feet to be so disrespectful! Makes sense—right? If that little person is getting up at the crack of dawn five days a week going to work for eight or nine hours, and paying all the bills, then I suppose they've got every right to call the shots. Right? I'm just asking.

Generally speaking, interaction between females sometimes can be a force to be reckoned with. At other times relationships between females can be a match made in heaven. We girls come in all attitudes, shapes, heights, sizes, and vocal ranges. Yet, we share a common thread. We were all created by God. Quite frankly, I think it's risky to want to be like someone else, or even worse, desire what somebody else has. Just because someone else appears to have it going on, you should never assume their life is so much better than yours. After all, if God had wanted you to be just like that person, He would've duplicated you.

Do I *really* want to look like so-n-so for appearance sake because I think she's prettier than I am? This next generation of females coming up behind us should be hearing that it's perfectly okay to be who God has created them to be. Telling young girls they possess a special kind of beauty on the inside of them will make all the difference later on. I can only imagine what it must be like for mothers with teenage daughters who are fascinated by the latest partially clothed female singing sensation. We have an obligation to teach our young daughters, grand-daughters, nieces, and cousins early on to accept, and be comfortable with them self. Don't misunderstand. There is nothing wrong with borrowing a few fashion tips, styles and ideas from each other. Females enjoy sharing clothes, make-up and shoes almost as much as we enjoy sharing every necessary and noteworthy detail in our conversations. However, when borrowing transcends into obsessing, these little girls, and teens are heading for identity problems as young adults. She can never be anyone other than who God has created—herself.

I'm all for glamour. Ask any one of my friends who *really* know me. They'll all tell you, I'm very fashion orientated.

SO, WHO DO YOU THINK YOU ARE

I love pretty clothes, jewelry, and shoes, shoes, and mo' shoes! But there has to be a balance. I can't let myself get so caught up in the life of another female (famous or not), that I neglect to flourish in my own beauty. Girlfriend, it's like I always say. Just because the grass appears to be greener in your neighbor's yard doesn't necessarily mean its real grass! Fantasying about the kind of life we might imagine someone else has, rather than embracing our own, I believe is offensive to our Creator. God made us exactly the way He wanted. Let's be very clear. The devil will always try to trip females up! He'll have us drooling and slobbering over what another female has, thinking *she's got it going on*, without having considered the possibility her life could be the complete opposite of our fantasy. In other words, the devil may have tricked this female into getting in credit card debt up to her eyeballs just so she can feel better about herself. Meanwhile, her husband continues to ignore her. She wishes they hadn't bought a five bedroom, three car garage house, and would give anything to get her husband to trade in his $55,000 luxury car. The funny thing is. You're wishing you were her because of what you've seen. She's married to a handsome man, lives in a large suburban house, wears stylish clothes, and drives a popular foreign car. However, unbeknownst to you, she fantasizes about being married to a man like your husband, who seems to absolutely adore you. You have three children. She can't have any due to health related issues. Your husband sends you flowers at the office for no particular reason. It's obvious he loves and appreciates you. Her husband gawks at every skirt that passes by, and he hasn't shown her any affection in a very long time. This woman leads a very unhappy and lonely life. If she couldn't shop, she doesn't know what she'd do. So you see. The grass isn't always greener in the neighbor's yard, is it?

    First and foremost, God doesn't make mistakes. I don't care what kind of situation you're experiencing today. God can turn your circumstance around if you'll take the necessary approach to renew your mind and fellowship with Him for clear, concise direction. Girlfriend, the struggle is in our mind! We'd probably be alright if we didn't let negative thinking get our mouths and hearts into so much trouble! I'm sure you've heard the phrase, "the mind is a terrible thing to waste." That's very true. Look at how much time is wasted when we sit around wishing our lives were like somebody else's. Look at how much time is lost strategizing (plotting) to get what somebody else has. As I grow older, time has become a very precious commodity. Therefore, I try not to waste too much of it. I think time should be used constructively. It should be put to use wisely because once it's gone...it's gone! Time lost isn't retrievable. I believe that's why the enemy starts lying to us in childhood. He uses family members to paint a picture less promising than what God predestined for us. The enemy conducts schemes to destroy us. Know this. The enemy has one purpose. It is to kill, to steal, and to destroy us! (John 10:10) A failure to understand who we are in God equates to never fully comprehending just how valuable or how significant we really are. The awesome wonder of God's almighty hands personally sculptured you into a living being—His living being.

Isaiah 64:8 reads:

"But now, O Lord, thou art our Father, we are the clay, and thou our potter, and we all are the work of thou hand." (KJV)

Please believe this. God wants only His best for you! He loves you! It's not His Will that any of His daughters walk around blinded to the truth. As adult children of God, we have covenant rights to receive an inheritance in the earth, as well as the eternal abundance that awaits us in Heaven. But girlfriend, if our heads are filled with bees, listening to everyone else's opinions and accepting bad advice, we'll surely miss what God has predestined. Speaking for myself, I want every good thing God planned with my name on it. In other words, what He has for you is for you. I think it's really nice that you have what you have. But it's even better that I receive what God says rightfully belongs to me. There's no need for me to fantasize, wishing I was anyone other than myself.

Are you aware you block blessings by longing for things that God didn't plan for you to have? Like-n-love who you are! Appreciate what you do have! Our Father in Heaven is the richest man alive! God's more than capable of giving whatsoever our heart desires, so long as that desire is in agreement with His desire for us, and comes from an honest heart. Girlfriend, don't be snared by thoughts of envy. Don't let what you're thinking from a materialistic standpoint open the door to a spirit of jealousy. Learn to reverse your thoughts by strengthening your heart in faith through God's Word. Start believing there's nothing you can't achieve, or overcome. Assure yourself (everyday) there's nothing wrong physically or mentally with being you! Begin telling that woman in the mirror how much you love her!

Here's a tid-bit. Regardless how another female may feel or think toward you, it's never as serious as the enemy would lead you to believe. Most times when one woman expresses negative disapproval of another female, she's insecure within herself. There are probably years-old issues that haven't been resolved. It's not you this female doesn't like. She's not pleased with the woman staring back at her from the bathroom mirror day after day. Unfortunately, she isn't aware God created her to lead a good, whole and blessed life. Unbeknownst to this woman over a span of time the enemy's lies have spoken louder than the Word (truth) of God. Her true identity remains out of focus. It's quite possible the spiritual and mental security you display, knowing who God says you are, triggers a spirit of jealousy in her. Sad to say, but another female not liking you is her problem—not yours! You can't *make* people like you! That's a fact of life. I think the sooner females grab hold of that revelation, the better off they'll be. Trying to make someone like you only steals precious time away from you. In the past while I was trying to figure out why so-n-so didn't like me, or why that person didn't seem to want to share the same air space with me, time kept right on moving. Meanwhile, I was running behind these women (at a previous job) trying to fit in, hoping they'd like me enough to let me be a part of their lunch-time social group. Over time as I sat among these women listening to them gossip about other co-workers, I realized not only was eating lunch with them a waste of my time, I finally recognized I shared very little in common with them.

Farrell Ellis

When I graduated high school in the spring of 1972, I was seventeen. Three months later I turned eighteen. At that age, naturally I was still living at home with a mother who didn't hide her low tolerance for laziness, coupled by idleness. For seventeen years I'd been solely dependent upon mommy. I began elementary school at age five, pretty much stayed out of serious trouble all throughout my school years, and managed to get decent grades. I was a kid, which meant I didn't have to be very responsible. I was 17, just graduated high school. Life was good! But life as I knew it was about to turn a new page. Being young and irresponsible was vastly approaching an abrupt end. The blank pages of adulthood were just waiting to be filled. With twelve years of school now completed, what was I gonna do now? In many respects I was still just a kid! Well, mommy was about to help with my somewhat unnerving dilemma.

Immediately on the morning following graduation mommy woke me up with the solution. "You're either going to college, or you're going to get a job! You will not sit around here doing nothing. Welcome to the real world!" Hearing those words were certainly enough to shake any teenager into reality. Not to mention that crooked smile of hers sent flashbacks of my childhood days when she enjoyed punishing me. One thing was for sure. I had a decision to make. But in the meantime, I wanted to go back to sleep!

Within a month's time I enrolled at community college for the fall semester. Looking back, I understand why mommy took that (I'm not playing with you), tone of voice the morning after graduation. I didn't get it then. The truth is. She hurt my feelings! Mommy hadn't raised me or my siblings to be lazy, so why wouldn't she think I wanted to do something meaningful with my life? Wasn't she the one who traveled back and forth with me to Baltimore for interviews with Eastern Airlines? Wasn't that proof I wanted to succeed after I graduated high school? I mean after all, I had *just* graduated the night before. Couldn't mommy at least have let me sleep till noon the next day? Knowing me, more than likely when she came prancing into my bedroom, I'm pretty sure I shot her one of my (are you crazy?) looks! I hadn't come home from celebrating till well after 2:00 earlier that morning. What was wrong with letting a Sista get some sleep?

My mother was trying to prepare me. I understand that now. She was letting me know then and there, time wasn't going to stand still until I could decide what I wanted to do with the rest of my life. This was her way of informing me life as I had lived and enjoyed at her expense for 17 years was about to change. And boy was she right! Seemingly in no time at all I went from being a 17 year old kid with no responsibilities to a grown woman with a lot of responsibilities that came with being a grown-up. So here I am at 50-something, and it seems the days are going even faster. Out of the forty years since high school graduation (can't believe it's been that long), I can honestly say the last twelve years have been my better years. How so? I have a different mindset. My mind is renewed and improved—glory to God! Prior to accepting Jesus Christ as my personal Lord and Savior in 1997, I wasn't living. Oh, I thought I was. The truth is. I only existed. There's a big difference.

Ironically, on that spring evening in 1972, when I strutted myself across the auditorium stage on graduation night, I felt like there wasn't anything I couldn't do! I was young. I was smart. I was going to conquer the world! Still, after hearing mommy's enlightening words, I figured a little more ed-u-ma-ca-shun probably wouldn't hurt. Three years later I graduated college. After talking to one of the counselors I decided not to return to school the following fall to complete my degree. The truth is I couldn't get pass 40 wpm writing shorthand. That's when I said to myself, "*Why waste time?*" I accepted a Clerical Certificate, wore the cap-n-gown, partied till the wee hours of the morning, and began working full time a week later.

I was now making my own money. I had stepped into the role of a young adult—self sufficient. Life was good! Eighteen months later I bought myself a brand new car. A couple of months after that I moved into my first apartment. It was an exciting time for me! All this happened before my 24th birthday. I was unstoppable! *I had it going on!* Then before I knew what hit me, I had recklessly accumulated a lot of credit card debt. No problem. I found a second job. It wasn't long before the part-time data entry job in the evenings began meeting the need to pay off the cards.

Then I met a nice young man. We dated for a while, and fell in love. I married, and divorced him all within two years. Following my 27th birthday I mysteriously slept through (figuratively speaking), the next ten years. And, if that wasn't enough, I blinked a couple of more times and forty was staring me in the face! By the time my 42nd birthday rolled around I resigned from the company I'd worked at for eighteen years. I was ready to go! Once again I met a nice man, fell in love, and got married. In the meantime, what had I accomplished in all this time? From where I was standing, not much! Life felt more like I was running in place. I had long since stopped writing. Yet, I still dreamed of becoming a published author one day. But the truth is. I continued to put writing on the back burner, even though it was never very far from my thoughts. In essence, I believed being a published author would always be a dream than believing I could actually achieve it.

By my mid-forties, I started asking, "Where do I see myself in five years?" Didn't have a clue! Yet, I knew I didn't want to go on living a hum-drum lifestyle with no sense of purpose, or direction. I was tired of feeling like I'd been born for a reason, but not understanding what exactly that reason could possibly be.

As time continued progressing along, I found myself envying other women who seemed to be able to grab life by the horns and flourish, while I sat on the sidelines wishing I were them. My marriage was starting to slowly crumble as I emotionally sank into a state of misery. Then something happened. One morning while I was getting ready for work I took a long hard stare at myself in the bathroom mirror. Undeniably, I was having a real problem with the woman staring back at me. Quite frankly, I was tired of seeing that dumb blank look on her face! Truth be told, I didn't like that woman in the mirror! At this stage of my life I was now a faithful church attendee. I was hungry for the Word of God. My daily prayers included asking God to help me to better understand how being single again was going to improve me as a person? Where was the future heading this time? I remember one morning tears were streaming down my face as I stood over the bathroom sink desperate for answers. *"God, this isn't fair! Am I ever going to be happy? I need you to help me! I feel like I just don't measure up!"* Following my morning cry, I heard a soft voice. *"I'll never leave you. When you're hurting, I'm hurting too. Trust me to bring you through this temporary pain."* I raised my eyes from looking down at the sink. I met the sad dark brown eyes of the woman staring back at me from the mirror. I'd forgotten whose child I was! God understood exactly what I was feeling. He'd seen my tears. He knew my heart was broken. My Father understood pain and misery. Yet, I became so caught up in my misery, I felt completely alone. But He'd been there all along! God had been there the entire time! As I finished dressing for work, I desired more out of life. But it wouldn't be until later that evening when I'd come to understand (by reading God's Word), if I couldn't allow myself to free myself, very little if anything was going to change.

John 8:32 reads:

"And ye shall know the truth, and the truth shall make you free." (KJV)

If I continued letting guilt cloud my better judgment, nothing would ever change—starting with those bad feelings and confusing emotions. The Holy Spirit brought to my memory something I'd heard my pastor say on occasion. One must learn the truth, and the truth would ***make them free!*** I'd remain in the same miserable rut if I didn't take responsibility for any future decision making. My life would continue running in place if I didn't do something. A year from now nothing would be any different than it was that morning. I wasn't exactly clear what I wanted to occur in the next five years, but I knew it wasn't doing me any good playing the victim. *"Look!"* I said to the woman in the mirror, *"if you don't want to see a repeat of 2003, then you had better get to doing something! Where's all that faith you're* *always talking about you have? Make it work! God is waiting on you to take your faith and make it work for you!"*

Long story short, I began to diligently read more of God's Word. I purchased taped messages that my pastor preached. I listened to his messages over and over each morning while getting dressed for work. I'd listen to them again at night as I lay in bed, allowing those faith messages to massage my heart and renew my mind. I can honestly tell you, it was hearing the Word (even while I slept) that enabled my spirit-man to grow stronger. My faith was also growing. I could feel myself gaining spiritual momentum. I was learning how to think differently not just about myself, but my circumstances too. The Word was teaching me not to be afraid. I also learned something very valuable during this process. Change would start to happen when I started opening my mouth. Well, the moment had arrived. Change meant expansion. I needed to open my heart to receive the Word of God. Then I would need to declare His Word out of my mouth. It was on that morning when life took on a new beginning—a new meaning. The time had come to stop giving permission to the enemy to beat my brains in. Granting him access to my mind with crazy, negative thoughts was over! Here is a Bible truth I'd like to share. This Scripture gave me hope for achieving real inner change.

I Chronicles 29:12 reads:

"Both riches and honor come from You and You reign over all. In Your hands are power and might; in Your hands it is to make great and to give strength to all." (AMP)

In God's hands was the power to overcome my situation. In His hands rested the power to heal my broken heart. He could supply me with both the power, and the might to overcome fear. Glory to God! I grabbed a hold of that Scripture with one hand and latched onto God's hand with the other. He pulled me up out of a spiritual and mental chaotic mess! I needed to read Chronicles to point me in a positive direction. Reading that verse of Scripture opened my blinded (natural) eyes to see the truth. God was more than able to supply the spiritual strength I desperately craved. With His help, I knew I was going to rise above a divorce, if it came to that. There were still unresolved issues from the past that I needed to meet head on. But at least now I could face myself in the mirror knowing God had my back!

The following Sunday my pastor delivered a message of confirmation. In his message he said. "Everything starts with the Word of God." WOW! When I came home from service later that afternoon, I removed my concordance from the book case, and retreated to the dinning room table. With pen and paper in hand, I began writing down every negative emotion I'd been experiencing before and during the break-up of my marriage. On another sheet of paper I listed any negative thoughts I had about myself as a wife, as a daughter, as a sister, and as a friend. When I completed both lists I searched the concordance looking for Scriptures that bore witness with my spirit. Taking the time—making the effort to do this for myself that afternoon was one of the best things I could've done. Suddenly I felt like my life wasn't running in place any longer. Girlfriend, the Word of God *can* and *does* bring about a change! If you're lonely, depressed, insecure, unhappy, miserable, doubtful, confused or fearful, God can deliver you from intrusive, nagging, condemning, and unproductive feelings. He can erase that distorted image you have of yourself.

Psalm 34:19 reads:

"Many are the afflictions of the righteous; but the Lord delivereth him out of them all." (KJV)

Living bound by distress day after day, isn't living the way God intended for His daughters to live. Constantly worrying whether your best doesn't seem good enough to please someone else stifles who God created you to be. A possession of faith (built on God's Word), is what it will take to bring about spiritual and mental transformation. Before you were blood, bone and flesh, you existed in the spirit realm. God had you on His mind long before your mommy and daddy came together. We are spirit first. The spirit-man is the real us. No one has the ability to see beyond flesh (except God), searching the deep corridors of the heart and the spirit.

Ephesians 5:9 reads:

"For the fruit of the Spirit *is* in all goodness and righteousness and truth." (KJV)

There's one thing none of us should ever forget. The enemy hates females! He hates men too, but my main focus is on females recognizing they are spiritually empowered. I gotta admit. I truly enjoy being a girl! But I'd be lying if I said since discovering I had a fetish for shoes at age 13, everyday has been sheer bliss. If that were the case, there'd be no need for writing this book. However, more and more a spirit of low self-esteem appears to be running rampant among the female sector.

I can't help but notice there are mothers being put in positions to raise babies alone. Many of whom are still children themselves. At 14, or 15 years of age these girls haven't been given the opportunity to figure out who they are before taking on such a huge responsibility of becoming a mother. Far too many young girls are easily influenced by their girlfriends, as well as the glitz and glamour of the entertainment industry. They wanna be like hip hop singers they idolize. On many covers of magazines I see while standing in the supermarket checkout line, women are portrayed as sexual beings instead of intellectuals. The models are half clothed, pouty lipped and photographed in provocative poses.

Is it any wonder why men critique females in a negative light? Men also play females against each other. One woman doesn't wear a long weave down her back, the other one does. Who do you think he wants to be seen with? You guessed it! The one who closely resembles a fashion model! I think it's fairly safe to say a large majority of men have been duped into believing beauty is what matters most when it comes to having a female on their arm. Men seem to have this crazy notion the prettier the woman, the more fly she appears to be (all that and a bag of chips mentality), that makes her a woman. That's just not true! Beauty resides within ones heart. Self-assurance, self-confidence, and high self-esteem are matters of the heart! Much like the brain sends signals to function throughout the body, the heart is an emotional function. The two go hand-n-hand. Together they predict how we behave outwardly.

Unbeknownst to a lot of females (young or old), the use of poor word choices become self-fulfilled prophecies. We end up having what we say. Taking the initiative to be more attentive to the ways we think while becoming cautiously mindful of what we say does not go without reward. In the past as a child, my mother told me on more than one occasion. "Think before you speak!" Gee. Wish I had five dollars for every time I tossed that piece of advice out the window. I'd be a multi-millionaire! Regardless whether we intend to or not, we give birth to what we say. It doesn't matter if it's good or bad wording. You will have whatsoever you say.

Over the years we absorb the words we hear from other people. That's one of the ways slang quickly spreads through the English language. We hear a slang term enough, and before we know it, we're saying it too. Most often what we hear starts right inside the wall of our homes—the environments we are raised in. Our parents speak things that can easily take root and manifest in the future. Sadly, parents don't understand what they say shapes our futures. A mother who is always telling her daughter how she isn't going to amount to much of anything is speaking mental and spiritual limitation into her daughter's life. A female's level of self-esteem is detrimental during her early development. There's some truth in the cliché, we're products of our environments. If mothers instill self-worth and value in their daughters while they're young, they're more likely to have success in leading whole, healthy lives by the time they reach adulthood.

Far too many of us are discouraged by life because of the words that have consciously or unconsciously hardened our hearts. If all you do is fix your mouth to utter, "nothing good ever happens to me," I'm guessing so far nothing good has. If you say you'll never be successful, then you won't. Words are seeds that take root in our minds and hearts waiting for the appropriate time to give life to what we've been saying. Negative words produce negative results. The Bible clearly states we will reap whatsoever we sow.

Galatians 6:7 reads:

"Be not deceived; God is not mocked; for whatsoever man soweth, that shall he reap." (KJV)

There's another part of the human body called the tongue that shouldn't be over looked in this chapter. The tongue (small as it is), has the ability to get us into all sorts of trouble. Whether you know it, or not, the tongue plays a prominent role in which direction we go in life—how far we go in life. If we're constantly mouthing words of defeat and failure over ourselves, our loved ones, our dreams, and our futures, then just settle back. Watch things spiral downward, or out of control. Girlfriend, saying something over and over again is a confession that becomes real in the subconscious of our mind. You confess fear you receive the results of those fears. You confess faith you receive the results of your faith.

Confession is meditation. What we cling to in our thoughts and then speak out will ultimately materialize because we've meditated over it for a length of time. That's what meditation is. If you continue to think about a particular thing long enough, you're going to act on it. Whenever, I found myself worrying over something. I'd wake up worried. I'd go to bed worried. Days would pass and I'd still be worried about it. You know why? I mediated on that situation! So what do you suppose happened next? That's right. I gave voice to what I was worrying over. Those words took flight and brought back what I'd been saying would probably happen. Bottom line. The problem didn't go away just because I worried (meditated) over it. Finally, I had to be big girl, suck it up, and confront the issue.

Once words are released they go on assignment to manifest those words. The words we speak will eventually come to fruition. That's why I encourage you to please read God's Word. Saturate your mind in it to help you develop a disciplined positive meditation. Fill your heart with a passion for housing the Word—the truth. Renewing your mind with the Word of God will also help you stay spiritually balanced and focused. You won't be all over the place questioning this, and doubting that. Instead by nourishing your spirit, you'll begin speaking God's Word more and idle words less. God told Joshua in Joshua 1:8, he should meditate upon His Word day and night. If Joshua would do this, he would *make* his way prosperous and *have* good success. Training and disciplining ourselves (on purpose) to think before we release words that are capable of hindering our future is wise. There truly is power in the way we talk!

That being said, I am far from being perfect. Nevertheless, I have no business saying any ole' thing just because I may have thought it. Crucial situations involving hardship or unexpected challenges have a tendency to stir up anger and frustration, mixed with feelings of anxiety. As a female, my emotions can quickly shift from calm to irritability, especially now that I'm enduring menopause! Still, it's what I say that will bring a positive or negative result. I can't blame every negative word that comes out of mouth on menopause, even though I'd like to use it as an excuse. *"Menopause made me say that."*

I'm learning when things aren't exactly going the way I had hoped they would, that's the time to put pressure on the Word of God. By that I mean the more I read (aloud) to replenish my spirit, it shows the enemy how serious I am about filling my mind, heart and spirit with God's infallible Word. The more positive my vocabulary, the stronger I can grow both spiritually and mentally. The more I fill my mind with positive thinking it increases the level of faith in my heart. Remember, these three things: (1) The enemy comes to steal the Word. (2) He comes to challenge the Word hidden inside your heart. (3) His attacks are deliberately aimed at destroying any chance of you believing God's Word will manifest in your life. But you know what I always say. *"The devil is a liar!"*

Whenever things get tough (speaking for myself), I'll admit, I sometimes complain and whine. I'm constantly reminding myself not to go there. Why? Because whining and complaining doesn't change one thing. All it does is delay the outcome. Carefree indulgence in negative speech paves the way to self defeat. I'm learning instead of talking the problem, I have to speak to the problem. Jesus said in Mark 11:23, that I can speak to my mountain (problem), telling it to move out of my way! Once I speak to my situation I usually get quiet. Actually I shut up talking about it! I allow God to be God believing (by faith) the problem will no longer be a mountain I can't climb over. One thing is for certain, without any doubt. God's Word cannot return void. Therefore, speaking His Word over any situation won't return void either! (Isaiah 55:11) **I CAN'T STRESS THIS ENOUGH!** Our words have the power to bring back *everything* we say—good, or bad.

As little girls I imagine a number of us probably mimicked our mothers. It's not uncommon for small children to adopt all sorts of behaviors that they are witness to seeing and hearing. The truth is. It doesn't matter whether it's our mother, our grand-mother, auntie, or a sister. Influence starts at home. What we learn behind closed doors initially becomes a part of us. I can only speak for myself, but a lot of my childhood influences have remained with me even as an adult. For instance, my home reflects what I was taught by my mother as far as housekeeping. Every thing in my home has a place. I keep my home neat and clean. Peace resides within the walls of my home. You won't find drama living with me like someone who has overstayed their visit.

The thing is. If we grew up experiencing a dysfunctional household, the disruption and discord probably became embedded in the back of our minds and settled within our hearts. If we came from homes where parents divorced when we were young, their divorce will likely play a part in how we seek a mate. If love was absent from the home, we probably don't have a clear concept of what it means to love someone, or how we want to be loved. Subconsciously I think little girls digest most of everything they see and hear. They're young and innocent. Therefore accepting what they hear. If mommy is always saying, "get away from me! You make me sick!" that little girl processes those words. She can easily associate any shifting in the tone of her mother's voice as an indication her mother is about to be sick. This young child's brain computes any sudden change in her mother's voice means she should quickly exit the room so she doesn't make her mommy sick.

Do you see where I'm going with this? Words have impact! This is why we should train ourselves to build a wall of protection around our mouth. It's vitally important for us to learn to discipline ourselves to think before speaking. None of us are immune from coming under attack by our own accord, byway of our thoughts and words. My mother used to constantly say, "don't let those words come back to bite you!" In the Bible there's a Scripture that pretty much sums up running our mouths with idle talk.

Proverbs 18:21 reads:

"Death and life *are* in the power of the tongue; and they that love it shall eat the fruit thereof." (KJV)

Is that profound, or what? This Scripture is informing us that we need to practice choosing our words very carefully. Saying everything we think, and doing anything we feel like doing as a result of wayward thoughts has the power to bring death (scarceness) or life (increase) to pass. Perhaps the next time you find yourself on the brink of murmuring or complaining about your husband, you may want to think before you speak. Have you noticed there are too many single women out here looking for good men? And if your man isn't happy at home because you're constantly complaining about what he doesn't do…need I go on? Start calling those things that aren't the way you like, the way you'd like for them to be. Begin speaking positive things you'd like to see your husband contribute to the marriage. I've been married before, so I know for a fact **everything isn't always his fault.** Please, don't close the book! I'm only trying to help. Okay girlfriend?

When we're constantly thinking and verbalizing how bad life is treating us, then we're bound to arouse negative spirits. Meet misery. It will show up prepared to move in for however long you might need for it to stay around.

Misery is a selfish spirit. It will isolate you from others, quickly becoming your best-worst friend. In fact, misery loves having you all to itself because misery loves company. Can I suggest finding a better companion? Don't allow misery to remain in your house a minute longer. If you don't show misery to the door, the next thing you know depression will stop by looking for a place to stay too! Open your mouth! Say what God says! If you start decreeing and declaring what the Word says, watch how fast misery will vacate the premises. Negative spirits cannot hang around where the Word of God is prevalent.

Unlike when we were children living under the guidance of our parents, as adults we can make our own decisions concerning the type of environment we want to live in. Whether those decisions are based upon familiarity from what we've learned or were taught, we should ultimately live in peace within the comfort of our own home. I'm not saying sometimes we may have to persevere in our environment, especially when peace is nowhere to be found. But it doesn't have to be that way. God wants all of His daughters to use their words wisely—able to turn around negative emotions and situations. God doesn't want us focusing more on our issues, and placing less emphasis in the power of His Word. Therefore, it's up to every female reading this book to speak to your problems. You can't run from them. You have to confront them. We cannot ignore or pretend they don't exist. Confrontation is a necessity. We're responsible for maturing our faith, instead of always talking to God about how heavy the load is. God is waiting on us to take His Word and begin applying it to our daily lives. No issue or problem is bigger than God!

Girlfriend, stop complaining and worrying about what isn't right about you, or your life! Everything you could possibly want or need to overcome years of deception can be found in the Word of God. Read it. Meditate on it. Believe it. Then open your mouth! Choose victory over defeat! Speak to your mountain(s)! If you want to change old behavioral patterns, say so! Psalm

SO, WHO DO YOU THINK YOU ARE

107:2 tells us as the redeemed of the Lord to say so! If you want to see strongholds torn down, start by changing the way you think. Then be mindful of what you're saying! I want to give you a few examples of things most of us say without any thought:

...life is depressing!

God says...if you allow My Word to minister to your spirit by meditating on it day and night, you will reach your divine appointed destination and you will have success in every area of your life. Joshua 1:8

...I feel so alone. Nobody cares what I'm going through!

God says...I'm right here. You can always count on me. I'll never leave you, or forget about you. Hebrews 13:5

...why is this happening to me?

God says...beloved, pass the test! Stop thinking what you're going through is uncommon or foreign. I Peter 4:12

...I doubt my dreams will ever come true!

God says...there isn't anything too hard, or difficult for me! Genesis 18:14

...it's useless to keep trying. I'm tired!

God says...do not be weary, I'll give you plenty of rest. Matthew 11:28-30

...I don't feel loved!

God says...I love you more than you can imagine! John 3:1; 3:34

...I just can't go another day being disappointed!

God says...My grace will sustain you! II Corinthians 12:9

...I don't know what I'm going to do!

God says...Your steps have been ordered. I will provide direction and guidance to help you along the way. Proverbs 3:5-6

...I'm not educated. Why bother?

God says...I've equipped you with the ability to do all things through Christ, who strengthens you. Philippians 4:13

...how can I ever forgive myself for what I did?

God says...I forgive you. Forgive yourself my daughter. I John 1:9; Romans 8:1

...I'm afraid!

God says...I did not create you to be timid, or to be fearful! II Timothy 1:7

...I'm really worried!

God says...give me your worry. Allow it to rest upon me. I Peter 5:7

...I don't know if I can do it!

God says...I will give you the wisdom to do what you do not know how to do. I Corinthians 1:30

Girlfriend, make yourself a list of negative things you've either thought about saying, or have given voice to what you were thinking. Find Scripture for those things. Begin to free yourself by tearing down those thoughts and those hindering words. Read the Scripture aloud everyday until you believe God's Word over everything that you've been thinking or

SO, WHO DO YOU THINK YOU ARE

saying. Let me encourage you to think positive, speak positive and to be positive in all of your endeavors! Your future is dependent upon the state of your mind!

SO, WHO DO YOU THINK YOU ARE

Chapter Three

Who Is That In Your Mirror

> To grant [consolation and joy] to those who mourn in Zion—to give them an ornament (a garment or diadem) of beauty instead of ashes, the oil of joy instead of mourning, the garment [expressive] of praise instead of a heavy, burdened, *and* failing spirit—that they may be called oaks of righteousness [lofty, strong and magnificent, distinguished for uprightness, justice and right standing with God], the planting of the Lord, that He may be glorified.
>
> Isaiah 61:3(AMP)

The next time you step up to the bathroom mirror, don't approach it casually, distracted by what you see with the physical eye. But rather, let your eyes linger over your reflection. Gaze deeply into the eyes of the woman staring back at you. Now, what do you see? Are you looking upon the face of a woman who feels hopeless, or helpless? Is the woman staring back at you uncertain who she is, thereby lacking a sense of real purpose? Do her eyes reflect frustration? Is the woman in the mirror a victim of mental stress compounded with worry? Do you see the face of a spiritually worn woman who believes she might never get beyond where she is at this particular moment in life?

Am I the only one who has seen these faces looking back at them from the bathroom mirror? It's my guess the faces like those I described have shown up in bathroom mirrors all across the country. More than likely there are women reading this book who have stared upon the reflection of one of these faces I mentioned. The truth is. No matter how hard we might try, we can't ignore the face looking back at us from the bathroom mirror.

When I read Isaiah 61:3, the word *diadem* struck me. I was unclear of its meaning, so I grabbed my Webster's to look it up. The dictionary interpreted diadem as a crown, royal power, authority, or dignity. God's Word promises to give us a spirit of praise to replace our heavy heart. He promises to place beauty upon our heads as a crown of authority to be worn with dignity. This Scripture reinforced what I wanted to convey in this chapter. Whenever we step up to the bathroom mirror, we shouldn't do ourselves a disservice by glancing quickly. Tomorrow morning try this exercise. Stand in front of your bathroom mirror for five minutes, or longer. Examine the eyes of the woman looking back at you. Observe closely. Does the woman in the mirror appear to be waiting to hear you say how much you love her?

I believe every morning when we awake, it's another day (opportunity) to make positive inner changes, as well as other changes within our lives. Why not begin each day by telling the woman in the mirror how much you like, love and appreciate her? Pause for a moment holding her gaze. After having heard those words, she'll probably give you one of her best smiles. If she does, I guarantee you'll return an even bigger smile. That woman in the mirror wants to know that she is loved. This is a simple daily exercise capable of boosting your self image. Start the day with an expression of love for yourself. If you're waiting to hear these words from someone else, you could be waiting quite a while. I'm speaking from personal experience!

Now, I might be treading on thin ice for saying this, but here goes. Girlfriend, stop waiting around for a man to tell you how much he loves you! You don't need validation from a man

SO, WHO DO YOU THINK YOU ARE

to love yourself. Females don't have to chase after a man (especially one that don't want you), to make yourself *feel* more like a woman. Just because he says he loves you doesn't make it so. I'm really going out on a limb now, but I am so tired of females thinking they're inadequate or incomplete because they don't have a man in their life. Pleeze! Girlfriend! God blessed females with brains! So how about we use them! Here we are in the millennium, and females are still pinning after a man who obviously doesn't want to be bothered with them.

There are women who make a career out of sleeping with another woman's man because they claim they can't find any 'nice' single guys. They have no problem, or conscience *sneak'n-n-cheat'n*. The enemy has convinced these females that *at least they got a man*! But what they fail to realize is this. Sharing a man with another female doesn't qualify as **having a man!** It's not the same thing. That's a relationship founded on convenience, deception and lies. The enemy has pulled the wool over her eyes. Females (young or old), have to believe there's more to life than the toilet seat being left in the up position by a man who doesn't even belong to them!

As for my divorced readers, and the female who's man just upped and left without so much as a note to explain why. **YOU CAN MAKE IT WITHOUT HIM!** I don't care if this man left you with a couple of kids. **GOD IS YOUR SOURCE—YOUR PROVIDER!** God will step in to help you finish raising those kids. If you'll allow Him to heal and restore you, God can even help you get over your feelings for that man, and, I say this in love. Girls! We have got to get a grip when it comes to relationships with the opposite sex!

The enemy has managed to rip apart more marriages, and bust up just as many potentially serious male/female relationships. But you know what? LIFE STILL GOES ON! If someone had told me, I'd be twice married; twice divorced, I would've said. "*I don't think so!*" The first husband looked good in a suit. This man was fashionably sharp! I'm talking G-Q sharp! From head-to-toe! Unfortunately, months later I would discover the suit had no substance—nothing to do with the man's character. Following my divorce, I remained single for fourteen years. Then I met my second husband. Seven years into the marriage he got a revelation. He decided he'd rather be alone and unhappy because he thought it was his fate. Please don't misunderstand. I'm not making light of my two marriages because God hates divorce. However, the point I'm trying to make is this. Divorce is never going to be easy. Usually one person takes the final separation somewhat harder than the other. And, believe it or not, I honestly think there are men who have had their hearts broken as a result of a divorce. They are, after all, still human with feelings and emotions just like us. There, I said it! Men have feelings too. However, in spite of the love-disconnection that is commonly associated with divorce, I believe God doesn't cast His children aside and abandon them when a marriage ends. God better understands the characteristics of mankind far better than we could ever begin to imagine.

Jeremiah 9:24 reads:

"But let him who glories glory in this: that he understands and knows Me [personally and practically, directing discerning and recognizing My character], that I am the Lord, Who practices lovingkindness, judgment, and righteousness in the earth, for in these things I delight, says the Lord." (AMP)

That face you see in the bathroom mirror every morning is the face of a unique and special female. She was fashioned in God's image—beautiful! While looking at her, you might notice the woman's eyes are pleading for something from you—change. Girlfriend, you are responsible for turning this woman's hurt and disappointment around. The woman in the mirror is powerless to do anything without your consent. She is counting on you to make sound decisions. Everyday she anticipates a new beginning filled with promise for unlimited possibilities. Don't you think the woman in the mirror has waited long enough for change? Can't you see she isn't afraid to take a chance on God?

Let me ask you something. Have you ever stopped to consider the woman in the mirror is ready to explore life beyond the hum-drum, day-to-day perimeters that you intentionally or

SO, WHO DO YOU THINK YOU ARE

un-intentionally constructed to keep her bound? This woman looking back at you from the mirror wants more out of life! She has a burning desire to move forward, pushing past the boundaries that have held both of you back. The woman in the mirror is excited about God's plans, but she knows you're afraid to take a risk! With her eyes, she is silently begging you to set yourself free from a poor self image. The woman in the mirror desperately needs you! And, whether you know it or not, you need her too! Morning after morning, and day after day, this woman has been witness to the same tired, unsatisfied eyes looking back at her. It breaks her heart to see you this way.

Girlfriend, will you dare to look beyond the bathroom mirror? "God can fix anything. He's God!" the woman silently cries out from the mirror. Yet another morning passes, and you barely notice her. The woman's eyes slowly look down on the sink with a troubled heart. She knows nothing will change today. Perhaps when the two of you meet tomorrow morning in the mirror, it will be the day you believe God loves you, and she does too!

The enemy doesn't want me to tell you this, but I'm gonna tell you anyway. Trust God! Then trust yourself to rise above the past hurt, pain and disappointment that were meant to keep you living in bondage. God created you to be a well able individual who can overcome anything! Whenever any of us face hardship(s) or adversity, God provides both the strength and the guidance to get through it. We must trust God at His Word, and let God be God! Under His infinite direction we are then better equipped spiritually to confront issues that plague our life. I've come to learn that the Word of God builds self-confidence. I have no doubt my God is more than able! This is where unwavering faith comes into play. To accomplish rising above situations we need to rely heavily upon faith. If we can get pass doubting, and begin applying trust to our faith, there's no telling what we can do. Nor is there anything we can't achieve, or overcome. The Bible plainly says. "Without faith it is impossible to please God". (Hebrews 11:6)

Faith possession is a requirement as a born again believer. It's not an option. Possessing faith takes patience—a lot of it! But I assure you developing a heart of faith will definitely pay off in the long run. I highly recommend reading God's Word daily. It helps to reinforce the mind that faith is real. It's not a question of maybe I need faith. No. You need faith to believe for the impossible! Faith makes us spiritually stronger and mentally we'll believe we're unstoppable. Faith also intensifies our 'want to'. It adds zealousness to a person's belief that change is inevitable.

Hebrews 10:23 reads:

"Let us hold fast the profession of *our* faith without wavering; (for he *is* faithful that promised)." (KJV)

An energized, high level of faith keeps the heart pumping with expectation that what you believe is possible, will indeed come to pass. You see, when we make the decision that we're going to fill our heart with God's Word in unwavering, undeniable faith, it will open doors of unlimited possibilities. Even though we might face heartache in life, faith can speak to that situation. Faith can transform disappointing segments in our lives into self-fulfilling moments. It's going to take a strong, determined heart of faith to know, that you know you can hold your head up high when passing by the naysayers. You know who *they* are, don't you? They're the people who said you were never going to be nothing. Regardless whether those words were uttered by a family member a friend, or a school teacher. They will not recognize you once you receive a faith heart transplant. Girlfriend, once you put your faith into action, you'll experience a spiritual makeover! With time and patience you can blossom into the woman God has created you to be! In the meantime, remind yourself, you can leap over any wall of despair and land on your feet victorious! Through Jesus Christ, you already have the victory! Hallelujah!

I Corinthians 15:57 reads:

"But thanks be to God, Who gives us the victory [making us conquerors] through our Lord Jesus Christ." (AMP)

SO, WHO DO YOU THINK YOU ARE

That's worth shouting about! As a matter of fact, put the book down for a minute. I want you to stand to your feet. Now start clapping your hands if you believe victorious living belongs to you—glory to God! Send up a clap offering to God for what He's about to do in your life! Hallelujah! I'm getting excited myself! Hallelujah to Your Name, Lord!

Girlfriend, it's imperative to develop a mindset of being a woman who is willing (unafraid), ready (mentally/spiritually), prepared and able (yes I can!), to fulfill God's plans for you! The Bible says, "I can do all things through Christ, who strengthens me!" (Philippians 4:13) And, that's precisely what I believe! YES, YOU CAN—GLORY TO GOD! Our Heavenly Father doesn't want to see His daughters burdened by a low opinionated spirit. He wants us to see what He sees. Every time we look into the bathroom mirror, we should see the face of a female who knows she is a child of the Most High God! Through enlightened eyes, we are able to see the spiritual beauty that rests on the inside of us. Ask God to improve your vision. Ask Him to open your eyes to see what He sees when he looks at you.

In the book of Numbers 13:33, The Israelites saw themselves as grasshoppers compared to the giant inhabitants of the land God had sought out for them to conquer. God instructed Moses to send men to take possession of the land in spite of what they could see in the natural. Caleb's faith gave him the courage and confidence as a united front backed by God they could defeat the giants to lay claim to the land. But instead of believing (by faith), they were strong enough to defeat the giants, the enemy distorted their eyesight. Sadly, the men were unable to see past their fear. Instead, the Israelites believed a lie over God's Word. One look at the inhabitants of the land and they immediately fainted within their hearts. They saw defeat. The men lacked the faith to believe God's Word was more than enough to equip them with the power to kill those giants and take possession of their land. They blew it! Because of their unbelief, the land of future wealth and opportunity was seen as anything else but achievable.

Farrell Ellis

This story in the Bible should serve as an example and a constant reminder to all of us that when God instructs us to move, we shouldn't doubt Him. We should move! Whenever we hear the voice of the master liar hissing in our ear, we need to shut him up, and shut him down by springing into action. The enemy tries to trick us into believing we're unqualified to walk in the victory God says belongs to us! He'll try convincing us the dreams we dream are attainable for other females. He'll lie about our dreams, wanting us to think they are never coming to pass. That's why you have to *see* yourself through spiritual eyes. Then you gotta open your mouth declaring the Word of the Lord by taking hold of what rightfully belongs to you! Through eyes of faith you will begin to see progress in the making.

I'd like to share a story with you, if I may. There was this family that consisted of a mother, father, and six children. Out of the six, two were girls named Gina and Lorraine. At age seventeen, the older sister Gina left home for college. Her childhood dream had always been to grow up and become a veterinarian. Gina was the eldest of her five siblings. Her parents openly doted on her. All throughout Gina and Lorraine's childhood there was sibling rivalry. Early on Lorraine sensed a different kind of love from her parents. She felt conflicted by their affection towards Gina, causing Lorraine to compete for their love and attention. As the two sisters grew older, the tension increased. All the while their parents seldom interfered in their constant feuds. They said nothing as the two girls constantly bickered between themselves. By the time Lorraine reached sixteen, she resented her parents for not thinking she was as smart as Gina. Her mother frequently reminded Lorraine how unpopular she was, and how popular Gina was in school. A year later Lorraine couldn't take the harsh criticisms from her parents any longer. At sixteen she quit high school. Who cared whether she stayed in school anyhow?

In spite of dropping out of high school, Lorraine was able to get employment at a shoe store in the local mall. It was a low paying job, but with the handy work of her father and brothers they converted the garage into a small living area for

SO, WHO DO YOU THINK YOU ARE

Lorraine. Needless to say, after years of being compared to Gina the straight 'A' student, the most popular girl in school, Lorraine viewed herself to be insignificant and worthless. Gina was off having a grand time in Boston living on her own away at college. Meanwhile, Lorraine thought of life as someone trapped. She hated who she was.

A few years later at age 23, Lorraine was still frustrated with life. She continued to watch the love her parents showered on Gina whenever she came home from college for a visit. When Gina announced she was going to make Boston her home following graduation, Lorraine noticed the grave disappointment in her parent's eyes. Silently she observed her parents try to sway Gina to return home. "I'm here! You have another daughter! I'm not moving away!" Lorraine wanted to scream to the top of her lungs. But she remained quiet almost glad Gina wouldn't be around. For years it seemed no matter what Lorraine did to try to win the love and affection of her parents, they hardly ever made her feel like she was good enough in comparison to Gina. So eventually she stopped trying.

Sadly, now at 31, Lorraine has given up on life by shutting out everyone around her. Over time feelings of unworthiness silently festered, which caused Lorraine to withdraw from society. She grew into a timid, quiet shell of a woman. Following years of rejection from both parents, shadowed by a deeply embedded resentment toward her sister, Lorraine's individuality suffered. Every negative word that passed through the lips of her parents and siblings attached themselves within the walls of Lorraine's mind and heart. Starting in her early teen years Lorraine created a world barricaded by hopelessness and depression. Lorraine was told she'd never be anything like her sister Gina. Her parents were quick to remind Lorraine how much prettier Gina was compared to her plain looks. It wasn't anything for their mother to take Gina shopping for new clothes while Lorraine was left behind. Lorraine believed the way she looked had become an embarrassment to her mother and from that thought was birthed a mindset of caring very little about her appearance, publicly or privately. In her youth instead of socializing and interacting with her peers, Lorraine intentionally kept her distance from the other kids, especially the girls in school. Following years of feeling like an outcast in her family, Lorraine developed a self image of a very unattractive woman. She had fully convinced herself, she didn't deserve to be loved, and no one would ever want her. Lorraine believed she was better off alone.

Each day Lorraine faithfully reports to work at the local mall where she has been an employee at the same shoe store since dropping out of high school. Recently, the store hired a new manager. He likes Lorraine's work ethics and often expresses his appreciation through compliments. To Lorraine's surprise she has found herself stealing glances at the manager when he isn't looking, or is busy assisting a customer. Meanwhile, the enemy has taken notice of the spark of life illuminating behind Lorraine's eyes. He quickly began whispering in her ear. "What man would want someone who looks like you?" This time Lorraine chose to ignore the voice of despair. Instead for the first time since she could last remember, Lorraine held on to hope.

The next day the manager happened to overhear derogative remarks exchanged between two female shoppers. "She's so ugly. Why do they put her at the cash register? They must be trying to deter people from coming in here!" they laughed exiting the store. A week later the manager felt pressured when his regional boss phoned stating he had received complaints from customers about Lorraine's appearance. The manager listened, but in his heart he didn't want to stop Lorraine from working at the register. She was his best employee. She'd been an asset to the store. The manager hated being put in such an awkward position. The conversation ended, but not before his boss reiterated the store was an upscale shoe store. If he couldn't handle the job, there was always someone else who would adhere to company policy.

With reluctance, the manager took Lorraine aside when she arrived to work the following morning. He could always count on her arriving before the other employees, which helped to make what he had to tell her somewhat less difficult. He gently explained as best he could about implementing a few changes within the store among the staff. From now on he wanted Lorraine to be head of sales. Her new position involved overseeing the weekly shipments of new inventory. Lorraine would begin working in the rear of the store where she could conveniently keep abreast of the stocked inventory. She would immediately begin working behind closed doors, out of sight in a musky smelling stockroom all day. Lorraine wasn't dumb. She could see what was going on, but she silently retreated to the rear of the store. The shoe store had been the one place Lorraine had been free to be herself for all these years. Now she was being forced to work in a secluded area without questioning the manager's decision or risk losing her job if she voiced her disapproval. His actions hurt Lorraine very deeply. She thought he liked her too. Feeling betrayed Lorraine pulled even further away from people. Day after day Lorraine limited her contact with the outside world—a world she could no longer trust.

Lorraine's true identity of a bright and loving girl became overwhelmed by insecurities. Unbeknownst to Lorraine's parents ignoring her all throughout the years when she needed them most as a confused and troubled young girl, they had only helped push her further and further into obscurity. In the meantime, the enemy dispatched certain spirits to invade Lorraine's garage apartment where they were able to gain easy access.

Lately when Lorraine settles down for the night, a spirit of suicide now makes itself comfortable next to her in bed. He keeps perfectly still waiting until she falls asleep. He then begins whispering in Lorraine's ear. "Why do you keep tormenting yourself? Why don't you put an end to the pain you've suffered? No one will miss you. No one will mourn. Do you think anyone cares if you live or die?" This cunning voice has been whispering in Lorraine's ear for months, yet she still clings to a ray of hope. She wants to believe that one day her life will be better. Lorraine has always believed there is a God. Recently she bought herself a Bible from the book store in the mall and started reading it. Lorraine asked God to save her from her fears of being alone. She didn't want to die, especially since she hadn't *really* lived.

This story is fiction, although, to some it may seem real. The enemy starts attacking us at an early age to try his best to destroy God's plans by putting people around us that mean us more harm than good. And, I can't emphasize this enough. The enemy uses those closest to us to help carry out his schemes and plots for destruction. My heart breaks for every Lorraine in the world who has been severely wounded (spiritually/mentally) by their past. These females don't have an inkling of who they really are. Many of them feel lost. They feel alone. They believe no one could possibly understand, or even cares that they are hurting. But the devil is a liar! Lorraine, if you're reading this book, I want you to know you have a friend who understands your plight. He knows what it feels like to be rejected—betrayed. He's felt the same kind of agony. This friend suffered unimaginable and horrendous pain as He was tormented, battered and ridiculed, just for being who God said He was. You have a friend who knows about caring and loving others, only to find they don't feel the same way. You have a friend who understands what it means to be dismayed. He understands the hurt and heartbreak you've had to endure. This friend I'm speaking of is named Jesus! Call on the name above all names! Lorraine, I promise you. Jesus will come! Open your mouth! Call Him! "*Jesus! Jesus!*" Now open up your heart to receive Him! Will you give yourself this life-rewarding opportunity for real change to take place within you—in your life? I'm praying for you!

I think an overwhelming number of females do not realize most everything they were taught or not, from their mothers during the early years (post kindergarten), has a lot to do with the attitude and mindset in which they measure themselves as grown women. If you and I fail to *see* ourselves as winners, the road ahead can go on being long, unrewarding and possibly quite lonely. Nevertheless, whatever the case result from our childhood might be. As adults we have choices. First and foremost, no one can make you and I do anything we do not want to do. We should however, accept this fact (the truth), that God created each of us for *His purpose* here in the earth. That's why we're here. That's why you're able to endure life's ups-n-downs in spite of everything you've had to go through. God loves you! He has great plans for you, and for your life! Granted, it may have taken some of us several years to discover exactly what our purpose is, but God never intended for any of His daughters to go through life experiencing so much misery, depression, loneliness, inferiority, rejection, unworthiness, despair, insecurity, helplessness, fear, isolation and hopelessness. I know no one said our journey here on earth would be easy, but I often think we bring a lot of unnecessary hardships on ourselves. We have after all, free will to do as we think and/or feel.

Girlfriend, usually it's not until we hit a low point in life do we decide change is needed. It's at this point when we make quality decisions for improvement. Out of despair, many of us understand something must be done if the same ole tired situations are going to stop occurring over and over again. Suddenly we wake up! We realize if we opt not to seek change, very little if nothing will change for us spiritually, mentally, physically, or financially. Looking to others isn't the answer. The responsibility is ours in making crucial life altering decisions. Change must start with speaking God's Word into our lives!

Matthew 21:21-22 (Jesus speaking to His disciples) reads:

"And Jesus answered them, Truly I say to you, if you have faith (a firm relying trust) and do not doubt, you will not only do what has been done to the fig tree, but even if you say to this mountain, Be taken up and cast into the sea, it will be done. And whatever you ask for in prayer, having faith *and* [really] believing, you will receive." (AMP)

Start looking to God as your source for overcoming all the junk that you've been carrying around, probably for years. The idea that a man or another woman has ***all*** the answers to solving the internal issues we face emotionally and spiritually everyday is being unrealistic. People are not liable for fixing what's broken on the inside of us—only God holds the true power to restoration. I don't want to step on anyone's toes, but I think it's delusional to put so much faith and trust in another human being. I know there are therapists we can consult to try to help work out the mental kinks. But there again, I still believe God holds the power in His hands—total complete restoration. Please don't misunderstand. I'm not speaking against medical professionals. Most doctors are good at doing what they do. Thank God for giving men and women the gift of practicing medicine. So please do not take out of context what I'm saying. Next thing you know I'll have doctors emailing my website all upset! They do what they do, and do it very well. I do what I do—write!

That being said, according to Bible Scriptures, God is our first physician. Therefore, we should be seeking His Word first and mankind second. God has imparted men and women all over the globe with the skills, the knowledge, and the medical wisdom to help heal the masses. But God will forever remain the Almighty Physician! Jesus lived and walked among mankind performing one medical miracle after another while He was in the earth. Jesus (God) has the power to heal us everywhere we hurt!

My question to you is this. Why wouldn't you believe Jesus is still in the business of performing medical miracles today? Don't you know by Jesus' stripes you were healed from every mental and physical sickness known to man? Glory to God! (I Peter 2:24) Divine mental, physical and spiritual health belongs to you! Jesus (laid down His life) paid a hefty price for your body to function free of sickness and disease. He also took worry and stress upon Himself so that you wouldn't have to carry the weight of those burdens. I think worrying is one of the main causes for not feeling 100% healthy in our bodies. Living in despair is a type of infirmity. The brain is the targeted area where the enemy likes to attack relentlessly over and over again. He's clever enough to know if he can get us thinking

SO, WHO DO YOU THINK YOU ARE

indifference toward what the Word of God says, then it will only be a matter of minutes before those thoughts are verbalized. And, once we open our mouths, what is spoken takes flight to bring back those negative words.

By faith each one of us must begin somewhere if we desire inner change. Talking to your reflection in the bathroom mirror is a huge first step! I imagine there are a lot of females who don't hold conversations with themselves while standing before their mirrored image. But girlfriend, if you're behind the privacy of the closed door to your bathroom, who's gonna know you're in there having a one-on-one with yourself? I never said speak to the top of your lungs. It should be done softly—discreetly.

Can I ask you something? If you read my first book, then you know there won't be a chapter where I don't ask a few personal questions. Why is it you and I seldom think twice about talking to ourselves all day long at work, or around the house? Yet, we shrink back from having a private conversation with the woman in the bathroom mirror of our home? Why is that? Ugh? Do you honestly think your co-workers haven't heard you sitting behind the desk talking to yourself? Guess again! You wanna bet they haven't wondered whether you're the sharpest pencil in the pencil box. Ugh? Well, if you're not embarrassed around your co-workers, why hesitate talking to yourself at home in the bathroom? The bathroom is a great place to start dealing with things that no one else knows about you, but you. In order to grow—to mature both spiritually and mentally, you must allow the need for a process to heal and restore the mind. It's the mindset that has to change first to get the ball rolling. If you continue believing the unproductive life you're leading right now is *the only way* it's supposed to be, you're setting yourself up to fail. You can't be looking to God as your source for everything because if you were, you'd know better. Girlfriend, if the mind remains unchanged, you won't envision a new-n-improved image of yourself. Aren't you tired of feeling like you're drifting through life, having to accept whatever comes along? I know I am!

Well, reading God's Word reprograms the mind. Females (me included) have got to learn to set a guard around their delicate minds, as well as protect their fragile hearts. Derogative thoughts hinder us from moving forward. In other words, spiritually we possess the ability (our will) to better control our thought life. I've found that when I'm consistently reading the Word, something starts happening. God's Word begins to drown out the hissing lies of the enemy. A commitment to read the Word of God everyday changes the way we think. Our thoughts begin channeling on the things up above. Our Father in Heaven is a good God! He's a merciful God! He's faithful to His Word to perform it!

Ezekiel 12:25 reads:

"For I *am* the Lord: I will speak and the word that I speak shall come to pass; it shall be no more prolonged; for in your days O rebellious house, will I say the word, and will perform it, saith the Lord God." (KJV)

Even if your busy schedule only allows you 15 minutes to squeeze in reading a couple of scriptures, don't beat yourself up. Just continue the process of replacing old negative thoughts with a new way of thinking—a positive way of thinking. One thing is certain. If you think small, you'll receive little. If you don't expect much, you'll probably get even less in return. Remember. The woman in the mirror is well worth fighting for! She is! You are! Make a commitment to yourself to break free from a poor, woe-is-me mentality. Girlfriend, please don't allow whatever may have happened in your past to prolong the kind of rewarding future God has planned for you. Trust God! This image you have of yourself can be transformed into a new person! Look what happened to Ruth! One minute she was gleaning the fields. The next minute she was marrying Boaz, living in a palace! Look at God! He's totally awesome! Letting go of past hurts and mistakes is a mindset. As you read the Word of God, not only will you notice yourself thinking and talking differently, you'll start believing you have every right to experience the goodness of God in your life! Your Heavenly

SO, WHO DO YOU THINK YOU ARE

Father desires that you accomplish great things here in the earth. He wants you to leave the ugly past behind!

Proverbs 13:19 reads:

"The desire accomplished is sweet to the soul." (KJV)

Your Creator has deposited unique gifts on the inside of you that are in dire need of being awakened—stirred up! These wonderful qualities are not meant to go undiscovered. Nor were they meant to go unshared with others. I believe God imparts visions, dreams and passions on the inside of us that match our personalities. The truth is manifested visions and dreams are meant to glorify the wonders of God. Dreams are also paths leading to abundant living. A wise woman will read the Word, get in sync with God's Word, and allow herself to be directed by God through her gifts and talents as a service for meeting the needs of others. The rewards of Heaven can be overwhelming if you're willing to seek God's guidance. Jesus said. *"Seek first the Kingdom of God, and all these things shall be added unto you."* (Matthew 6:33) Only then can you build up your strongest faith. You must believe that change is possible for every area of your life! Girlfriend, you are a female who is capable of doing all things! Stop letting the enemy fill your head with nonsense! I didn't say it. God said it. He says "you can do all things through Christ Jesus, who will strengthen you!" Therefore, receive this truth into your spirit! By faith, believe it! The next time you're standing before the bathroom mirror tell that female looking back at you, she's a winner! God created you to be victorious. You can overcome anything, even a poor self image!

Identity theft cripples the mind. The enemy doesn't want you to discover all of the wonderful ideas that exist on the inside of you. That's why he starts lying to us early in childhood because he wants to destroy every good thing the Father has for us. The enemy will do anything to keep every female from recognizing the potential she possesses, even at a young age. He knows should we fail to recognize or understand the depth of God's love for us, we're destined to believe his lie that God doesn't care anything about us. And, we'll undoubtedly believe

God can't possibly love us because we won't feel, or think we'll ever be good enough to receive it. But the devil is a liar!

Every female (me included), is a daily work in progress. That's why it's not easy trying to change ourselves all by ourselves. By faith, we must rely upon Jesus for healing on the inside whereby the beauty of His light can shine through us! That being said, a couple of things need to be addressed. Ask yourself. Do I really want to be changed? Do I really want God to fix me? Have I bought into the lie that I'm perfectly fine just the way I am? If you answered these questions yes, then you must believe unlike ever before that (by faith) change is going to manifest itself. Another thing, don't condemn yourself if you loose your footing every now-n-then. Who hasn't taken a spiritual slip? You're not perfect! I'm learning a set back is only temporal. It doesn't mean I'm returning to my old way of thinking. The smart thing to do is not add fuel to the fire by opening the door for the enemy to try to gain access to my mind. So I pick up my Bible. I encourage myself to keep believing, and I keep moving forward! Please be encouraged. Do not become discouraged. Don't be tempted to throw your hands up in the air like you just don't care! You're not the first female who has slipped and you definitely won't be the last. The key is learning to recognize the areas where you can improve. No female has any room to speak against the other when we see a sista slip up! You and I individually must reach a complete awareness of who we really are by attaining a higher level of self-love. Until then, we can't talk about anyone else!

Girlfriend, this fabulous life God has given you is meant to be lived—enjoyed! Love it! Embrace it! You are valuable, and highly valued in the eyes of God! It doesn't matter how big of an issue you might have. It's not how you measure them its how you determine to free yourself once and for all. God is so much bigger than any of our problems or issues. He's able to suddenly deliver you right now—today!

SO, WHO DO YOU THINK YOU ARE

Psalm 34:19 reads:

"**Many are the afflictions of the righteous, but the Lord delivereth him out of them all.**" (KJV)

God is waiting. Call Him! "Daddy, I need you! I can't do anything without you!" Do you want to know one of the things I love about God? As a Father, He protects my integrity along with my reputation. He always shows up, and shows out on my behalf just to prove naysayers wrong! I'm telling you, our Father will avenge us of our adversaries! Every negative word that has been spoken against you behind your back, or to your face, God can cause those same deliberate nasty words to fall to the ground. Those words are immediately null and void! Our Heavenly Father helps His daughters in ways we can't begin to fathom—glory to God! But we must call upon Him. Don't we have to pick up the phone to call our natural daddies whenever we need, or want something? Well, I'm not ashamed to admit I constantly call my Heavenly Daddy. God has shown Himself strong in my life over and over again. He has continued rescuing me whenever I call.

I've often wondered why females have this tendency to settle for so little in themselves and their lives. Girlfriend, **WE'VE GOT TO ARRIVE TO THE PLACE WHERE WE UNDERSTAND THERE IS GREATNESS LIVING ON THE INSIDE OF US!** Unfortunately, more times than not, too many of us settle (compromise) for whatever comes along instead of waiting until we know that we know. I think what many of us have done is, we've unconsciously convinced ourselves that it's okay to settle. The Word of God (The Bible) is a life saving, self-help handbook for righteous living. Reading the Bible increases your knowledge. You learn how to begin implementing God's instructions into your life for nourishing your spiritual needs. His Word also helps us apply the teachings of the Bible to our daily lives. The substance in God's Word can overturn a private self imposed prison sentence. Did you know you could be living incarcerated by the thoughts of your mind? That's no kind of way to live. The Word (the written Word; the logos Word) releases minds that have been imprisoned in years of untruths. Best of all, the Word of God shows us how to begin living and enjoying ourselves through true spiritual and mental freedom.

Matthew 4:4 reads:

"But he (Jesus) answered and said, it is written, Man shall not live by bread alone, but by every word that proceedeth out of the mouth of God." (KJV)

I believe a major instrument in strengthening our faith is to educate ourselves in preparation for change. Read and study God's Word. Girlfriend, overcoming generational curses, mental strongholds, or people bondage can not be achieved without help from Heaven. Clear and concise direction is a must-have. You have to comprehend where God is trying to take you. He doesn't do things like we might think. Therefore, humble yourself before God by being transparent. I think there's a risk of losing fundamental growth in our faith when we remain where we are (complacent) for too long, especially when a season has ended, but we're the only ones who haven't discerned it's over.

If there is one thing I've learned it is this, change requires doing more than what I've been doing. More importantly, I've learned change may also involve doing something that I've never done before. Nevertheless, the key to change is to *do!* Being emotionally driven by a negative mindset operating off low self-esteem, limits you from taking possession of your God-given dreams. Any type of negative energy whether stimulated by the mind, or activated out of a discouraged heart, prevents a person from enjoying life—the good, blessed life God intended for them. It's time to throw out the collected junk along with the accumulated baggage you picked up over the years. Throw them out with the kitchen trash! God says you already have the victory! Stop thinking of yourself as a victim, but rather a victor! Do you know the enemy likes nothing better than making you feel like you've somehow been done unjustly wrong? Have you ever noticed those same individuals go on with their lives? Meanwhile, you wander aimlessly stuck between the past and the future playing the role of victim. Girlfriend, that's an empty life—an enemy set up! He wants you to *think* and *believe* you don't deserve to move on. But the devil is a liar! This is not what God desires for you. He doesn't want to see His daughter leading a poor, woe-is-me lifestyle. So let me ask you this. Shouldn't this be what you want for yourself as well? Don't you want to lead a meaningful, satisfied, good, and blessed life? You are blessed and highly favored of Almighty God! Accept that as truth, and nothing but the truth!

Luke 1:28 reads:

"And the angel came in unto her, and said Hail, *thou that art* highly favored, the Lord *is* with thee; blessed art thou among women." (KJV)

I honestly believe females have a lot to offer this world. I also believe that's why as little girls the enemy lurks about trying to destroy God's divine plans and purpose for our life. He plots to keep us from receiving what God says has been made possible through the Word of His promises. The enemy attacks young minds because he knows little girls are trusting and vulnerable. Children can easily be influenced by what they hear and by what they see. Prime example: How does a young girl not believe her parent(s) when he or she tells them something? After all, surely mommy and daddy want what's best for their child—right? How does any child not trust their parent, even when he or she is physically violating them? Mommy and daddy love her—right? They wouldn't deliberately say and do things that could possibly scar their child for the rest of their life—would they? A dysfunctional household quite often is the direct result of a generational curse that hasn't been broken over the next generation. Have you ever stopped to consider perhaps it's *you* God has chosen to destroy those curses!

Ecclesiastes 1:4 reads:

"One generation goes and another generation comes." (AMP)

Long before I accepted Jesus Christ as my personal Lord and Savior, I had no idea, nor did I have any concept of having what I say. Throughout my teens and into young adulthood I was busy having fun. I was doing my thing! How about you? Do you think we might've passed one another coming off the dance floor at one of the dance clubs on a Saturday night? It's highly possible! Anyway, now that I'm born again (thank You, Jesus!), I understand how words can either perform, or operate against me. So, I've learned to choose my words more carefully. Ironically, I knew that I didn't want to see my siblings or myself dealing with a generational family disease, hypertension. I'd find myself constantly saying. *"We will not have high blood pressure!"* I had no idea what I was speaking out in the natural realm was destroying a curse that had plagued the Ellis family generation after generation. Family members on my mother's side have suffered premature stroke-related deaths. My grandmother (whom I would've loved to have known), died of a massive stroke when my mother was only 12 years old. My mother and her nine siblings were at a high risk for developing hypertension. Naturally, the foods they ate while growing up didn't help either. My mother told me as a child she ate hog maws, chitterlings, pig's feet, ox tails, possum, rabbit, and a lot of ham. Her relatives also cooked with an ingredient used in most of their foods, called lard. My mother was born and raised predominantly in the south. She witnessed Jim Crow laws, segregated schools and churches. She worked in cotton fields. She picked beans, tomatoes, corn, and potatoes. As a young girl my mother saw the aftermath of a couple of men hanging from trees, who tried to stand up for themselves. She would tell us stories how she had to enter establishments through back doors. Mommy often shared a number of interesting stories about her childhood upbringing with my siblings and me. Because of her own childhood mommy provided each of her four children with more material things than she ever had, or might've thought about while growing up. But in spite of us having things, she taught each of us how to appreciate and take care of what we received. Thanks mommy!

My grandfather Tom, mommy's father, produced twelve children. The fact is. The large Ellis household gave way to unhealthy eating habits. What they ate and how it was prepared only added fuel to a silent disease. My mother, along with her other siblings were diagnosed with hypertension as young adults.

SO, WHO DO YOU THINK YOU ARE

When it came time for mommy to teach me how to cook, I was determined I wasn't going to prepare foods like I'd seen her do. At age 13, I got pulled into the kitchen (not without argument), to observe mommy cooking certain meals. She used Crisco grease in her cooking. And, how can I forget the infamous hamhocks mommy used to help season green vegetables. Whenever my mother cooked chitterlings for my father, I had the urge to run away from home! Between the way those things looked, and that awful smell, I promised myself I'd never, ever cook anything like that for my husband when I grew up! And, I didn't either!

Long story short, by the time my mother was diagnosed with hypertension she was in her early thirties. At age forty-something, she began taking prescribed medicines everyday to help regulate her blood pressure. I suppose over time mommy probably resolved herself into accepting hypertension as something she was going to have to live with for the remainder of her life. In the meantime, I repeatedly declared high blood pressure would not have its way with my siblings, or me. And you know what? My adult siblings and I have not been diagnosed with hypertension! Praise God! I believe the power of my confession destroyed that horrible curse for future generations to come!

Now that I better understand what words can do for and/or against a person, I refuse to live bound by generational curses. God's Word says by faith and on the authority of Jesus Christ, I've been given the power to break them! I don't care if those curses involve family sicknesses, social diseases, mental health, and physical abuse, children born out of wedlock, divorce, or financial lack. I will open my mouth! I will decree and declare what the Word of God says. You and I have the power (in our mouth) to tear down generational curses!

Proverbs 18:21 reads:

"Death and life are in the power of the tongue; and they that love it shall eat the fruit thereof." (KJV)

The same principle applies to speaking the Word over ourselves. We shouldn't accept the negative way we feel or think about ourselves as being the norm. It's not. Negative thoughts and feelings are traps set to cause spiritual and mental infirmities. Girlfriend, walk with your head held high knowing who you are, and to whom you belong. Females must no longer be deceived into thinking that they don't count for much. On the authority of Jesus Christ, you can speak into your life for whatsoever you desire to see manifest in the lives of your loved ones, your dear friends, and your own life.

I'm learning in order to experience true freedom of the mind one must start by respecting themselves, regardless of any faults and imperfections. Ask yourself this. How can anyone respect me, if I don't respect and love myself? Girlfriend, look into your bathroom mirror every morning. Learn to rejoice with that woman staring back at you! Together the two of you must agree your desires are one in the same. Then form a bond of allegiance. The two of you must share a genuine love and utmost respect for each other. Together, you and the woman in the mirror will be unstoppable!

No female is perfect. I repeat. Not one of us is perfect. After all, let's face it. Females have issues. And, I say this in love. I wouldn't be at all surprised if every female reading this book has something she doesn't like about herself or her life. Quite frankly, I don't like that my hair grows very slooooooooow! But you know what? I still love Farrell in spite of it. Stop stressing over the small stuff! If you've got similar hair issues, might I make a suggestion? Go out and buy some! I can change my hair color, the length of my hair, and the style anytime I want. It's fun! The hair problem is solved. Whatever your personal dislikes are, find a solution. Lord knows I think I have my fair share of female issues, but I can't go around beating myself up! God is nowhere near finished with shaping you and me into the women He created us to be! Not one thing can either one of us change (spiritually/mentally) without consulting God for guidance and direction on how to go about it.

SO, WHO DO YOU THINK YOU ARE

John 15:5 reads:

"I am the vine; you are the branches. If a man remains in me and I in him, he will bear much fruit; apart from me you can do nothing." (NIV)

Granted, the results may not be quick, but just know (by faith) God is reshaping and preparing you everyday for who He has called you to be—an example of His likeness in the earth. No matter how much we mess up (thank God for His mercy and grace), His ears are attentive, listening for His daughter's call upon Him for help. (Psalm 94:9; 116:2; I Peter 3:12) I'm very grateful He's a loving and forgiving Father. God is a God of second, third, and fourth chances. He values His daughters.

You and I mustn't allow anyone to undermine our self-esteem or self-worth, especially when we run up against certain people who treat us like we're insignificant. Learn to recognize negativity. And, once you see negativity for what it is, put some distance between you and it. The Bible says if everybody rejects you, God will not. He loves us for who we are. (Ephesians 1:6) We are His priceless treasures. We are God's own specially crafted masterpieces. He knows *everything*! Don't think He doesn't know about the bad stuff or the really ugly stuff that you manage to hide from others. Still, God loves us unconditionally. Praise God! You may not be exactly where you want to be spiritually, mentally, or physically at this particular time in your life, but you can thank God that you're not where you used to be! Hallelujah! Thank You, Jesus!

The most proficient way in succeeding in becoming who God says you are, is by not becoming easily discouraged in the meantime. What God has planned for our lives isn't predicated on the past, or what's taking place at this very moment. God knew your end from the beginning. This tells me that God is well informed about the middle too. However, He has promised to bring you and me to an expected end.

Jeremiah 29:11 reads:

"For I know the thoughts *and* plans that I have for you, says the Lord, thoughts *and* plans for welfare *and* peace

**and not for evil, to give you hope in your final outcome."
(AMP)**

Read His Word. Renew your mind. Be spiritually transformed. Your path to empowered greatness will shine brighter and brighter each passing day. You've got God's Word on it! He is a man who cannot lie. (Numbers 23:19) I want to share something with you. Whether you know it or not, when we walk around feeling sorry for ourselves, having private pity parties, and complaining about what we think is wrong with us, God isn't pleased. Thinking and operating out of the flesh has consequences. That's why consistently reading the Bible helps in correcting negative behavior, nasty attitudes, patterns of speech and unproductive actions.

Out of all the things I've written in this chapter, the bottom line is this. Learn forgiveness. Forgive the people who may have hurt you in the past. Let it go! Move forward! God told Moses. *"Why do you cry to me? Tell the people of Israel to go forward!"* (Exodus 14:15) In other words, stop whining to God to do for you what He has equipped you to be able to do for yourself! God asked Moses. *"What's that in your hand?"* (Exodus 4:2) He then gave Moses power through the rod he was holding in his hand. Whenever Moses raised this rod toward heaven, he was able to perform signs and wonders before Pharaoh, the Egyptians, and the Israelite people. Like Moses, we too have been supplied the necessary tool in which we can use to move forward. God has given us the authority through Jesus Christ (the Living Word), to speak His Word, and watch it manifest into existence! I enlist you to please, go forward with your life. Stop harboring un-forgiveness! Ask God to deliver you from thinking harshly towards another for what he/she did, or didn't do. Get on with the good, blessed life God has planned for you! Stop letting the past control you by murmuring and complaining about what *they* did to you! Go forward in God!

One thing is true, and I'm sure you know this for yourself. Family, friends, and people in general are quick to tell one another what they can and cannot do. However, be aware that the majority of time folks don't like seeing someone pull themselves up. Once you make a quality decision to no longer accept the status quo, you become a threat. Oddly, people will pride themselves on trying to keep you right where you are—doubtful and running in place! Our Heavenly Father desires to see His daughters not only living out their dreams, but He wants to see them spiritually set free. He knows there is greatness on the inside of you! You were born with purpose! The Bible says God's ways are so much better than ours. His thoughts are higher than anything we could ever begin to imagine.

Isaiah 55:8-9 reads:

"For my thoughts are not your thoughts, neither are your ways My ways, says the Lord. For as the heavens are higher than the earth, so are My ways higher than your ways and My thoughts than your thoughts." (AMP)

One of the wonderful promises of God is that He will never leave us, nor will He toss us aside when we screw up. (Joshua 1:5; Hebrews 13:5) Whatever you do, don't ever give up on God, or yourself. The past is behind you forever. Look ahead. Speak to the woman in the mirror. Tell her how much you love, respect and appreciate her. Remind that woman how much God loves her. You're going to find that no one can encourage you the way you're able to encourage yourself. Therefore, learn to motivate yourself! You're responsible for stirring up the gifts that lay within you! Begin to prophesy over your life! **OPEN YOUR MOUTH—SPEAK LIFE!**

I dare you starting tomorrow morning to strike up a conversation with that woman in the bathroom mirror. Allow your eyes to linger over her beautiful face before speaking. Don't be afraid to share ideas with her. Confide in her about your desires and aspirations. You can trust the woman in the mirror to be discreet with all of your dreams. After a week or so of doing this self-love exercise, go to my website: www.gbydfarrellellis.com Send me an email. I'm anxious to hear how this exercise is helping you to like and love yourself more. I'm serious! I'd be very interested in knowing if you were open and honest with the woman in the mirror. Remember, she can see through you. If your words aren't coming from your heart, she will know it.

I'm not saying this exercise will help every female reading this book, especially if you're not serious about inner change. I'm sharing this suggestive exercise because it helped me to face (no pun intended) some hard truths about myself. Following a short period of indulging in lengthy talks with myself, emotional bondages were broken over my life. The very idea that I could shut the bathroom door and hold a private pow-wow with that woman in the mirror didn't seem like a strange thing for me to do. Partly too, I knew she wasn't going to judge me. She was there to listen while I expressed what lay in my heart during some of the most difficult moments. When we come together she reaffirms that she has my best interest. One thing is certain as I gaze into this woman's dark brown eyes, she knows how much I love, respect and appreciate her for the woman she is!

Chapter Four

Value The Value In You

> So don't be afraid! You are worth more
> than many sparrows.
>
> Matthew 10:31(CEV)

While drafting the first, second, and third chapters for this book, my outline pretty much went unchanged. However as I prepared to write this chapter, I was thrown a curve. My ideas took a slight detour. As usual, God funneled new text to my brain. You see, it's my personal belief most everything I write is inspired from My Heavenly Father, byway of the Holy Spirit. How else can I explain completing an entire chapter, let alone an entire 200 page (or more) book—to God be the glory!

Quickly let me share. I'll start off by saying by the time this book is published, we would have witnessed a history making milestone in this country. A man by the name of Barack H. Obama will have been re-elected to be our 44th President.

Mr. Obama seemingly stepped out of obscurity to participate in a politically energized race that would conclude at 1600 Pennsylvania Avenue in Washington, DC. Early on Mr. Obama set the tone for his campaign, proving it was plausible to promote an idea of hope, while asking the voters of this country to believe change could launch us into a fresh new direction—a better direction. The first presidential election of former Senator, Barack Obama was unprecedented to put it mildly. It was, in my personal opinion—phenomenal!

Before Mr. Obama entered the race to the White House, I will admit. I hadn't shown him or his candidacy a lot of interest. Truth be told, I vaguely recalled that he had spoken at the 2004 Democratic Convention. I didn't know he was a Senator from Chicago until he started running for president. Just keeping it real—okay? And, my guess is, I'm not the only one who hadn't heard about him. But let's stay on point. Something unusual occurred during Mr. Obama's 21 months of campaigning. This man possessed a great magnetism, which drew thousands upon thousands of Americans together all across the country to start believing our country could turn around, if we all came together to make it happen. In my lifetime I had never seen anything like this before! Mr. Obama's campaign rallies increased in potential voter attendance everywhere he went. His speeches were simplistic, yet powerful. Mr. Obama will forever be remembered as the candidate who used three words to create a history making political frenzy. He simply said. "*Yes we can*!" Those words raised awareness such as the political race for president had never known in times past. Those three words propelled the least likely candidate to the forefront, while inspiring hope in the hearts and minds of voters all across the United States. Mr. Obama's creative plan and prepared approach to running his campaign proved quite unsettling for a number of voters. He also incurred strong resentment from his Washington colleagues, some of whom had started out in the race with him. "Who did this Junior Senator think he was to run for President?" "Did he really think it was possible for him to win?" I can only imagine those questions were on the lips of almost everyone on the opposing side of the political circuit.

Meanwhile, it wasn't long before I jumped on the Obama bandwagon too. I followed the presidential race via TV, newspapers, magazines, and the internet. I quickly recognized that Mr. Obama had '*IT*'. Senator Barack Obama had the '*IT*' factor working largely in his favor. *It* was destined for him to be

SO, WHO DO YOU THINK YOU ARE

elected President of the United States. During one of the many television biographies I watched, one evening I sat listening as he explained the meaning of his name, Barack. He smiled broadly with pride. "It means blessed." Need I say more about his destiny?

Each day as I observed Mr. Obama's demeanor (charismatic), and studied his body language, I couldn't help but notice his tall, lean stature openly displayed a man of confidence. I suspect to some observers he often appeared arrogant. I'm learning there's a very thin line that coexists between arrogance and confidence. All too often the two characteristics can be misconstrued, especially when a person is fully aware of whom he or she is as a person. When Mr. Obama came to Wilmington, Delaware (where I live), on a campaign stop, mommy and I rushed from church service that Sunday afternoon to get to the area where he was scheduled to speak. I just wanted to catch a glimpse of the man, if I could. But more importantly, I wanted to hear his speech. Amongst the excitement of the huge, supportive crowd, it was tough trying to get close to the grassy area of Rodney Square where he was speaking. Mommy and I tried to get as close as possible. I finally spied a narrow opening where she and I could squeeze in with the other excited voters. We were scrunched together, shoulder-to-shoulder, anxiously waiting to listen to a man who had managed to arouse thousands of people across the prejudicial borders and racial divides of this country. At the time while standing in the square, I strongly suspected Mr. Obama would become our next president. Of course I know I could just as easily have been wrong in my summation, but there was something about Barack H. Obama— different from presidential candidates of the past.

Three months later as I sit glued to my bedroom TV, I was proud as a Black American. I hung on every word of Mr. Obama's eloquent speech. I watched misty eyed as he stepped up to the microphone poised and seemingly ready to accept the grueling two-man race that now lay ahead. I'll always remember that extraordinary night in August of 2008. Mr. Obama stood tall (shoulders back), before the people of America. We were hopeful. We were proud for him to accept the elected nomination for the Democratic Party. Barack Obama demonstrated a quiet strength, which often was mocked by the other opponents throughout the campaign. The opposition interpreted his somber demeanor for a direct indicator as a sign of weakness. Earlier in his campaign when Barack Obama wouldn't stoop low, or get down in the mud with the other Democratic opponent, that's when I had no doubt this man was very comfortable in his own skin. Mr. Obama knew exactly who he was. For me personally, this presidential race was taking elections to a whole new level. I do not want to sound deep, but there was so much more happening around this country during the 2008 presidential election. It was more than a black man campaigning for the top position in government during one of this country's most challenging, economic declining moments in history.

On November 4, 2008, as I sat on my bed (pillows fluffed behind me), talking on the phone with Jeannette, crunching chips in her ear (love my chips!) I wondered if anyone else had actually grasped the magnitude of this race. Barack Obama was going to have a significant impact around the world should he defeat the opposition. In the months leading up to Election Day, this hadn't been an ordinary run of the mill political campaign from the moment Mr. Obama announced he was running. An astounding record-breaking number of voters stood for hours in lines stretching two and three miles long to cast their ballots in this presidential race. Everything about this election was astronomical, even for the history books. From the beginning Mr. Obama hadn't presented himself as the usual kind of mud-slinging and trash-talking campaign candidate. That in it self should've been the first clue to the final outcome. All during his campaign (once I got into it), I observed this man endure a lot of skeptic from candidates in his own party, as well as from the opposing side. But what I admired most about him was his perseverance. Mr. Obama rarely, if ever shifted away from remaining committed to the race, while staying focused on fulfilling his vision. In a nutshell, Barack H. Obama's overwhelming nomination for president would leave a memorable, profound effect upon just about every eligible voter, whether they voted for him or not.

At the start of his campaign, Mr. Obama's platform was grounded by his faith, which he acted on by having the courage to trust his faith enough to step out. He believed winning the highest government position in the United States was possible even for an unknown junior senator. It was clear to me. Mr. Obama believed two things were doable for the future of this country. (1) Hope (2) Change. I recall waking up the following morning tired. On the night before I refused to go to sleep until I could watch and listen to Mr. Obama's acceptance speech. The election of our 44th President impacted me with a new attitude— a fired up attitude! Barack H. Obama demonstrated what it meant for one to be in touch with who they are. When someone knows that they know, it's hard to penetrate their shield of confidence. When someone is walking by faith, believing can't no-thing or no one stop them from fulfilling their dream, look out! If God be for us, who then can be against us? Barack H. Obama's life story had been written long before he was a baby in his mother's womb. He was destined to become the 44th President of the United States. Thank you, Mr. Obama for having the un-staggering faith and the determination to follow God's plan and purpose for your life! You were born for such a time as this!

One of my favorite Scriptures I decree quite often is, "I can do all things through Christ, who strengthens me." (Philippians 4:13) Within the very depth of my soul, I believe what I'm saying is true. However, for any female who is struggling with that Bible truth, I want to share another example that God's Word is true. Throughout President Obama's campaign I couldn't help but to notice there was power in the words he released. He spoke from a heart of faith. Girlfriend, our God is no respecter of person.

I said all of that just to say this. If Barack H. Obama could evolve out of obscurity and overcome opposition, you can too! He had to turn a deaf ear to the voices of negative comments. He had to stand tall, head held high despite the degrading remarks coming from the naysayers. This man challenged a well liked high profiled powerful political couple. Still, Mr. Obama believed he would receive the nomination as the Democratic Party's choice to continue running in the presidential race. People all across the globe were definitely keeping an eye on the outcome of the election. Had you ever seen so many newspapers from foreign countries reporting on the election of an American president in the past? All I can say is, you better believe **there isn't anything by faith we cannot accomplish!** I hadn't intended to use President Obama as an example. But that's where my writing detour took me.

However, let me get back to discussing female issues. Far too often our thoughts and expectations don't line up. Usually we'll think one thing, while actually expecting something else. Somehow either one or the other gets lost along the way. Still, one needs the support of the other for power and influence. That being said, I understand females don't always get what they want. But the bottom line is this. God will always know (better than we do) what's best for His daughters.

Jeremiah 21:5 reads:

"Before I formed thee in the belly I knew thee." (KJV)

On the other hand, if our mindset has been programmed not to expect much out of ourselves or our lives, we will receive little. It's simple. Like it, or not. You and I can only receive what we believe belongs to us depending on what, and how we're thinking. If our thoughts are positive (acting in faith), then we correspond with expectation. However, if we lack in the area of having faith there can be no expectation. When our frame of mind revolves around 'woe-is-me' that kind of thinking will only work against us—not for us.

There's an issue that commonly exists amongst a lot of females, which is the dreadful inner personal character struggle. Women (me too), constantly beat themselves up. Usually if something doesn't go the way I thought it should've, I can be very hard on myself. But can I suggest something? Instead of giving yourself a black eye, why not start learning from these personal challenges? I think failing to understand what makes us tick only continues to fuel the fire for inflicting spiritual and mental abuse upon ourselves. Reacting to our own behavior, whether it's good or bad is generated by what we're thinking.

When my second husband and I separated, emotionally all sorts of self-incriminating thoughts ran through my mind. Had I done enough to try to save the marriage? What was the church folk going to think when they found out hubby had left me? Had I been a good wife? What was his family going to think of me now? Where did I mess up in our relationship? Had I expected too much from this man? What did I do to make him fall out of love with me? My head was spinning! The questions just kept coming! I was so busy trying to figure out where things went wrong, I forgot to eat! I dropped over ten pounds. If I wore a skirt, I had to pin it up. If I wore pants, I had to put a pin in them too! None of my clothes fitted properly. Then I went on the defense when a woman asked if I was losing weight. "*No! I'm not!*" I growled back!

What I needed was a quick work from the Lord because I was experiencing mental and spiritual turmoil! But the thing I finally realized was that I was inflicting this agony upon myself. Jesus said I could cast *all* of my cares upon Him. But during that particular time in my life, the only thing I thought about was my situation. I wasn't thinking about what Jesus said or what would Jesus do. I'm keeping it honest because I'm trying to help the next woman who could very well be experiencing the same situation. Girlfriend, when the head and the heart are sick, the spirit suffers too! My husband was gone! Moved out! I could've cared less about girding my loins. Instead I was consumed by 'what were people going to say'. But you want to know something? In the end, none of the worry mattered anyway. My husband wasn't coming back. The marriage was over.

Self-induced abuse isn't anything new. It's been around for decades. No one will ever be harder on a person than that person will be on themselves. My sense of self-worth got wiped out by all the craziness that occurred during my separation and divorce. I didn't understand it was going to take *real faith* to believe I could rise above it. Rebuilding my self-worth rested upon the way I thought and felt about myself.

God promised to give me beauty for ashes, and a garment of praise for a spirit of heaviness. (Isaiah 61:3) One night while I was sitting on the side of the bed in the stillness of my bedroom, the Holy Spirit began ministering to me. He reminded me of a number of God's promises. I began to believe joy was coming in the morning! You know why? Because for the first time in days, I thought about food! Suddenly I was hungry! I wanted something to eat! I hurried downstairs to the kitchen!

I've since learned that my head must be in complete and total agreement with my heart. The two working together are dependent upon each other. I've also come to learn the enemy uses ignorance as one of his weapons against us. He's counting on God's daughters to forget who they are, and who He says they are. If need be, you and I should remind ourselves everyday, God loves us! We belong to Almighty God!

There are three things required for moving forward: (1) Acknowledgement, (2) Identification, and (3) Awareness. Instead of concentrating on the things that cause displeasure with who we are inside/outside, we should try focusing on our better qualities. I don't think it is conceited or arrogant to tell ourselves that we are special. I'm speaking in terms of building up ones self-esteem. I can't stress enough how vitally important it is that you see yourself as God sees you! Then adopt a new vocabulary. Speak positive words over yourself. Girlfriend, by faith you must transform the mind, the will, the emotions, and the mouth. Each of them has to get in line with God's Word. In the Book of Ephesians we've been given the instructions to put on the whole armor of God. When you get dressed in the morning you need to include God's armor to your wardrobe.

Ephesians 6:11 and 6:13 reads:

"Put on the full armor of God so that you can take your stand against the devil's schemes. Therefore put on the full armor of God, so that when the day of evil comes, you

SO, WHO DO YOU THINK YOU ARE

may be able to stand your ground, and after you have done everything, to stand." (NIV)

Faith—real heart generated faith (that changes things), allows God to show up on your behalf when you need Him most, especially during difficult moments when what appears to be an impossible situation is staring you in the face. An act of faith also helps to make you strong (spiritually/mentally) in times of emotional challenges. Quite often the way females respond to certain situations causes their faith (or lack thereof) to become transparent to others. How do you view yourself? What does your life look like to you? Positive? Negative? However you answer those questions, you can probably bet other people have seen what you feel.

Girlfriend, no one can ever have enough faith for themselves and you too. Why? Because faith possession is as individual as you are. Building a strong heart of faith is something one must attain for oneself. The only person who can make a decision to believe (by faith) is you! God has equipped you with the ability and the power to take authority over your life! Do you need a right now miracle? Exercise your faith! Do you desire inner change? Put a demand on your faith! Do you want peace, joy, and prosperity to manifest in your life? Speak in faith!

The woman in the bathroom mirror has been waiting on you to start believing not only were you created for successful living, but you are well able to achieve it! Past mistakes and/or failures shouldn't have any dominion over your future! Let the past be just that—the past! With God on your side, the future will ultimately grow brighter, if only you can believe! Paul said in Philippians 3:13, "but this one thing I do, forgetting those things which are behind, and reaching forth unto those things which are before."

Unfortunately, I'm going to have to burst your bubble when I tell you this, but only you can have faith for you. Family and friends may have a strong show of faith in you, but it's up to you to acquire faith on your own. It's time we stopped blaming mommy, daddy, sister, brother, boyfriend, husband, ex-husband, church folk, and anybody else we can think of for what's unsatisfying in our lives. I'll even take it a step further. You and I can no longer point the finger at other people for our lack of self-gratification. Sure, life may not be a bed of roses right now, but so what! Get over it! We are responsible for taking charge of our emotions. The devil will beat our brains in if we don't get in line with God's Word!

Faith does bring about change, but first you must believe beyond any doubt that change is possible. Our God is an able God. Having a strong heart of faith does bring results, if we faint not! By consistently feeding our spirit on God's Word, we receive nourishment to the mind and heart. By meditating on God's Word, we believe we are who He says we are. God says I'm more than a conqueror. (Romans 8:37) That's a truth I had to eat every day until I could believe it was the absolute truth!

Between trying to accept my mother's death and left to handle her financial affairs, plus make the necessary preparations to vacate the condo, I certainly didn't feel much like a conqueror! As the eldest sibling the task of finalizing our mother's affairs was placed upon me. But I managed to hold it together—thank you Lord! At least I was eating. However, the people around me had no idea I was spiritually depleted. My faith level was also very low. Truth be told, I resented that my mother had fallen sick unto death. People awake from comas, why couldn't she open her eyes? Each passing day I would smile as though all was well within my soul. However, those smiles couldn't have been furthest from the truth. Outside of opening my Bible during Sunday and Wednesday church services, I had no desire to read God's Word. My heart was grieved. It ached from brokenness. Within two and a half years life had dealt me what I considered had been unfair hard blows. But our Father is a compassionate God. In spite of the hurt and despair I was feeling, God was right there the entire time.

In the weeks following my mother's funeral, I busied myself with packing. I tried thinking about mommy as little as possible because when I thought about her, the tears were uncontrollable. I asked myself (not God) what more could I do to ease the pain, the resentment, and the emptiness that lay within my heart. Well, while I may have been confused, I wanted to feel alive—a part of the living. That's when I began frequenting a casino in Pennsylvania. Going there didn't have anything to do with trying to hit a million dollar jackpot at the slot machines. It had everything to do with trying to escape my grief. Traveling to the casino Saturday after Saturday quickly developed into an emotional crutch. At least while I was at the casino I didn't think about abandonment, or loneliness. For over a period of two months I visited the casino every weekend. I had lost well over $2,700 before I finally came to my senses.

Once the fall weather arrived I had moved into my new residence along with my spoiled cat. In the chilly evenings I gradually began reading my Bible again. I created a list of Scriptures to read daily. As the year approached the final calendar days of 2008, my heart was still heavy, but the resentment was starting to subside. One of the Scriptures on the list that I began confessing everyday was Roman 8:37. It reads:

"No, in all these things we are more than conquerors through him who loved us." (NIV)

The start of a new year was quickly approaching, and more than ever I needed faith to believe I was indeed more than a conqueror! I desperately wanted to believe I could go on living a full and meaningful life without mommy. I prayed asking God to mend my broken heart in the days ahead. I requested the kind of peace His Word said would surpass all of my human understanding. (Philippians 4:7) *"Father, please restore me spiritually. Heal my mind and heart as only You can!"* Then one evening in the quietness of my bedroom, the Holy Spirit reminded me, 'greater is He who lives on the inside of you than he who is in the world.' (I John 4:4) I started to believe!

There's a reason why I shared this with you. Girlfriend, what we choose to believe about ourselves and about our lives has everything to do with how far we will go in life. So please be very careful about what you allow to turn your heart from God.

For a minute I allowed feelings of resentment and self-pity to cloud my better judgment. The enemy planted seeds of incompetence within the corridors of my mind. He had me thinking life without mommy was no longer as important as it had been prior to her death. The indescribable happiness mommy contributed to my life was gone forever, or so I thought. I felt somewhat less than a person. My biggest cheerleader had been silenced. The enemy had me right where he wanted me—hopeless. My self-esteem was running on fumes. But through it all, had I not experienced those days of mixed emotions, feeling I had reached my lowest point in life, the enemy could easily have won. But thank God, a small measure of faith still remained in my heart. It was enough to draw me back to God, and His Word—again.

    May I ask you something? Do you honestly expect change to begin taking place from within? Can you believe God for restoration and the healing of your mind, spirit, soul and body? If you answered yes, then I have another question. Are you capable of forgiving someone for what they did to you, or didn't do for you? This became a poignant question I had to ask myself when it came time to move forward with my life. After all, healing requires a starting point. Healing begins from within. I needed to forgive myself for being resentful towards God. I believed He had the power to raise my mother up from that hospital bed fully recovered, but she never regained consciousness. Following her death, I lost the faith to believe God was the almighty physician. In my resentful state of mind, the enemy seized an opportunity to whisper untruths. "God let your mother die. How can you have faith in Him if he didn't do anything to heal her?" In the months ahead, when I began reading God's Word again, I realized something. God didn't *let* my mother die. In death, just as in life He was with her all along. Mommy's life-span had been decided even before she came into the earth. I asked God to forgive me for hardening my heart against Him. Since that time, I've come to understand a critical piece of knowledge. It doesn't matter what kind of a negative image you or I might have, with God Almighty's help He can erase that poor self-image away. I am living proof!

SO, WHO DO YOU THINK YOU ARE

Can I quickly share another story that forced me to forgive someone, when all I really wanted to do was cling to my hurt so I could feel justified in my un-forgiveness. At the time I actually thought harboring a heart of un-forgiveness made me the better person. Boy, talk about being clueless! So here's my story. During my late 20's (before I accepted Jesus), I dated a married man. I'm not glorifying what I did. Nor am I proud of what I did. But I'm making this confession because I want you to know God is in the repair business. If He could fix this messed up female, He can certainly fix whatever ailments you have too! Besides, His Word says we're to confess our sins one to another.

James 5:16 reads:

"Therefore confess your sins to each other and pray for each other so that you may be healed. The prayer of a righteous man is powerful and effective." (NIV)

In the Book of James, it is written that if I act as if I am without sin, I not only am living in deception, but I make myself to be a liar. However, if I'm woman enough to speak openly and honestly about my sins, He (God) is faithful and just. He will forgive me of the sin and cleanse (heal) me from committing that sin again. (James 1:8-10) Therefore, I hope what I'm about to share will help another female who may be where I once was.

I'd gotten a divorce from my first husband and swore off men (no dating) for over two years. Needless to say, I was quite vulnerable. The thing is the devil knew it too. After being celibate during this time, out of nowhere a co-worker seem to notice me. He and I had worked in the same office day after day for a few years. We constantly passed each other in the halls. Now, he notices me? Oh really? Anyway, he invited me to join him for lunch. Each time I declined. Finally after weeks of asking me out to lunch, his persistence won over my resistance.

Long confession short, it wasn't long before I found myself falling head over heels in love with this man. I'm vulnerable, remember? Well, I had my own apartment so it wasn't hard to find privacy for us to be together. Call me dumb, but I loved and breathed this man! For six years! One evening on the ride home after having a romantic night out in Philadelphia we got into a heated argument. It had to do with a broken promise. I was livid! So much so, I had the audacity to tell this man it was either me, or wifey-n-the kids! I performed real ugly, screaming and hollering! I probably could've been nominated for an Academy Award! However, it was in that heated moment when an alarm went off inside of me. I was no longer comfortable being the *other woman*. And, you probably already guessed. The relationship shifted to a whole new direction. I was putting this man in a position he hadn't expected to be in. He said I was asking for more than he was able to give—at this time. He questioned after six years why had I decided to place demands on him and our relationship. Hadn't things been just fine? Well, Mister Man, I was tired, that's why! This man became the center of my life! I was demanding more because I honestly thought I deserved more from him!

Well, it wasn't too many days after I laid out my list of demands when the phone started to ring less and less. If he did call, it was to give me another excuse why he couldn't stop by. All of a sudden his family became very important. Mr. Man even began inventing clever little ways to avoid me at work. I don't want to get ahead of myself because in chapter nine I write about the things we girls do for love. But I wanted to take this moment to be transparent about my past because during that time I didn't understand that I didn't need this man to make me feel significant. What I actually needed was deliverance!

Anyway, as our relationship drifted further apart I literally felt like I'd been kicked to the curb. Plus my emotions were outta control! It would be months before I developed a healthier mindset. Getting that man out of my system didn't happen overnight. It was hard, but I had to come to a decision about what I wanted for myself and my life after the break-up.

Upon deciding I needed to feel better, I began allowing myself one day at a time to get it together. It had taken over a period of time to fall in love with this man; it would take time (for however long) to fall out of love with him. Later I would discover those mental emotional ties had been self-imposed. The struggle to let go had been in my mind all along. The way I was thinking at that time—what I was feeling had a lot to do with the miserable rut I found myself stuck in. Instead of dealing with the root of the problem—lust, fornication, and believing I wanted someone who wasn't mine to have, I blamed that man for taking advantage of me. Isn't it funny how when things get into disarray, we start blaming other people? Not only did I blame him for the miserable way I felt, I hated the fact that he'd had his fun, and now he was hiding out at home with the wife and kids. He behaved as though he and I were never intimately linked together. I also hated the fact that his conscience didn't convict him for walking away. The fact is our relationship was over. It may have ended rather abruptly, but nevertheless it was kaput! Mister Man went back to his life. So I made up my mind that I would never, ever forgive him for what he'd done to me!

Psst! He could only do whatever I willingly allowed to transpire between us. Did you catch that? Girlfriend, the truth of the matter can't be overlooked. I made a decision to go on lunch dates with this man. I made irresponsible choices to have this man in my life. I gave him permission to feel welcomed to visit my apartment knowing full well he belonged (legally belonged) to another woman. I knew precisely what I was getting myself into. Nobody was twisting my arm to take those friendly lunches past 'caution'. I'm not using this as an excuse, but when he and I got involved my church attendance was sporadic at best. It's not like I was full of God's Word. I seldom opened my Bible to read it. So how could I know it was a sin to be sexually involved with a man who wasn't my husband? That's because I was ignorant. I had to go through some heartache, embarrassment, and a whole *lotta* pain to come to myself! Let's face it. When a female's head is filled with bees buzzing around confusing her even more, life can get real messy! Anybody feel me? Sadly, that's also when many of us tend to make some of our worst life-altering decisions. Then again, maybe I should just speak for myself, ugh?

I've learned a feeling of low self-esteem does one thing. It increases. It grows heavier each passing day. Misdirected self-worth creates an inferiority complex. And, you know what? The enemy tells himself, "my work here is done." I should know because I was hopelessly wandering around in the dark! The lights could've been on, but I still couldn't see the truth! The sun could've been shining high in the sky, but darkness was all around me. After about a month or so of being alone again, I realized I didn't have to settle for being the other woman ever again. I was better than that! I didn't have to sneak around town with someone else's man. My mother hadn't raised me to be a home wrecker! How could I be content being number two, always having to adjust my schedule to revolve around his availability? Following our break-up, I didn't like myself much because of what I'd done. Perhaps Tina Turner summed it up best when she asked, "*What's love got to do with it?*" Exactly!

Unfortunately, I didn't know the first thing about the various kinds of spirits that attach themselves to people. I had not a clue a spirit of fornication had grabbed hold of me. Unbeknownst to me, this spirit had taken control over my mind, and my body. Neither was I aware the devil is a deceptive liar. Thank God! I know better now!

Again, I tell you, this is why it's imperative for a female's way of thinking to line up with the Word of God. A daily reading of His Word helps to change spiritually destructive ways in which we think. The scales will fall from our eyes allowing our vision to become spiritually clearer. You'll be able to see precisely what's going on around you, as well as what's happening on the inside of you. Gradually, you'll start to see through the darkness living on the inside of you. Spiritual eyes reveal the ugly stuff that keeps you bound. But however, ugly or unsettling it might be, once you begin to *really see* yourself you can then begin to work on freeing yourself by changing what you do not like. The best antidote for progressive change is reading God's Word and allowing it to renew your mind, as well as massage your heart. A constant thought of not being good enough, or always feeling like a failure are slowly replaced by thoughts of being a whole (nothing missing; nothing broken) person. You'll start to believe you are more than able in accomplishing whatsoever you set your will, and mind to do. I learned a very valuable lesson from that relationship in spite of getting my heart broken. It had come to the point where I was tired of pining over a man who obviously had moved on. And you wanna know something? He had every right to do so! Almost a year later I decided to forgive that man. I had to, if I was going to leave what happened in the past. Equally as important, I forgave myself too. I was cordial to him in the presence of our co-workers, but if he and I happened to be coming down the hall at the same time, my eyes would shift in another direction, and I said nothing. But be that as it may, I grew stronger. Life had pretty much returned to normal. Yes, I had forgiven him. But on the off-set chance that his eyes remained on me a second or two too long, memories of what happened crept into my mind. I'd be a liar if I told you being in his presence at work had no affect on me whatsoever. No! On the contrary, there were occasions when I had an urge to bust him up side his head! I still wasn't born again—okay?

Seriously though, reprogramming thoughts, feelings and emotions through God's Word has the potential to bring about change. The Word speaks of leading victorious lives. I don't believe God ever intended for His daughters to live in continual despair (mentally), or experience so much defeat (spiritually). Girlfriend, forget you ever heard the word **can't**. Yes you can! Females in general harbor negative images about themselves, about other females, about their imperfect lives, and so on. I have too! I am far from perfect. If there were a pageant for crowning the Queen of 'Whatmademethinkthat', I'd be wearing a huge diamond stud tiara, okay? I have unflattering thoughts just like you!

Therefore it's vital to our well-being to learn how to stop sabotaging ourselves by operating in old habits that are channeled by distorted mindsets. God speaks truth.

As human beings we want to believe in the Word, but our natural eyes see one thing, while our contaminated minds compute the complete opposite. Self-affliction starts in the head. The mind is the battlefield that you and I must war against everyday. There can be no down time. You can't take the day off. You can't bury your head in the sand when it comes to destroying negative thoughts and behaviors. Sure, people and/or situations may lead to unproductive scenarios in our lives, but there's great news! God says we don't ever have to settle for life *as is*. The Bible clearly provides us with instructions for productive and successful living. All females have the option to choose life or death, curses or blessings, positive results, or negative results.

Deuteronomy 30:19 reads:

"I call heaven and earth to record this day against you, that I have set before you life and death, blessing and cursing; therefore choose life, that both thou and thy seed may live." (KJV)

You and I are faced with making choices everyday. Stop listening to the lies fluttering around inside your head. Choose to accept and believe God's Word—the truth. Focus on all the good qualities you possess. Now granted, a negative image will still try to sneak its way into your thoughts. After all, we're not immune from regressing back now-n-then. However, that can't be used as an excuse, especially when we know right from wrong. Choose to think good thoughts (on purpose) about you. You may not be able to block every negative thought from coming to your mind, but at least you can learn how to pick up the arsenal (The Word) that has been made available for fighting back! The Bible warns against growing weary and fainting in our minds.

Galatians 6:9 reads:

"And let us not be weary in well doing; for in due season we shall reap, if we faint not." (KJV)

You and I have to make conscientious and wise decisions when it comes to winning over the daily war raging in the battlefield of our minds. You'll be in an on-going spiritual fight till you go home to be with the Lord. I don't care how spiritual or religious some females proclaim they are. I repeat. **THE MIND IS A BATTLEFIELD!** It takes a whole *lotta* faith, and just as much courage to defuse negative self-images. You should be on guard at all times because the enemy won't stop dredging up memories from the past, reminding you how you used to be, and lying about how a person can never escape their past. Girlfriend, not only can you escape from it, you've been equipped to overcome it! The enemy wants the past to infiltrate your re-born spirited image. He knows as a child of God, you are valuable! According to the Bible, the enemy is the accuser of the brethren. (Revelation 12:10) One of the characteristics about the devil you'd better recognize is he thoroughly enjoys throwing the past up in our faces. Nevertheless, our Father has a solution—peace.

Isaiah 26:3 reads:

"You will guard him *and* keep him in perfect peace *and* constant peace whose mind [both its inclination and its character] is stayed on You, because he commits himself to You, leans on You, *and* hopes confidently in You." (AMP)

There is nothing like having inner peace or surrounding yourself in a peaceful atmosphere. It didn't matter what I did back-n-da-day while I was sowing my wild irresponsible oats. God *still forgave me.* I could live in peace instead of being tormented by the past. I'm grateful that He's a forgiving God. If He could forgive me of the sins from my youth, surely He will forgive you too. If we allow God to start the process of healing our mind, heart and spirit, we begin to look at the woman in the mirror very differently. By faith you're required to do your part trusting God at His infallible, incorruptible Word.

Aren't you tired of condemning yourself for things you did in the past? Are you uncertain whether the image staring back at you from the mirror might never want to change for the better? If you answered yes, do something for yourself. Take the first step toward victory! Don't waste another minute feeling sorry for yourself. Don't let another day leave you trapped by old habits from the past. Get free! Even if you don't feel any different right away, stick with it! Know in your heart by faith, God is at work to bring restoration to the woman He created you to be. If you can trust God, it will only be a matter of time before you'll be gazing into the confident eyes of a woman feeling more assured of who she is. Read God's Word daily to help renew your mind. Allow His Word to marinate within the walls of your heart where faith resides. Your walk of faith must be deliberate. Through faith, with every step you and I take is a step in the right direction to overcoming years of deceptive and nonproductive self-images. God values all of His children whether male or female. Therefore shouldn't we value ourselves too? Females need to know that they know they are worthy vessels, deserving of God's goodness and His many blessings.

Luke 12:7 reads:

"But even the very hairs of your head are all numbered. Fear not therefore, ye are of more value than many sparrows." (KJV)

Please understand something. The enemy's strategy is to whisper enough lies into our ears while we're young so by the time we reach our teens we believe those lies. He wants to lead young girls off the designated path of their God-ordained destinies. Before they can have a chance to learn about themselves as valuable children of God, or educate themselves with a clear understanding of who He says they are, the enemy is already working behind the scenes. Our mothers might've dragged us to church every Sunday when we were little girls, but probably once most of us became teenagers, we stopped attending. I'm guessing I am not the only one the enemy whispered convincing untruths into their ears. You and I started believing his lies, and thought we were too grown for church. Am I right? I certainly bought into his lies. At sixteen, mommy stopped telling me to lay my church clothes out the night before—grown! Well, I didn't know it at age sixteen, but I'd later learn those negative thoughts and feelings being influenced upon my young fragile mind by the enemy were primarily aimed (on purpose) at keeping me separated from God. The lies and deception was meant to put distance between me and the people (other than my mother) who might've been in a position to

SO, WHO DO YOU THINK YOU ARE

minister to my spirit. In the Book of Proverbs 18:14 it reads:

> "**The spirit of a man will sustain his infirmity; but a wounded (broken) spirit who can bear?**" **(KJV)**

Once the teen years ended and the twenties rolled in, I started taking notice what other people said could sometimes leave me feeling and thinking some crazy stuff! Why? Because, instinctively females have this mechanism built on the inside of them for wanting to keep everybody else happy. I think we suppress our real selves for that very reason. Let me give you a couple of examples: Example (1): You don't agree with what you heard fall out of hubby's mouth. You think it was the dumbest idea he's had thus far. But you'd rather not disagree with him, so you keep silent. You don't want your teenage daughter staring back at you like you're the meanest mother on the planet, so you keep quiet instead of forbidding her to 'hang out' until she's ready to come home from being with friends you don't know. Example (2): You don't want Sista-usher to be irritated with you in church even though you're tired of always sitting directly behind Sista Necey, on the second row blocking your view of the pulpit with her outlandish wide brim hats.

Girlfriend, we have every right to speak up when another person causes our spirit-man to become uncomfortable. Whenever I'm faced with uneasiness—something not setting well within me, I make my feelings known. Grant you, as females probably most of us need to learn when to speak and when not to. But on the other hand, verbalizing personal objections is not always out of line. Neither is speaking up for oneself an indication of being disrespectful, or rude. Speaking up is simply another way of defending your feelings and your convictions in spite of the feelings, actions, opinions, or suggestions of someone else. I think shrinking back from being more comfortable within ourselves opens the door to identity theft.

Using a diplomatic tone, calmly inform hubby you're not going along with what he suggested about giving your teenage daughter more freedom. Tell hubby you disagree that treating her like an adult will make her more responsible. Quite frankly, if you remember how immature you were at her age, then you know there should be limitations and certain boundaries set in place, especially with a female teenager. Now be honest, could you strut up to your mother, introduce new friends then pass her a look like you were daring her not to like them? I seriously doubt it. My mother would've knocked me into the middle of next week! I might not be alive today! If she said she didn't like my friends, guess what? I severed ties quick!

As for Sista-usher, speak to her in your most loving Christian voice as she approaches you next Sunday. "Please do not seat me behind Sista Necey. Her large, bright neon colored, rhinestone hats are a distraction. Every time she jumps to her feet to assist Pastor in preaching his messages, I can't see around her." Smile. Then go seat yourself in another pew where you have a better view of the pulpit.

I think every time we ignore a twinge of resentment (no matter how slight), we do ourselves a disservice. When we say nothing a spirit of offense could easily raise its ugly head. Personally, I don't want to miss anything God has planned and purposed for my life because I've been spiritually blindsided by the enemy using people to do his underhanded dirty work. I don't want negative experiences from the past replaying over and over in my head. Nor do I want unforeseen circumstances to arise that could've been prevented had I spoken up for myself. As a female there are three things to consider. **FIRST,** you have an obligation to be true to yourself. **SECOND,** as an individual, it's up to you to take control over what you allow to pass through your ear-gate. Didn't like what you just heard? Speak up! **THIRD,** it's important to recognize when tactics of the enemy are being aimed directly at your heart to deflate your spirit.

In most cases a poor self image is birthed from wounds of self infliction, or attacks (verbal/physical) imposed by someone else. Sadly, over time these experiences can impoverish our spirit. Much of what occurs during our young years spills over into adulthood. But there's good news! God is available, accessible and willing to restore you and me! He wants to turn our mourning into dancing! (Psalm 30:11) He wants to see you and I living out our days in peace—real peace. (Philippians 4:7)

Psalm 29:11 reads:

"The Lord will give [unyielding and impenetrable] strength to His people; the Lord will bless His people with peace." (AMP)

Girlfriend, confront the woman in the mirror. Make a commitment to her. "From this day forward I will not entertain thoughts of unproductive images! God says I'm His masterpiece! I've been wonderfully made! I believe what God says! There is greatness living on the inside of me!" If you begin speaking words of life (by faith), your heart becomes receptive to what it hears you saying. Those words will become a reality to you. Confessing the Word of truth will take root inside your heart. As the Word feeds your heart you'll flourish spiritually, as well as mentally. Having faith requires doing something. Faith demands taking action. By opening your mouth, rejecting what you've been led to believe all these years gives faith something to work with. Your faith will not only grow stronger (increase spiritually), but it will drown out any untruths. Before long you'll be walking shoulders back, head held high, no longer bound by a poor self-image. Tomorrow morning when you look into the bathroom mirror tell that woman, "We're going to a whole new level in God! Our way of thinking is changing!"

In addition to your new attitude, ask God during your prayer time to enlighten your eyes so you can see the beautiful female He sees. By faith, God will reveal her to you. He'll remove the scales from your eyes that have blurred your vision for far too long. With every passing day, you'll start noticing there's hardly any trace of the old you. How so? Because the new woman smiling back at you from the bathroom mirror is undergoing a spiritual heart transplant! Her mind is being deprogrammed! God is so awesome! Therefore, be encouraged! Stand strong in your faith! Trust God, who is able to provide whatever you have need of. Through clearer, restored, fresh eyes of faith, observe how God is doing a new thing in you, as only He can!

Farrell Ellis

Isaiah 43:19 reads:

"Behold, I am doing a new thing! Now it springs forth; do you not perceive *and* know it *and* will you not give heed to it? I will even make a way in the wilderness and rivers in the desert." (AMP)

I can understand another woman's dilemma when she's not pleased, or unhappy with herself. Unfortunately, this often results in verbalizing things we do not mean. We *think* we mean what we're saying for the time being. I remember my high school days like they were yesterday. Okay—I'm stretching it a little! But there are still a few events that occurred during high school, I can recall to memory. I think that's pretty good considering it's been forty years since I graduated high school. That being said, I'm entitled to have a memory lapse or two, or three. Can I tell you about one of my high school memories? It was my junior year.

I desperately wanted to be a cheerleader! The fact that I had my eye on one of the football players had nothing to do with it. Well, that's not entirely true. I figured if this boy got to see me out on the football field wearing that pleated short skirt, kicking up my cute legs, cheering, clapping, and waving my pom-poms in the air, it just might qualify me for a phone call. Better still, a date! I wasn't the most popular girl in school. Nevertheless, I still wanted my classmates to like me. Some did. Some didn't. That's the way of high school.

Anyway, I had issues with gym. My mother asked, "Farrell, how can you fail gym?" as she looked over my first semester report card. I saw no need to lie. "*Mommy, I hate gym!*" She narrowed her dark brown eyes (like only she could), and didn't blink. "If you bring home another report card with an 'F' from gym, it's going to be you and me! Do you understand?" My shoulders shrunk. "*Yes mommy.*" I gave her my most pitiful look. However, by the time I got upstairs to my room I was already thinking to myself. I'm not going to participate! I didn't care what she said!

SO, WHO DO YOU THINK YOU ARE

Well, on the day of auditions for the junior cheerleading squad, who do you think was conducting try-outs? My gym teacher, whom I'll refer to as Miss. Anonymous was sitting there watching while other hopefuls and me came inside the gymnasium. So what! I didn't care. I wanted to be a cheerleader! I pretty much thought Miss. Anonymous would forgive my non participation in her gym class. Besides, this was different. I was trying out for the cheerleading squad. This had nothing to do with gym class! I couldn't imagine why it should have any bearing on what I wanted. After all, it was no big deal if I preferred to sit on the bleachers twice a week in my school clothes and be a spectator during gym class. Right? With that in mind, I ignored the stares from the other girls there to audition. I paraded myself pass Miss. Anonymous and took a seat on the bleacher to wait my turn. I was excited to show my stuff! I was pumped!

I'd been practicing at home for weeks down in the basement. I secretly dubbed myself the princess of cartwheels. I was a shoe-in for sure!

Needless to say, later that afternoon when I left the gymnasium I was crushed! My heavy heart had nothing to do with getting any of the cheers wrong. I nailed every one of them. Even my cartwheels were performed with precision. Upon my grand entrance inside the gym that afternoon, I felt most confident watching the other girls I was competing against. I sat on the bleachers putting my best face forward (waiting to hear my name) with my chin up. There may be a lot of things that slip my mind about good ole' high school, but I'll never forget the afternoon I tried out for cheerleading. Having a nonchalant attitude taught me a valuable lesson that day. When it came my turn to shine, I opened my mouth giving those cheers everything I had. Afterwards I joined the other girls sitting on the bleachers feeling like I had performed just as good as they had.

I anxiously waited, believing I'd be chosen to join the squad. What I hadn't counted on happening was *who* had the authority to make that decision. Not only did I think Miss. Anonymous got back at me for not suiting up in her gym class, the entire time while I was auditioning she had this smirk on her face! Miss. Anonymous leaned over exchanging whispers with the senior captain and junior squad co-captain who were judging try-outs along with her. Now mind you, these two girls were quite popular. They were a part of junior and senior clicks that included other popular girls who were also cheerleaders. These girls had cute boyfriends who were either football or basketball players.

As I left the gymnasium fighting back tears, it occurred to me why I hadn't been selected to join the junior squad. Outside of being an unpopular girl, I had nothing in common with them. And, I certainly didn't have a boyfriend on the football or the basketball teams. Then I concluded perhaps I wasn't pretty enough to stand along side of them cheering at our school games. I was devastated to say the least. My feelings were hurt! It's my suspicion this sort of thing still persists in the lives of our young daughters, granddaughters and nieces. They probably encounter rejection and embarrassment because their peers judge them according to what they perceive to be as different, or undeserving. That afternoon was a life lesson. I learned if girls think they're the cat's meow, they can make it tough for other girls who aren't.

There are many young girls selling themselves short because of what someone else has said, or might think about them. I realize it's possible what I was thinking following cheerleading try-outs was a slight stretch of my imagination, but I was fifteen. As an adult I know it's highly probable I simply hadn't been chosen to join the junior squad because I hadn't cheered loud enough. There's every possibility my cartwheel was a tad off from being as perfect as I thought it was. But at 15, my teary eyes perceived Miss. Anonymous and her two cohorts had conspired against me because they didn't like me. From the snide looks exchanging between the three of them, I honestly perceived they thought I wasn't worthy of being a cheerleader. Girlfriend, my feelings were hurt!

When I got home from school, naturally, I told mommy I didn't make the squad. One look at my face and she already

SO, WHO DO YOU THINK YOU ARE

knew. Mommy gave me a 'sorry' motherly smile, which started me to crying all over again. But what happened that day turned out to be a good thing. It taught me that in spite of what someone else may think about me, or how they might feel towards me because of what they perceive with the physical eye, is their loss. And, you want to know something? The following morning as Jeannette and I were walking to school that awful feeling of rejection had subsided. When I passed those same two snooty girls in the hall later at school I overheard them snickering, but it didn't bother me.

The night before my mother had given me some wise motherly advice that would stay with me forever. I'd gone to my room earlier than usual. Mommy could see I was still upset. She came into the bedroom and sat down on the edge of my bed. Mommy smiled. "Years from now those same girls are going to look at you differently. You want to know why?" I shook my head fighting back the tears. "Because real beauty isn't what we can see. It's what on the inside that makes someone beautiful. Real beauty shines inside out. Those same girls are going to see you a few years from now and resent the woman you've grown into. Farrell, don't ever let anybody make you feel like you don't matter. Don't ever let someone else make you feel like they're so much better than you are." Those words stuck! When mommy left the bedroom I understood I should never accept the way someone else might try to make me feel about myself. That's why I could go to school the next day with my head held high. Thanks mommy!

No female should be deceived into thinking that she's not good enough because of the misperceptions that are formed by someone else. Instead of accepting what they say as truth, turn what they've said back on them. Take a deep breath. Hold your head up high (don't let'm see you sweat) and girlfriend, prove them wrong! You are someone very meaningful—special in the eyes of God. He loves you! You are His peculiar treasure! Don't coward back from being who He has created you to be! You are a valuable masterpiece! Always value the value that resides on the inside of you!

Chapter Five

You Must Chose to Be Happy

Happy *is* he that *hath* the God of Jacob for his help, whose hope *is* in the Lord his God,

Psalms 146:5 (KJV)

Are you aware that you're blessed to receive another opportunity to implement change in your life every morning the good Lord wakes you from a nights sleep? Let me ask you something. Do you welcome each morning with gratitude? Are you thankful? Well if not, may I suggest you begin embracing the morning? (Lamentations 3:22-23) It's because of God's mercy and His grace that you and I have been blessed to see another day, which He has created. Girlfriend, the alarm on your clock radio doesn't have anything to do with stirring you out of your sleep. While our ears (hearing is the last thing to cease functioning when we die), may hear the alarm going off, it doesn't necessarily mean we will rise up from our bed. Ponder over that for a minute.

Lamentations 3:22-23 reads:

"It is of the Lord's mercies that ye are not consumed, because his compassions fail not. They are new every morning: great is thy faithfulness." (KJV)

I believe it's God's Will that all of His daughters thoroughly enjoy their lives right now—each day. The thing is. I've come to learn we have a choice in how we greet the morning. We can welcome it with joy, by opening our arms wide giving God praise and thanksgiving. Or we can start the day grumpy and miserable. Waking up with an attitude of gratefulness is a choice. As we swing our legs over the side of the bed and place our pretty pedicure feet on the floor, instantly the choice becomes ours. Whether you realize it or not, starting the day off thinking and feeling miserable won't change anything for the better. Personally, if I start my morning off in an irritable mood (for no reason), my mood only gets worse as the morning progresses, especially if I choose to do nothing to pull myself out of it. Truth be told, by allowing negative feelings to have their way, my attitude can stink for the entire day! But what I found out is this. The enemy is glad to oblige our sour moods. He assists us in our mood by increasing a negative thinking pattern. Then our stinking-thinking lasts throughout the rest of our day. We just go from one unproductive thought to another, which ultimately affects the course of our behavior, and not one positive surge of energy can get past that negative thinking and bad attitude.

It's up to us to shake off nasty moods immediately. Don't allow them to follow you around in the morning while you're starting your day. Shake them off and declare in the name of Jesus you're going to have a great, blessed-God day! By the time I finish making my bed, I want moodiness off me! After all, I live alone. I sleep alone. So why should I be waking up in a foul mood anyhow? It's a clear signal the enemy is trying to set me up to have an unproductive day. Girlfriend, tomorrow morning if you should wake up feeling lousy dreading the day before it even gets started, I want you to shake yourself and perhaps ask yourself. "Why am I feeling this way?" It could be for any number of reasons you're feeling moody first thing in the morning because the enemy likes catching you off guard, especially at the start of your day. If you're moody, you're not thinking about giving God praise for waking you up, are you? Difficult situations, other people, close relationships, places of employment, and many other things contribute to how we think and feel. Waking up with a negative mindset is a much bigger picture than what many females are able to discern.

SO, WHO DO YOU THINK YOU ARE

However, it comes as no surprise to God whenever one of His daughters experiences a spiritual melt-down or mental challenge. He understands better than anyone how despair can cause us to feel discouraged, or unhappy. But keep in mind. God never intended for His daughters to feel over burdened or held captive by their emotions. God observes each of us closely (closer than we realize) waiting for you and me to reach out to Him whenever we need help. By faith, we should get to a place of calling upon Him more frequently because God has promised never to leave our side. He'll be there when no one else is. You and I don't have to go through life feeling alone, nor helpless. We've got to recognize a bad attitude for what it really is. These emotions are traps set by the enemy.

Romans 10:11-12 reads:

"The Scripture says, No man who believes in Him [who adheres to, relies on, and trusts in Him] will [ever] be put to shame *or* be disappointed. [No one] for there is no distinction between Jew and Greek. The same Lord is Lord over all [of us] and He generously bestows His riches upon all who call upon Him [in faith]." (AMP)

When your Heavenly Father created you, there wasn't anything omitted that He didn't want left out. You are exactly who God made you to be. But sometimes the mind will deceive a person into believing another person's life is better than their own. I can easily admit it's happened to me a few times. But let me tell you something. Girlfriend, regardless whether the life of another appears to be all that and a bag of lightly salted chips, ***assume not***! Appearances are not always how they seemingly look. More and more since losing loved ones so suddenly, I've learned not to concern myself with what somebody else has, or what they're doing, because life is too short! And life is definitely too short to have my spirit-man in a constant state of discontent, although the enemy would prefer I believe everybody has it going on, except for me! The devil is a liar!

Psalms 37:1 reads:

"Do not fret because of evil men or be envious of those who do wrong." (NIV)

Negatively charged emotions usually stem from insecurities we keep hidden from others. Prime example: We find ourselves having an issue dealing with family, friends, church folk, co-workers, and strangers we pass on the street! That nasty attitude doesn't have anything to do with them. On the contrary, this attitude is demonstrating a lack of self-knowledge. Not understanding and knowing who you are as a child of God keeps the door open for the enemy to come in to steal, kill, and destroy your identity. Let us agree concerning this. Together we're going to express love for ourselves by choosing to embrace each morning from a grateful heart! Will you make this commitment with me? Come on, let's decree it together.

"Starting today I am determined to be the best of who God has created me to be! I am the blessed seed of Abraham! I am blessed and highly favored! I am blessed coming in and blessed going out! I am more than a conqueror! I am the head and not the tail! I am first and not last! I am well able to overcome insecurities because I already have the victory through Jesus Christ, the Anointed One! God is doing a new thing in me, and through me—today! Therefore, I embrace this day with Jesus joy!"

Is it me, or lately does society seem to have grown overly obsessive about beauty and wealth? Somewhere along the way the idea of living the 'good life' got out of control—twisted! As many times as I've gone to the grocery store (my cat eats a lot!), it wasn't until most recently when I began noticing the check out aisles were running over with magazines basically discussing the same topics—who's the most beautiful? What do the rich-n-famous enjoy spending their fortune on? The competitiveness that exists within the fashion/celebrity magazine industry is increasingly creating negative personas and images for most young females. Of late, females under the age of 20 lean toward doing unhealthy things to their bodies trying to look like the top model of the month. Often females are pitted against one another. For example: *Fat v. skinny; weaved hair v. natural hair; youth v. maturity, abstinence v. sexual freedom*, and so on.

SO, WHO DO YOU THINK YOU ARE

Whatever happened to people accepting one another based on integrity and character? Is it any wonder why young girls are growing up way too fast? They're being swayed by glitz and glamour. My guess is many of these young girls probably don't lift a finger to help around the house with chores. How about getting a part time job? Are you serious? This young female millennium generation is looking for easy living at the expense of others—especially their parents!

As Christian women, we should be teaching young girls it's not about being the most popular girl in school. Nor should they expect mommy to buy her all the latest fashions or every new technological gadget. Christian women need to be setting godly examples for young females instead of letting them witness ungodly attitudes associated with carnal behaviors. I think the next generation coming up behind us, are in for more heartache, struggle and disappointment beyond what you or I may have experienced when we were their age. Unfortunately, this generation is running out of time. No doubt, we're living in perilous times. It's the end time. Therefore we need to step up our Christian walk. We must educate ourselves in fully understanding who God says we are. It's important that valuable information be passed on to the next generation. If we're going to teach little girls and adolescent females to love themselves and to be happy with who they are as an individual, it has to start with you and I being proud godly women. Each of us must be comfortable in our skin as Christian women.

The Bible says we have not because we ask not. (James 4:2) I've heard this Scripture used during conversations as well as used as an illustration relating to material things. Okay, maybe so. But couldn't this Scripture also be interpreted in relation to spiritual knowledge and understanding? Is it possible too many of us lack knowing who God says we are because we haven't bothered to ask? Perhaps we've gone to our Father for other things yet, neglect to ask Him for clarity concerning what His Word says about females. I can only speak for my self when I say this, but there are times when I forget I'm not my own property. I belong to God. I'm His property. He's my Heavenly

Father—my divine Creator. Jesus Christ paid a very hefty price for my salvation. I am not my own! (I Corinthians 6:19-20) Jesus was crucified. God raised Him from the grave so that we might live (to the full) and have life (overflowing) abundantly. Seeking God's wisdom in learning why I'm here, and who I am according to His divine Word and purpose should be a priority. Negligence opens the door for the enemy to send havoc into our lives.

John 10:10 reads:

"The thief cometh not, but to steal, and to kill, and to destroy: I am come that they might have life, and that they might have it more abundantly." (KJV)

Girlfriend, it matters little how fly we keep ourselves looking, where we live, what designer clothing we wear, or how far we've gone in our education. If we fail to fully grasp hold of, or comprehend the depth of God's love, I think we can miss the mark on being truly happy. More and more I understand everything should begin with the Word of God. In the beginning, this planet came into existence because God spoke out what He envisioned for creating a family. (Genesis 1:1) That Scripture couldn't be simpler. To see change, one must speak change (by faith) before they *see* anything.

One of the greatest assets God provided mankind is the ability to speak. Whether we're speaking up for ourselves or against ourselves, there is power in the mouth. Our words can either delay or speed up the results we desire to see come to pass. Therefore, you and I should learn to discern whether our mind and eyes are trying to pull a fast one over on us when certain things occur. The enemy can have us thinking some of the weirdest stuff not only about ourselves, but about other people too, especially other females. It's his attempt to dim our eyesight and trash our minds. He doesn't want any of us to know our true identities.

I think a vast majority of ill feelings females have towards themselves (low self-esteem, lack of self-worth, no self-acceptance) don't have to dominate their lives when God is but a Scripture or prayer away.

Psalm 119:33 reads:

"Order my steps in thy word; and let not any iniquity have dominion over me." (KJV)

Maybe it's safe to say most of us have believed untruths. Unconsciously the enemy was permitted to get away with whispering all sorts of lies into our ears. But get ready! Get ready! The time has arrived to shake ourselves loose from the ways we've been thinking! It's time to destroy negative behaviors that inflict harm upon us mentally as well as spiritually. Females must *choose* to educate their minds in the things of God. If you possess strong faith built upon God's Word, you will receive spiritual strength. It's going to take the God-kind of strength to see changes manifest for our well-being. But that won't happen until we know, that we know we're completely happy being our true selves.

God doesn't want His daughters walking around feeling defeated from the weight of a woe-is-me spirit hanging about their necks. No! He wants us enjoying each day—making the most of everyday! You have God's grace (unmerited favor) to live for today. While tomorrow hasn't been promised, you can surely take advantage of what God has given you today. One of the most thankful ways you can express out of an appreciative heart is by expressing joy for the precious time you've been allotted.

Psalm 42:11 reads:

"Why are you downcast, O my soul? Why so disturbed within me? Put your hope in God, for I will yet praise him, my Savior and my God." (NIV)

If you're always worrying about tomorrow, and what's going to happen if things don't work out, or what's to become of you if a particular situation doesn't resolve itself according to your plan, you can miss what's happening today—right now. But I won't pretend I've always thought like this. While I say this to you, I'm speaking to Farrell too. With certainty, all of us make plans for the future. We set goals we'd like to achieve. We have visions of brighter days ahead, and dream of seeing those visions come to fruition. Well, we do this because we're supposed to dream and plan for a productive future.

Females who lack vision or don't dream, are merely existing. Each one of us needs aspirations, visions, goals, and dreams. They offer hope. They give us something to get excited about. Visions keep us looking forward instead of constantly turning, looking behind us. However, while trying to achieve these things, we mustn't forget to appreciate what we have today. Embrace the moment—the now. I don't know about you, but once my day comes to an end, I can't get it back. But if you can, please go to my website www.gbydfarrellellis.com because I want details on how you're able to do this!

Girlfriend, greet tomorrow morning as a new beginning—a fresh opportunity. Life is too short not to try your best to enjoy every day the good Lord sends. Today is what you have right now! Live it! Discover your utmost joy living for today!

Psalms 118:24 reads:

"This is the day which the Lord has brought about; we will rejoice and be glad in it." (AMP)

Dare I mention this again? Seeking happiness is a personal decision. Quite frankly, I think acquiring peace, joy, love and happiness is more of a mindset than an emotion, or feeling. If you stop to reason, other people *really* don't make us happy. They do, but they don't. How can I say this? People actually aren't the source to obtaining joy and happiness. Jesus is. He is the way to receiving and keeping true joy in our hearts and spirits.

SO, WHO DO YOU THINK YOU ARE

John 15:11 reads:

"These things have I spoken unto you, that my joy might remain in you and that your joy might be full." (KJV)

Probably every female reading this book has fallen in love at one time or another. You could be in love right now. Isn't it something how for a while that man can make us feel special and as giddy as a school girl? But when the newness starts wearing off, we usually fall back to where we were before Mr. Makesmesohappy came along. We allow negative feelings accompanied by unproductive thoughts to begin to creep into the relationship. All of a sudden Mr. Makesmesohappy can no longer do anything right! He stops saying the words that used to make us happy. Am I right about it? It's basically the same scenario with material things. We're just as thrilled as we can be when we first buy a new dress. But once we've worn that dress a couple of times, it just doesn't quite do it for us anymore. Like clock work, the monthly credit card statement arrives in the mail to pay for that temporary moment of happiness. Then you really aren't smiling like you did on the day you were happy to say, "Charge it!" Do you see where I'm going? Girlfriend, lasting joy won't be found in other people. Joy isn't accessible through material things. Unfortunately, the world's idea of joy is fleeting. It's only temporary. Real joy is sustained by getting in touch with our spirit. The true you (your spirit-man) will bring a far greater reward of joy, peace love and happiness than you could ever imagine. Why not get to know the real you? Introduce yourself to the woman in the bathroom mirror. She won't judge. She will accept you as is. She's waiting to become your friend.

I'm learning the enemy can't steal my joy unless I let him. Now, I want to ask you something. Would you intentionally leave the front door to your home standing wide open when you left for work, knowing full well when you return home most (if not all) of your belongings are likely to be gone? I doubt it! So why is it that we leave the door to our mind open for all kinds of negative thoughts to enter in, giving them permission to rob us blind of our joy? Why is that? I'm just asking.

I'm speaking for myself when I say this. Over the years a large majority of what I've learned, or was taught from a child became second nature. I was taught to lock the front door behind me whenever I left the house. Yet, no one taught me how I could protect myself from intrusive thoughts and images gaining access to my mind. In my failure to discern the schemes of the enemy, I continued to face one hardship after another. The bottom line is this. The enemy doesn't want you or me to experience real happiness in the Lord. No way! What the enemy wants to do is hold us hostage, functioning out of a manic depressive state of mind. That being said, the first thing every female had better know (unequivocally) and recognize (beyond a shadow of doubt), is that the devil is a liar! We're not without options—glory to God! We can choose to lead happy, fulfilled, whole lives allowing God's Word to flow within us by educating ourselves. The Bible holds the answers for attaining true joy—God's kind of joy—soul passionate joy!

Jeremiah 15:15 reads:

"Your words were found, and I ate them; and Your words were to me a joy and the rejoicing of my heart, for I am called by Your name, O Lord of Hosts." (AMP)

I believe seeking the kind of joy that is available once our minds are disciplined to maintain a good attitude the second we wake in the morning, until we return to our bed at night can be conquered! I realize endeavoring (by faith) to maintain a joyful attitude, regardless of what may be going on around us isn't easy. I've been there a time or two or three… Nevertheless, anything worth having is worth fighting for! Christian women, ought to be willing to roll up their sleeves, ready to fight for what God has said is available to them, and for them. The Word says the battle is the Lord's, but that doesn't mean we can't get into a shoving match with the enemy and his cohorts when we see what they're up to. Don't kid yourself. There will be times when we're going to have to get into the fight for our Kingdom inheritance. The devil comes prepared, armed for a fight. He's determined to make sure that we never receive it! You and I are not without the ability to discipline ourselves to be happy.

SO, WHO DO YOU THINK YOU ARE

Things I can change about myself I do, but that which I can't (a stronghold), I pray asking God to do what I cannot do on my own. Girlfriend, if necessary, put the power of persuasion into play. Wear a smile on your face, even though you may not feel like smiling. Stand with both feet planted securely on the ground. Hold your head high (by faith), trusting and believing God is working in you regardless if you don't feel any different. (Psalm 3:3)

Make a daily declaration to maintain a good and positive attitude on purpose. Remember, a bad attitude doesn't produce positive change. A nasty attitude stunts the development of faith. A negative attitude stifles trust. I think a bad attitude runs contaminated interference for believing God's Word is true. Like you, I too understand we live in an imperfect world, which means challenges and problems are apt to occur. That's life. The Bible speaks about trials, tests, and tribulations. Therefore, how can we think we'll escape them? However, while that may be true, we still don't have to allow problems or circumstances to manipulate us. Remember the number one rule to the change factor is this: **WITH GOD, ALL THINGS ARE POSSIBLE!**

There isn't one married female who is immune from facing marital problems. No mother is exempt from her children rebelling. Lots of females work at jobs they hate. Young single women will grow older and live alone. Females who are dating will experience problematic relationships. A 50-something female will deal with hubby going through a mid-life crisis. There are going to be times of financial lack, and the list goes on. As a matter of fact, I'll take this a step further. I bet every woman reading this book has experienced one of those scenarios at one time or another. You very well could be going through one of them right now. All across the country there are females who are possibly involved in turbulent, violent relationships. There's a woman somewhere up to her pierced ears in financial debt with no idea where the money is coming from to pay her creditors. Some females have never been married. They grapple with trying to understand why they haven't found a man, or why men don't find them attractive. There are women who are married, but don't know what it's like to receive a compliment from their husband. Some wives feel unappreciated. I even suspect there's a woman constantly being ridiculed like a small child by an overbearing husband. Perhaps you're involved with a boyfriend who uses manipulation as a means of keeping you in check—controlling you. And, I can't begin to tell you the number of sexually abused females who silently struggle with self-love because they can't stop blaming themselves. But if it's any consolation, I don't want any of these women to think it strange what they're going through. Meaning, you're not the first, nor will you be the last. The Bible speaks of this very thing.

I Peter 4:12 reads:

"Dear friends, do not be surprised at the painful trial you are suffering, as though something strange were happening to you." (NIV)

Somewhere out there is another female who can relate to your situation. She is going through it too even if your problem might differ, however so slight. The difference being, if the other female doesn't believe God loves her, or Jesus is the answer, she might not survive her ordeal. There are too many instances to point out that contribute to the ways females think, feel, and behave as adult women. That's why I'm thankful our God is a loving God. He's a forgiving God. He's a mighty, mighty good God! Can I get an Amen? Girlfriend, dry your eyes. Stop wringing your hands in despair. God promised they who sow in tears shall reap in joy! (Psalm 126:5) He promised to give us beauty (restoration) for ashes (hardships). We can rely on His promise to bestow garments of praise for a heavy spirit. I'm telling you there isn't anything our God can't fix! He can take brokenness and transform it into wholeness—wellness. God's Word can increase you spiritually as well as replenish you mentally. God is able to restore the mind, spirit, soul, and body. He wants to give his daughters life filled with His joy; the kind of joy that no man or woman can take away; the kind of joy that can't be spoiled by today's problems and situations. By faith, you and I have to believe God is able!

SO, WHO DO YOU THINK YOU ARE

Isaiah 61:3 reads:

"To grant [consolation and joy] to those who mourn in Zion; to give them an ornament (a garment of diadem) of beauty instead of ashes, the oil of joy instead of mourning, the garment [expressive] of praise instead of a heavy, burdened, *and* failing spirit—that they may be called oaks of righteousness [lofty, strong. And magnified, distinguished for uprightness, justice, and right standing with God], the planting of the Lord, that He may be glorified." (AMP)

Yes, God will do the fixing, but He expects us to be doing something while we're under spiritual construction. I think during this transformation it should also be a time for sharing what's going on in our life. In other words, when we recognize God is doing a new work—a better work in us, sometimes we shouldn't keep it to ourselves, especially if we know of another female who is being challenged in the same area. We shouldn't act like since we're being delivered, now we have it all together. No, it's not always about us. Let another woman know you understand her plight. Show her some empathy. Express to her that you've been going through the same thing; talk to her about it. Together the two of you can combine your faith in a prayer of agreement that both of you (by faith) are coming through this temporary hardship (trial) victoriously! Perhaps the two of you could fast together. Set a designated time you can pray together. Join forces! Become each other's allies in recovery and restoration! Together the two of you can help each other to demolish the walls of defeat!

Leviticus 26:6-8 reads:

"I will grant peace in the land, and you will lie down and no one will make you afraid. I will remove savage beasts from the land, and the sword will not pass through your country. You will pursue your enemies, and they will fall by the sword before you. Five of you will chase a hundred, and a hundred of you will chase ten thousand, and your enemies will fall by the sword before you." (NIV)

Inform another female how God delivered you out of a negative situation for the better in your life. Share how He removed feelings of anxiety and misery. Testify as to how reading God's Word has reprogrammed the way you think. The Word instructs us to share trials of misfortune with one another. In doing so, it brings a cleansing (healing) and restoration (from brokenness) to our spirit. Any woman who wants God to help her, but once she's delivered, won't share her victory with another female is selfish, especially when someone she knows is experiencing the same kind of a problem. Well, here's a newsflash! Girlfriend, your deliverance isn't about you! What He did for you was for His glory—not yours! Did you think He healed you everywhere you were hurting just so you could keep silent? We're supposed to be examples that the Word of God works! He wants to use us as living testimonies! *All* the glory belongs to God! Whew! I don't know where that came from, but sometimes my fingers take on a life of their own across the computer keyboard! Let's move on, shall we?

Most every female will experience awful circumstances and situations they might not understand. The truth is. They may never understand why. Nevertheless, when trials come along joy is normally the furthest thing from our mind. Let's be real—okay? Do you want to know a fact of life? No matter how difficult or crazy that situation might appear to us, there's always going to be another female somewhere who would gladly trade places. I can probably count on one hand the number of females who haven't encountered problems. That's a fact. Some are probably worse than others. This too is a fact. So how do we rise above problems when they present negative feelings, thoughts and attitudes? We learn to overcome them by tearing problems down with the Word of God (our sword) one day at a time. It's going to take a while to untangle and dismantle all that junk you've been carrying around all these years. You're not going to instantly change overnight just because you read a few Scriptures from your Bible. Change insists on diligence, commitment and a lot of hard work!

SO, WHO DO YOU THINK YOU ARE

In the meantime try practicing patience. This way you won't beat yourself up. If you still notice a few old habits rearing their ugly heads, remember change takes time. You have to allow yourself a little leniency. Those behavioral patterns that have been part of your character for all these years deserve the necessary time to be corrected. Can I let you in on something? Whenever, we have joy in God, the enemy goes nuts! He can't stand it! Who are we to be happy in the midst of a raging storm? The enemy realizes he's losing the battle. As we grow stronger spiritually, he can no longer make us feel sorry for ourselves, depressed or thinking we're losers. Girlfriend, I encourage you to kick'em in the gut! While you're giving God praises of joy, turn up the volume! As a born again Believer, you must take full responsibility for operating (by faith) with an attitude of joy.

I'd like to share a quick testimony with you. During the winter of 2009, I lost my joy. It was so bad I barely wanted to get out of bed. It wasn't so much that the winter temps were brutally cold as much as I felt like the life was literally being sucked out of me. For days I lingered over why I was feeling this way. I even went to the woman in the bathroom mirror, but one look into her eyes told me all I needed to know. It was obvious she was in no shape to help me. She looked like I felt—emotionally drained. I couldn't understand what was happening to me. It would've made perfect sense if I had a case of the flu, or I was dealing with a nasty cold. However, I knew I needed to get to the root of this issue, and be quick about it.

Once my joy was gone, I moved about like a spiritually depleted robot. I'd attend church Wednesday nights for Bible study, and again faithfully on Sundays. Regrettably my heart wasn't in it. The Word coming forth from my Pastor was not sustaining. Every Sunday following service, by the time I reached my car in the parking lot my mind had already retreated to the bedroom for the remainder of the day. I wanted to be left alone. It was rather easy for me to place the blame for these lousy feelings on the winter weather. After all, gotta blame some one or some thing—right?

Farrell Ellis

Maybe I should explain what led up to this. Following what had been a nice way to end year 2008 surrounded by family and close friends, I sank into a mild case of depression. A qualified doctor would probably disagree with my self prognosis, but it's my story, and I'm sticking to it. My joy was gone. It moved without giving any notice. In joy's absence, I managed to smile on the outside, but inside I was absolutely miserable! I had no desire to pray. I certainly wasn't in any mood to read God's Word. So you know what? I didn't do either! When I returned home from work in the evenings, I did the exact same thing I'd done the previous evening. My routine consisted of changing out of my work clothes, washing the makeup off my face, preparing dinner (or not), and sitting in the middle of my black wrought iron canopy bed clutching the TV remote and channel surfing. I didn't have the energy to do anything else. Don't you feel sorry for me just hearing this?

Spiritually these mixed emotions of negativity were draining. Then one night out of nowhere it struck me. I hadn't begun to feel this way until Jeannette left to return home to Atlanta. Bless her heart she came up from Atlanta the week before Thanksgiving to stay with me. I was thrilled, considering I had recently lost my mother that summer. During one of our prior phone conversations I was able to admit to Jeannette that I wasn't sure how I was going to handle the upcoming holidays. It had been ten years since I had actually lived alone. Seven of those years I was married. The other three years mommy and I lived together. So once she was gone I had to adapt to living alone all over again. Unlike in the past, living alone had been my decision. This time it was quite different. I hadn't recognized anger was cohabitating with grief. I figured I was coping with mommy's death pretty well. Needless to say, by the time the phone conversation ended between Jeannette and me two hours later, Jeannette was coming to spend a month with me. She and I have shared a lot of ups-n-downs throughout our 40+years of friendship. I'll forever be grateful for what Jeannette did. She literally put her life on hold, though I'd do the same for her in a *New York* minute! Meanwhile, I was happy as a clam. My dearest, life-long friend whom I love like a sister was coming to spend the holidays!

After Jeannette returned home I didn't want to get out of bed. Things got so bad that I had to force myself to leave the house to go to work. I was in a mental and spiritual rut. Then something happened. Ironically I was scheduled to have oral surgery in the month of February. I would need to be out of work for a couple of days following the procedure. I know this is going to sound weird, but I was looking forward to the surgery just so I wouldn't have to leave the house for a few days. At least this provided me with a legitimate excuse to stay shut in.

Prior to the days leading up to oral surgery, I asked God. "*What's going on?*" Well, God didn't answer. Still, it didn't stop me from asking Him again. At this particular moment in life I should've been deliriously happy. My first book was weeks away from going to the final print. But I wasn't. I should've been especially happy that my dream to become a published author had finally come true. But I wasn't. Girlfriend, when I say I was miserable, I mean miserable in the worse sort of way! The book wasn't important! Not to mention, keeping up the façade that I was okay when it was becoming much harder to do. My spirit level was very low. It was undernourished from a lack of being fed the Word. And, my mind was all over the place! I kept having one dumb unproductive thought after another. Yes, I said dumb! Whenever what I'm thinking isn't constructive, those thoughts become idle, and meaningless. It seems all I could focus on practically 24/7 was the fact I couldn't wait to get back in bed. That's dumb thinking! There were plenty of productive things (like praying) I could've been doing with my time. I know myself well enough to know when I'm not myself. The devil doesn't have to lift a finger. He just sits back watching me do self-sabotage. One of the things I've come to learn in my Christian walk is this. Not every bad or unfortunate episode we experience in life automatically is an indication the devil has his hands in it. Let's be honest. Often there are instances we bring hardship upon ourselves. But that's a whole other subject.

Following the surgery my time at home alone sitting around with an ice pack pressed against my swollen face couldn't have come at a more appropriate time. On the third day of being shut-in, the Holy Spirit revealed what was taking place within my heart. "Joy has a difficult assignment to fulfill when it's not welcomed." WOW! HELLO! Suddenly the light bulb came on! *I didn't want to be joyful.* Somehow I had pushed joy away. The Holy Spirit also informed me unconsciously I was feeling guilty for having enjoyed the holidays without my mother. I quietly laid across the bed recuperating, attempting to rewind the past few weeks in my mind.

My sister Renee and I decided she'd have Thanksgiving diner at her house. For as long as she and I could remember, mommy always cooked for Thanksgiving. Jeannette and I volunteered to prepare all the trimmings. Renee cooked her first turkey, which I might add was absolutely scrumptious! Mommy would've been very proud of her baby girl! I don't do turkey. I eat it, but I've never cooked a turkey in my life! I think I do better cooking the other foods that go with serving turkey. Anyway, the week after Thanksgiving I was faced with mommy's birthday. December fourth came on Friday the calendar year of 2008. I had to work, so it helped to make the day less painful, even though I did think about her off-n-on throughout the course of the day.

Then Christmas came. I excitedly shopped with Jeannette and Monica. We visited the local mall buying gifts in one store after another. The three of us started cutting up like we were kids. Variations of Christmas music played inside each of the crowded stores as we laughed, enjoying the gleeful atmosphere of the approaching holiday. I bought plenty of food for Christmas dinner (mommy always cooked Christmas dinner) in preparation for sharing the day with our dear friend, Monica and my younger brother Avery. Naturally, the four of us over ate, but eating heavily goes hand-n-hand with the holiday—right? Afterward we exchanged gifts, laughed a lot and shared our fondest memories of past Christmases with family members who have passed away.

SO, WHO DO YOU THINK YOU ARE

It had been a blessed and beautiful day. I was happy! I got through it. Then New Years rolled around. It was January second. The next day Jeannette would board a plane for home. It was time to return to her life in Atlanta. She'd been living at my house for six weeks. Yet, I selfishly didn't want her to go, but I said nothing. What a true friend! I was going to miss having her around—a lot! But it wasn't until a couple of weeks later after Jeannette had gone home when I began experiencing feelings of uselessness.

I'm sharing this because I want you to really understand how taking possession of joy and happiness must become a choice. It's imperative to your well-being that you learn to discipline yourself to think inspiring, encouraging, motivating thoughts. I'm not ashamed to admit. My attitude stunk! And, you know what? I wasn't happy because I had chosen misery instead. However unconventional it might seem, having oral surgery brought me back to my senses. I believe God has a sense of humor! Not only that, my pastor also mandated a corporate 21-day fast, which started a couple of days prior to the surgery. Meanwhile, on day three of being home from work I found myself wanting to read God's Word. I wanted to give God praise. I had an urge to sing praises of gratitude to Him. I even felt like praying. I could feel my old self slowly reviving itself. I began feeling refreshed—rejuvenated! God has His own methods of getting through to our thick skulls. Or should I say my thick skull. The thing is, I don't want to have such a hard head that it becomes difficult for the Holy Spirit to relay a word of wisdom to me.

Well, since that time I've learned it's important that we pay close attention to emotional red flags when they start waving back at us. I figure those flags are there to alert me a potential problem may lurk ahead, should it go unchecked. Therefore, whenever you notice you're not functioning in a positive state of mind, that's probably an indication (red flag) you need to address the issue. Should that be the case, ask yourself a few simple questions: Why am I suddenly feeling this way? When did I start feeling like this? What can I do to get my joy back?

The enemy doesn't want you to be happy or joyful in the Lord. Please remember that. The longer we ignore those red flags, the more ammunition we give to the enemy. He takes satisfaction in knowing he's got the upper hand. But the devil is a liar! On the other hand, the devil may not have anything to do with your present situation. Unknowingly, you could have invited a spirit of sabotage upon yourself without realizing what you've done. This is why we must consistently pray in spite of how we feel so that God can shine light in our dark places.

You have a right to be happy here in the earth, enjoying life to the fullest because you are a daughter of Almighty God. A female's attitude greatly revolves around feelings, emotions, and her thoughts. How we handle them can either shut down negativity or prolong productivity. Constantly complaining solves nothing. Always pointing the finger resolves nothing. Not recognizing there is possibly an inner problem, is a problem. Regardless whether we bring these miserable feelings on ourselves, I still think when the enemy sees an opening, no matter how slight, he will eventually get involved. The enemy will use any means necessary to keep you and me off balanced and disheveled.

The first couple of wintry months in 2009 are a prime example of giving place to the enemy. The enemy knows I'm not a fan of cold weather. What better time to aid me in my lousy mood than winter? I say assist, because my woe-is-me moment wasn't all the enemy's doing. He did have a hand in planting the idea of me not wanting to leave the house. Nevertheless, I still had a choice. I didn't have to entertain his suggestion. This was my decision. I chose to feel sorry for myself. I wasn't naïve. I knew the enemy will use every opportunity he can to plant negative seeds in the mind of a Believer. But too many of us walk around powerless instead of whipping out our sword (God's Word) so that we're able to slay those thoughts by opening our mouths! Saying what God's Word says is more than enough to strike back against whatever might try to attack us first! Regardless whether we come under attack in the mind, or the body, you and I have to hold fast to the truth of God!

SO, WHO DO YOU THINK YOU ARE

Psalm 37:31 reads:

"The law of his God is in his heart; none of his steps shall slide." (AMP)

Girlfriend, it doesn't matter what anyone of us might have to endure in life. Never forget. God is still in control! You're not going to understand everything that happens to you, or why. But have you ever stopped to consider God may be doing a new thing in you by allowing you to experience sudden discomfort? Have you considered it could be His way of forcing you to step up, or step away from complacency, or remove yourself from certain associations? Have you bothered to ask Him if a season has drawn to an end? If not, may I suggest you read the Book of Job? Besides, I don't think we have to always try to prove how intelligent we are by trying to solve all of our problems. Actually I think it just goes to show how merciful God is to forgive ignorance by thinking we're the only one who can resolve these problems on our own. I think one of the best ways to demonstrate intelligence is by trusting God will always know far better than we ever could!

Before I bring this chapter to an end, there's one other area I'd like to mention. By the way, 2009 did get better. It was a very good year! Praise God! Now you may wonder why I'm bringing up mediocrity, but I want to show you how mediocrity ties in with making a decision to seek happiness. First, let's clear up a misconception. Living paycheck-to-paycheck, or frequently feeling like what you have now is about all you're ever going to get, isn't God's Will. Living below God's ways and means for you is apt to steal your joy. Living a mediocre lifestyle is the enemy's way of keeping you from possessing joy in the Lord. Another thing too, whenever we're unhappy the people we come in contact with can usually detect what we're feeling. It's called human nature. You won't have to open your mouth. Your emotions of despair will show on your face. I've also found that negative driven feelings spill over into ones physical appearance.

Pause here for a minute. Can you honestly say you *feel like* getting all dolled up when you're in a miserable frame of mind? I know I don't! Bad feelings cause us to experience spiritual, mental and physical fatigue. Regardless how hard a female might try concealing bad feelings, they're likely to be exposed on her face and in her demeanor. On the flip side, much like a negative attitude, a positive attitude is also visible to others. When you're happy, and filled with Jesus-joy, smiling comes naturally, doesn't it? Your demeanor exhibits the joy residing on the inside of you. I'll admit. Sometimes adult life can be stagnant or routine. Most of us probably do the same things habitually day after day. Nonetheless, I think one of the keys to maintaining joy is by not allowing ourselves to become too comfortable. Boredom is a hindrance to obtaining joy. I'm gonna say that again. **BOREDOM IS A HINDRANCE!** I seriously doubt there's a female on this planet who hasn't gotten bored with some one or some thing at some point in her life. Surely you didn't think you were the first female to get bored—did you?

      Frankly speaking, I bore somewhat easily. From time-to-time I get bored on my job. I get bored watching TV. I've grown bored with a car not long after buying it, and so on. Okay. Maybe you don't get bored. But when I do find myself getting bored, I make this strange sounding sigh. Then I go from sighing to mumbling and complaining under my breath. Boring moments rob me of my joy. Therefore, I'm careful not to let dullness invade my space for too long. I look for productive ways to snap me out of boredom so that my time isn't wasted doing nothing and there by robbed of my joy.

      Everyday is meant to be embraced with joy! Try greeting each morning with exuberance. Learn to motivate yourself by speaking positive words to the woman in the bathroom mirror. Get into a habit of speaking into your spirit before leaving the house in the morning. Girlfriend, look up encouraging Scriptures. Write them down and tape them in a place where you'll see them everyday and say them aloud. I have faith confessions, declarations and Scriptures taped on the walls of my bathroom that I read aloud while I'm dressing for work. Starting tomorrow why not invite joy to come along with you? Granted, you're not always going to have something fabulous or exciting happening in your life that will warrant gleeful joy, but you can *still be joyful in the Lord* starting with the fact He woke you up this morning! That in itself is something to be more than joyful about! The best thing you and I can do each day is try our best to find joy even in the midst of a storm. Choose to make yourself happy in spite of what may be taking place around you. Exercising bad attitudes or demonstrating nasty behavior toward innocent people doesn't help change one single thing—nadda not one thing!

Whether you're in need of a spiritual make-over, an attitude adjustment or a renewing of the mind, first and foremost you must determine within yourself that you *want* to make inward changes for the better. In other words, you have to **want to** do this for you, and only you! Inner change can usher in favorable advantages. As you begin demanding (verbally) to have more peace and joy, your words will transform negative images and/or attitudes. You'll look differently at yourself. Your life will reflect itself with a whole new perspective. Everything about you will begin to look brighter! Areas in your character that seemed impossible are now being transformed (spiritually) through the renewing of your mind.

If you've ever had a goal, a vision, or a dream, you will need to maintain a high level of enthusiasm. I want to challenge you. The next time you find yourself in the company of someone who expresses one negative sentence after another—run! Please stop giving negative people (talking to myself too) permission to bring you down. Stop accepting what *they* say, or how *they* feel about you. Who are *they* anyhow? Don't allow anyone to prophesy strong winds and torrential rains over your future! It's not God's Will for you to go through life miserable. The enemy is lying when he whispers there's no hope. The truth isn't in him! God wants to bless you with the desires of your heart. He wants all of His daughters to joyously live in divine health filled with love, peace, and prosperity.

III John 2 reads:

"Beloved, I pray that you may prosper in every way and [that your body] may keep well, even as [I know] your soul keeps well and prospers." (AMP)

You can best believe that when God steps in the midst of situations and circumstances (by faith) you're going to receive wisdom unlike ever before. Along with wisdom you'll experience an unexplainable kind of joy. Make a conscientious decision to be happy with yourself. Discover the joy in knowing who you are, and to whose you belong. Tomorrow morning greet the woman looking back at you from the bathroom mirror with a big smile. Tell her, "We're going to have a blessed and joyful day!" And mean it when you say it!

When it's all said and done, each of us must learn how to trust God, even in the hard places. Use the lemons in life to make lemonade. Be happy with who God has created you to be! Adapt to living the best of the life you have right now, and be joyous about it! None of us can predict what tomorrow will or won't bring, but we can be confident knowing that no matter what does or doesn't happen tomorrow, **GOD IS STILL IN CONTROL!** He gave us a promise. God will not allow any female to suffer beyond what she can bear. (I Peter 5:10) You deserve to be at peace, living in joy!

James 5:11 reads:

"As you know, we consider blessed those who have persevered. You have heard of Job's perseverance and have seen what the Lord finally brought about. The Lord is full of compassion and mercy." (AMP)

I'm thankful to the Holy Spirit for bringing the root of my miserable mood to light. He opened my heart to receive a clear understanding of unconscious guilt that was causing me to feel I didn't deserve to enjoy spending the holidays with those I love because mommy wasn't there to share in it with me. The truth is, I know my mother does not want me to be unhappy. Let me end this chapter by saying esteem to become the kind of female that when your feet touch the floor each morning, the

SO, WHO DO YOU THINK YOU ARE

enemy says, "Oh no! She's up!" Girlfriend, go take your joy back!

Chapter Six

Female Acquaintances (Friendships and Relationships)

God's Spirit makes us loving, happy, peaceful, patient, kind, good, faithful, gentle, and self-controlled

Galatians 5:22-23(CEV)

Are you a people pleaser? Do you show more concern for what people think of you, and about you? Can you in all honesty say that your relationship with family, friends and acquaintances are strong, good and healthy relationships? Do you knowingly use manipulation as a means of control over others? Are you in the habit of taking advantage of another's good nature? Strangely enough, some of our actions can easily go undetected in relation to the agendas behind our thoughts and feelings. Seldom do many females consider how much, and often others play influential roles in their daily lives, especially when it affects the image they have of themselves. The more frequently we nurture our spirit by reading the Word of God, the more we will begin to see ourselves in God's Word. Developing a spiritually healthy mindset is very important for inward change.

James 1:22-24 reads:

> "But be doers of the Word [obey the message], and not merely listeners to it, betraying yourselves [into reasoning

> contrary to the Truth]. For if anyone only listens to the Word without obeying it *and* being a doer of it, he is like a man who looks carefully at his [own] natural face in a mirror. For he thoughtfully observes himself, and then goes off and promptly forgets what he was like." (AMP)

In other words, when you and I gaze into the mirror, the female staring back at us will either survive in this big ole' world, or she's going to get lost in the shuffle. It's as simple as that. But there again, we have choices. **Life is choice driven.** Whether you know it or not, everything you need is neatly tucked away on the inside of you for leading a rich (spiritual/mental) and self-rewarding lifestyle. Our Heavenly Father has equipped each one of us with visions and dreams. God's dreams for His children are filled with spiritual insight and the potential in finding prosperity, as well as receiving joy throughout the process. One of the things that helped me in overcoming fear is to remind myself, I am the daughter of Almighty God! There is greatness built on the inside of every female! Never forget that! God created you with the capacity for achieving success in every area of your life. Nothing was done by osmosis when He put you together. We're told in Psalm 119:73, God's hands made and fashioned us. (Emphasis is added)

I believe what I John 4:4 reads:

> "Children, you belong to God, and you have defeated these enemies. God's spirit is in you and is more powerful than the one that is in the world." (CEV)

Far too often most females think they *need* to rely upon others. This is a half truth. Yes, we need one another. But there are some females who take needing to the extreme. And, I say this in love. Whenever she has a need, regardless how big or small, before she'll try to handle her business, she reaches for the cell phone. As Believers, we should learn to rely more heavily upon God for His help. Then sit still long enough to listen to Him tell us how to do it, instead of imposing upon someone else as a means to a quick-fix. Guidance from God can assist you in making the right decisions and better choices in situations.

SO, WHO DO YOU THINK YOU ARE

Girlfriend, I know you may not want to hear this, but people are not your source for everything. God is! He should be your every thing! Allow Him to be your Jehovah Jireh! (Genesis 22:1-14) I'm pretty sure God understands the needs of His children. If He didn't, how could He make a way of provision to handle those needs? He knows, and like a good father, He's a provider. However, you and I have to stop relying on people so much until they become a crutch. There's no reason (according to God's Word), why we can't stand on our own.

Ephesians 6:13-15 reads:

"Therefore put on the full armor of God, so that when the day of evil comes, you may be able to stand your ground, and after you have done everything, to stand, stand firm then, with the belt of truth buckled around your waist, with the breastplate of righteousness in place, and with your feet fitted with the readiness that comes from the gospel of peace." (NIV)

Please don't misunderstand. There is nothing wrong with asking for sound advice or tangible help on occasion. But when these needs become more of an obligation placed upon another person, then the generosity of others gets twisted. Constantly expecting family members or friends to bail us out of difficult situations, or expecting them to be available at our every beck-n-call is an indication that we need to check ourselves. We shouldn't assume people are readily accessible to help us, especially if the situation is grave. Often it's during some of the most pressing moments when our level of faith needs to rise above the circumstance. I think you and I have to get to a place (spiritually) within ourselves where we know beyond any shadow of doubt (by faith) God is able. Our God is above any problem. He's bigger than any circumstance. God has the power to stir the hearts and minds of people to assist us, who otherwise might not be so willing. But nevertheless, our main focus should always remain on Him (Jehovah Jireh) first. Now, I said all of that to get to the meat-n-potatoes of this chapter—female friendships and relationships.

As I briefly noted, we all *need* someone. God didn't create mankind to live isolated or apart from one another. Nor does He want to see us alienating ourselves when trouble arises. Although I think it's safe to say, I'm probably not the only woman who has ever felt like distancing herself from the masses for a day or two every now and then. Then again, maybe I ought to speak for myself. Girlfriend, I'm not ashamed to admit there have been numerous times when I've wanted to stay as far away from people as possible. I don't say this in a mean-spirited way. Let me explain myself before you start second guessing my Christian walk. *Is this woman really a Christian? Aren't Christians supposed to walk in love?* Yes, I am born again. But there's no denying the fact, I'm also a human being. If I'm going to be transparent and candid writing this book, I want you to know I'm far from being a perfect and flawless Christian. I'm an on-going, daily work in progress.

I may be the only female Christian brave enough to say this out loud, but sometimes people get on my nerves! Can we be real for a minute? I bet you've had a few folks get on your nerves too! Are you married? Do you have children? Do you work? Do you go to church? Do you drive? Do you walk down crowded streets? Do you shop at the mall? Do you shop at the grocery store? Are you getting my point? Where can you or I go that doesn't require interacting with people? NOWHERE! So even though you may not want to admit it, I suspect I'm not the only one. But for the sake of time and argument, let's move on.

Several years ago Barbra Streisand (one of my favorite singers), recorded a song titled, *'People'*. The lyrics include: *people who need people are the luckiest people in the world.* This song pretty much transcends the entire human race. We all need somebody because we all want to be loved. That's the way God made us, because He is the embodiment of love. God imparted His love for mankind on the inside of each of His creations. You and I can't help ourselves from wanting to share our love with another person. I think the love emotion is released the instant a baby is placed in his mother's arms, following delivery. Right then and there mother and child form an everlasting bond. Our journey begins with an immediate human physical instinct for dependency upon love. Even though babies are small, they are intuitively aware of this emotion and the need to be loved in return. It's within this fragment of life (infancy) the human connection starts to develop.

Young girls are exposed to all sorts of people. A vast majority of households include a mother, father, and possibly siblings. Most of what you and I have learned can be traced back to the type of environments we were raised in. Let's use a few hypothetic examples: A little girl's parents were disrespectful of each other. Over the years while growing up, she heard a lot of yelling and cursing exchanged between her parents. As an adult, this has resulted in her possessing a hostile demeanor to those around her. Next there's the young female who was raised in a home where her parents openly displayed love and affection toward each other. They also showered an equal amount of attention and affection on the children. This female is caring and loving towards others. Another female was raised in a home where her single mother was constantly introducing Mr. Somebody to her and her four siblings. Her mother frequently left them home alone so she could spend time with Mr. Somebody. Unfortunately, at a very young age this female was forced to grow up rather quickly so she could take care of her younger siblings in her mother's absence. And last, there's the female who grew up in a home where she witnessed her father use her mother for a punching bag whenever he drank too much. But when he was sober, he could be the sweetest, loving daddy any little girl could want. In the back of this female's mind she grew up assuming it must be okay to let a man physically abuse her, because beating her is an expression of his love.

These are only a few of the many scenarios that as young girls you and I might've been exposed to behind closed doors. However, it's worth mentioning what takes place within these walls is detrimental to a young female's self-image, and self-esteem. Family ties bind and shape us throughout the early developmental years. Little girls, teenagers, and young women retain most of what they learn inside of their homes. If mommy let Mr. Somebody sleep in her bed, then it must be okay for me to sleep with *any* boy I like too—right? If my mother struggled to take care of five kids after daddy just up and left, then I'm determined I'm going to make something of myself so that I don't end up with a bunch of kids to take care of. If my parents were always smooching when they thought us kids weren't looking, then I want to marry an attentive, loving man like my daddy.

Do you see where I'm going with this? Whether voluntary or involuntary, inside the home, or outside the home, people shape one another. One person can have the ability and influence to affect someone in many ways, and on various levels. How you feel about yourself, or see yourself usually starts with the way you were raised. Wouldn't you agree most little girls mimic what they see? I know I did. I was constantly playing in my mother's high heels. Ask the women who know me and they'll tell you, I absolutely love shoes! Youthful experiences whether they were good or not so good, have an adverse effect on us as grown women. A miscarriage at age 15 was an agonizing price to pay later as a grown woman desiring to have children. Right, wrong or indifferent, personalities are developed throughout the stages of child-hood. Now we're adults seeking inner change, but this is where God and *only* He can change distorted self-images from the inside out. Naturally, we're required to do some of the work, but ultimately God will do the majority of it. Let's face it. As humans you and I are incapable of repairing areas that have been severely damaged. Far too many females are walking around unaware they're even in need of damage control. God knows His creations better than we *think* we know ourselves. Who then is more qualified to fix us? (I Kings 8:39)

SO, WHO DO YOU THINK YOU ARE

I Samuel 16:7 reads:

"For *the Lord seeth* not as man *seeth*; for man looketh on the outward appearance, but the Lord looketh on the heart." (KJV)

I'll probably get myself in trouble for this, but I'm going to take the risk. The way a large majority of females feel about themselves usually affects their relationships. Feelings reflect how well we interact with others, especially relationships that involve the same sex. Females can be quite emotional. Then again, maybe I should just speak for myself. At 50-something, I'm experiencing menopause. This unavoidable fact of life is commonly referred to as 'going through the change'. I cope with menopausal mood swings. But trouble doesn't last always. That's the way I look at it. On certain days when hot flashes repeatedly fire my body up seemingly every five minutes, it takes everything in me to concentrate. It's hard to stay focused! One minute I'm fine. The next minute an unwelcomed surge of heat shoots through my upper torso and doesn't stop until it reaches my scalp! This excessive heat leaves me dabbing away beads of sweat. Hot flashes are very, very, very, very, intense! Ladies who are also going through menopause, do you feel me?

Whenever a younger woman smirks at me, "are you hot?" I think to myself, you'll be finding out soon enough, Missy! Then I'll be the one asking. *"Are you hot?"* Laugh now, but your day is coming! But instead of saying what I'm thinking, I bite my tongue and smile. Miss. Youngthang has the nerve to give me a blank look while I frantically fan myself trying to cool down. Sure, she has no idea what I'm going through, but one day she will! Hot flashes are enough to make a woman uncontrollably emotional! Okay? And, if being heated up isn't enough, my mind gets on board by slipping these 30 second memory lapses in on me! Well, that's enough about menopause. I can feel myself getting warm just talking about it. Where was I? Oh! Now I remember!

Girlfriend, whether the other female is our mother, sister, daughter, grandmother, auntie, cousin, co-worker, or a woman at church, we're going to be involved in all types of emotionally driven relationships. The thing to remember is, each relationship will be unlike the other. We're all different. Female relationships require different things one from the other. That's what individuality is—no two alike. God purposely planned it this way. You are you. I am me. Unfortunately, if some females aren't cognizant of certain behavioral patterns there's always the risk of wanting to be a carbon copy. In other words, you'll be too busy wishing you were more like her while the real you is struggling for attention and recognition. One thing you never want to allow happen, regardless whether it's a male or female relationship is to lose sight of yourself. You must learn how you can truly be confident in the person God has created you to be— uniquely, wonderfully different! You were not created to desire the life of another female more than you do your own. Therefore, might I suggest stop putting unnecessary pressure on yourself by trying to be someone you're not!

Deuteronomy 11:16 reads:

"Take heed to yourselves, lest your [minds and] hearts be deceived, and you turn aside, and serve other gods and worship them." (AMP)

In female relationships a major no-no is to remain friends with another female who makes you feel inferior to her. If she isn't making positive deposits into your life, you need to move on! Girl-friendships that lead to manipulation do not produce spiritual edification. I think it's fine to share certain similarities with another female, but that's as far as any relationship should go. You should lead a whole enriched life by being completely acceptable and pleased with who you are. Originality sets us apart.

Another thing we girls have been known to do in our friendships/relationships is compare ourselves to one another. Whether it's done consciously or unconsciously, it's my guess we've all done it. I'd be lying if I told you that I've never made a comparison of myself to another female. Sure I have, especially when a sista in church appears to have a speed-dial connection to heaven. In my mind, I'm thinking that woman *sho* can pray! I don't pray as good as she does! This woman even speaks in tongues better than I do! Well girlfriend, I had to be delivered from that inferior thinking. Thank you, Lord!

Can I give you another example? A stylish, attractive woman enters the room. Right away one female starts eyeballing this woman, and her mind shifts into jealousy. Come on, girlfriend! Be honest! You're never given another female the once-over with thoughts of jealousy running through your head? Okay. If Not, YOU'RE SPECIAL!

Don't you know your Heavenly Father didn't leave a single thing out (that He didn't intend to leave out) when He created you? God has blessed all of His daughters with talents, creative ideas, visions, potential, intellect, skills, abilities, wisdom and dreams. There isn't any reason for you to envy or compare yourself to another female. Awesome distinctions, wonderful characteristics and exceptional qualities exist on the inside of you. Be secured in who you are! The truth is you can only be *the best* at being you! Stop wasting time and energy on thinking about being anybody other than yourself. Can I say this? True friendships flourish and mature as time goes by. If you have girl-friendships that haven't grown, perhaps you should re-evaluate them. I'm just saying.

Personally speaking, every one of my female relationships have made positive deposits into my life. Not one of these women has taken anything away from me while allowing me to be the best of who I am. A few of these friendships began with simple pleasantries, but have now matured into unconditional love relationships. My girlfriends accept me for who I am without trying to change me into who they think I should be. And because of this, I'm able to be comfortable in my own skin without experiencing feelings of inferiority or envy. We each possess our own special and unique personalities. Where I might lack in some areas, one of these women has the component I need to keep the friendship in sync, and vice-versa.

When my mother suddenly became ill, Monica rushed to be at my side. Twenty-one days later after mom went home to be with the Lord, Jeannette, whom I've known since the age of ten immediately dropped what she was doing and flew in from Atlanta. Monica, who I've known for almost fifteen years, literally put her family on hold. From the first day I phoned Monica with the disturbing news mommy had been hospitalized, she put her daughter in charge of taking care of matters at home. Regrettably, both Jeannette and Monica also lost their mothers. They completely understood what I was feeling. The need for encouragement and sound thinking came through these two women, who were spiritually and mentally equipped in helping me keep it together during this ordeal. Monica and Jeannette unselfishly gave of themselves because of the relationships we've developed and nurtured over time. Both of these women poured love and inspiration into my spirit, helping me to get through the difficult days that lay ahead.

Over a span of twenty days, Jeannette and Monica truly blessed me. I believed I would get through the pain of losing my mother. I told myself in spite of the sadness, I'd be able to cope with her death, so long as I had them by my side. But that thought was somewhat misleading. Losing mommy was very hard! I began feeling the after-effects of my loss taking its toll on my physical body. In my grief I quickly dropped a noticeable amount of weight, which I definitely did not need to lose.

The other women that make up my elite circle are Carla, Joan, Traci, Michelle, Lynnette, Faye, and my biological sister Renee. These beautiful women meet my needs time and time again in their own individual special way. I remember one evening when I returned home from being at the hospital in dire need to hear Renee's voice. I dialed her number praying she had a minute. Renee is a wife and mother. I respect she has a family, even though she always makes time for me. Renee answered. I lost it! I sobbed into the phone, feeling the hurt and sorrow subsiding. I appreciated Renee so much that evening because she was hurting too, and I knew it. She provided the strength I needed in a moment of weakness. I thank God for surrounding me with genuine love in these friendships. Each of these women unselfishly provided me comfort in the days leading up to mommy's home going service. Ladies, I love you so much!

Girlfriend, if the enemy has his way, he will manipulate our every thought and feeling. He can plant misconceptions in our mind leading us down the path of prejudging another female. Why? Because he's hoping we'll miss out on becoming part of what may have been a divine connection. Have you ever stopped to consider God quite possibly is trying to connect you to a new friendship because it's part of His plan for where He's taking you? I'm a firm believer that not only is God every where, but He is also in control of everything! The Bible tells us that God is Omnipresent—everywhere. (II Chronicles 16:9; Psalms 34:15; Proverbs 5:21; and Jeremiah 16:17)

Job 34:21 reads:

"For [God's] eyes are upon the ways of a man and He sees all his steps." (AMP)

The Bible is the truth of God. Therefore I'm absolutely persuaded (by His Word) He will always know what's best for me. God cares about you beyond your human (natural) comprehension. It's not His Will any of His daughters get themselves involved in friendships (male/female) that will do them injustice, harm, or ill-gotten gain. When it comes to friendships/relationships, you should also understand God may bring a female into your life for a season. I know what I'm talking about. In 1996, a complete stranger entered my life shortly after my second marriage and relocation to Atlanta. God is so awesome! He knew far in advance what was going to take place months later. After all, God is my beginning. He is my present. He is my future, and He is my end. I didn't know it, but I was going to need someone spiritually sound and filled with a mother's wisdom since I was living miles away from mommy. Unbeknownst to me from the moment I arrived in Atlanta, God had already set the stage.

It was May when I first met Marion. She and I were hired through the same temp agency for work. God orchestrated a simple exchange. "Good morning." From that morning on,

Marion and I quickly developed a friendship. Marion was in her 60's. She was born again and married to a minister. As I eagerly shared that I too was born again, our friendship grew closer. God brought us together for a season. I would need to lean on Marion in my mother's absence, 8,000 miles away back in Delaware. I'm not clairvoyant, so I can't say what would, or might not have happened differently had I not reciprocated Marion's friendly greeting that morning. But I can say this. Having Marion in my life certainly helped ease the longing pains I had for my mother living so far apart. Living in an apartment across town from mommy definitely wasn't the same thing as residing in another state. This was a brand new experience.

    Well, ten months after making Marion's acquaintance, I learned I was pregnant. However, seemingly as soon as I surprised my new husband he was going to be a daddy, he was rushing me to the doctors. I began having pains in my abdomen. As he and I sat in the waiting area of the doctor's office an un-explainable feeling fell over me. This feeling gripped every fiber of my being. Suddenly I was afraid I might be losing another baby. It turns out this would be my third miscarriage.

    At age fifteen, I got pregnant and loss that baby. Nine years later, I got pregnant again in my first marriage. I was in my early twenties when I loss that baby too. Ironically, like the previous two miscarriages, this one also occurred during the very early stages (8 weeks) of pregnancy. Following my miscarriage, I slipped into a state of depression. I desperately wanted my mommy! But God is a good God. Marion assumed her assignment as surrogate, knowing exactly what to say and do in place of my mother. She comforted me with words of encouragement the way any wise and loving mother would do for her hurting child. Soon afterwards I started referring to Marion as my surrogate mother. She told me the sound of hearing it warmed her heart.

    In the meantime, the following spring my husband and I decided to return to live in Delaware. Marion didn't want to see us move away, but she understood how lonely I'd been living in Atlanta. I promised to call often, as well as write to her. My relationship with Marion didn't end upon moving back to Delaware. She and I frequently communicated by phone. I introduced her to mommy (by phone) after telling mommy about this wonderful woman I'd met while living in Atlanta—my surrogate mother. I wrote Marion as promised. Although we were miles apart, I treasured her friendship.

Staying in touch with her was important to me. I missed seeing her more than I thought I would. Marion became a very good friend. I had grown to love and appreciate her. If memory serves me correctly, I'd been back in Delaware about five months when Marion called one afternoon. Her voice sounded a little strained. I thought she might have had a bad cold. Never in a million years was I prepared to hear the devastating news she'd been diagnosed with lung cancer. My heart dropped! I started to cry into the phone. Marion calmly tried assuring me she was going to beat this horrible illness. Then she quickly changed the subject asking how I liked my new job. There was never any doubt in my mind that Marion knew who she was in the Lord. Unfortunately, later that fall I received a call from Marion's husband. He informed me Marion had passed away in the early hours that morning. I expressed my condolences to him and his family as I felt my eyes swelling with tears. A couple of weeks later I received an un-expectant call from Marion's daughter. We never had an opportunity to meet, but Marion spoke of her daughter and grandson often. She was at her parent's home helping her father to go through some of her mother's things when she found the letters and cards I had sent. Marion's daughter openly shared that her mother's disease had been a violent attack against her body. As I listened, trying not to cry, I was taken aback to hear her say she was relieved that her mother had died. At the time I thought, how could a daughter part her lips to say such a thing? Wouldn't it be better to still have her mother with her, even if she was sick? Years later, I too would express similar words.

Marion went home to be with the Lord shortly before the Thanksgiving holiday. I was deeply saddened. Still, I was grateful for the kindness this woman had shown a total stranger while living in Atlanta. So the next time another female speaks to you, return the salutation. You just never know. She could be a divine connection—someone God has crossing your path for unforeseen reasons. Matthew 6:8 explains that God has knowledge of what we need before we even ask. That's how awesome our Father is!

I tend to think successes as well as failures in life share a common thread. They too play a part in the choices we make in developing friendships. God brings people into our lives for good. But be not deceived. The enemy can bring people into our lives intended for demise. I call them counterfeit friends. Ponder over that for a minute. Then ask yourself whether you feel stifled whenever you're in the presence of your friends. Are there areas where both parties have matured since first starting this friendship? This is why being spiritually discerning is a necessary attribute. You could go back-n-forth wondering when is the appropriate time to end relationships that do nothing to stimulate you. Generally, there are two kinds of friendships people develop: (1) Non-productive, and (2) Productive. Now, I know what I'm about to say next may not go over well. But non-producing relationships are like wearing heavy chains about the neck. It's like trying to walk in a pair of cemented shoes. This type of friendship weighs a person down and prohibits them from going forward. In other words, as long as you and I continue to surround ourselves with negative females who have no dreams or desire to rise above the status quo, we hold ourselves back from becoming who God wants us to become. More than likely those friends see images of themselves as defeated. They will not change. They fear being made to feel uncomfortable, or they aren't willing to let go of familiarity.

Girlfriend, have you ever heard the phrase, guilty by association? There's a lot of truth to that old catch-phrase. Might I suggest you take another look at the kinds of female relationships you truly want to invest in? Make no mistake. Anything or anyone you devote time and energy into is vested time. I think one of the most common errors many people make is being unaware when to let go in order for true freedom to exist in our lives.

Can I share how I equate female relationships? Perhaps afterwards you'll be able to better relate to your own friendships/relationships. (1) **Acquaintances:** These are females that you know of, but not well enough to grant access to areas you deem private. They fall into the cordial, but at a polite distance category. (2) **Associates:** These are females you know fairly well. These friendships are more likely formed through school, social activities, church, or someone you met through another friend. There is little or no social contact outside of those perimeters. Seldom is there any private information exchanged on your behalf. These females fall into the limited category. (3) **Good friends:** These are females you know rather well. They're trustworthy, and use discretion with other females outside of your friendship. These females respectfully know their position within the boundaries of your relationship. They can be trusted to honor what is discussed between the two of you. You can rely upon them because you know they have your back! These females fall into the valuable category. (4) **Best friend(s):** This female has been a part of your life for a long time. There's history between the two of you. What you know about each other can be trusted to never be discussed with someone else. She is there when times are good, and when they aren't. This friend guards her confidences that will accompany her to her grave. This female not only has your best interests, she will go beyond measures as an expression of her love in this relationship. This female is like having a sister. She falls into the treasured category.

At every opportunity I get, I do all I can to show each woman in my elite circle how much I appreciate having her in my life. I never want to take what we've established in our relationship for granted. My friends and I share many of the same positive thoughts about one another, our lives and our futures. I'm proud to say, I'm part of an elite circle of beautiful, strong, inspiring and empowering women! The way I see it, if inner change is what someone is aspiring to achieve, then they must be responsible for taking the first step. But be prepared. Sometimes the process means distancing yourself from a friendship/relationship that isn't going anywhere, thereby preventing you from stepping onto a path in a new direction. I've been there; done that. Over the years there have been a few friendships that I've had to walk away from. It didn't feel good. I really didn't want to stop associating with these women. But the bottom line is, the friendship was stagnant. After a while it was obvious those particular friends and I were traveling on different paths spiritually, mentally, and socially. It hadn't been easy to sever those ties, especially since I genuinely cared for these women. However, I couldn't continue getting up each morning and going to bed at night with the same ole' influenced unproductive mindset either. Some of my decisions involved conversations with the woman in the mirror. She asked. "How can you expect things to be any different if you continue to stay the same?" It wasn't like I didn't already know that, but I finally got it. Character changes don't work by magic. My desire for inward change required making a few unpleasant decisions. But there again, life is choice driven. Some decisions that I've had to make in life, forced me to step out of my comfort zone. I'll admit. Moving away from familiarity is scary. But once you convince yourself to keep it moving, the fear of the unknown holds less and less power over you. From time to time whenever I bump into former friends, the second they open their mouths I'm hearing nothing different. Usually they're still complaining about the same old stuff. Not one thing is any different from when we last talked, however long it might have been.

Girlfriend, if you've come to a place in life where you feel like you've been on pause too long, you may need to re-evaluate a few of your friendships. You may want to reconsider your position in those relationships. Why not take a moment to make a list of your female relationships by category. For example: Do your **good friends** have best friends? If so, this means you're not number one. There's probably a certain criteria between the two of you that doesn't exist between you and your best friend. There are going to be private conversations and moments shared between your good friend and her best friend

SO, WHO DO YOU THINK YOU ARE

that she may never discuss with you. Can you accept your position as the good friend in this relationship? Are you sure? What if she explains you were unable to reach her on Friday and Saturday because she and her best friend jumped in the car for a quick weekend get away. Will you take offense because you weren't invited to join them?

Does your **best friend** have lots of other friends? If so, then you probably should understand that while you may be first in this relationship according to rank, and seniority, there may be times you will have to resort to being number two, three, four, or five depending on the nature of the need of one of her other girlfriends, even though she's your best friend. Are you mature/secure in your position in this relationship to not be jealous of her other friends? Sadly, too many females don't quite know how to avoid unnecessary offenses and misunderstandings. Therefore, I think we owe it to ourselves to periodically take self-personality exams by asking ourselves a few pertinent questions.

1. Have I out grown this friendship?
2. Would I be very disappointed if our friendship were to end?
3. In what capacity (acquaintance, associate, good, or best friend) is my relationship with _____?

Now I want you to write down the name of every female who makes up part of your circle of life. Then make up your own set of questions that coincide with your friendships/relationships. Read each question aloud. Afterward having created a list of questions, on a scale of one (being the lesser) to ten (being the greater) place a number next to each of those names according to your question. **BE HONEST!**

If any of the names on your list end up with a total less than number ten (10), perhaps it's time to re-evaluate that friendship/relationship. Girlfriends outgrow each other everyday! Let me assure you, it's going to be alright. Breathe slowly. Now inhale. And, exhale.

It's a known fact of life, people who start out on this journey with us, may not end it with us. Sometimes it isn't necessarily anything either of us has done to cause the friendship to deteriorate. It could very well be something as simple as it's just the time. You must learn to spiritually discern times, and seasons in your life. Unfortunately, if you're not sober minded (spiritually discerning), you very well could miss God's timing intended for propelling you closer to your destiny. A divine connection can also go unrecognized due to your failure to understand everything has its season.

Females should continuously check themselves, especially when it comes to forming friendships, regardless whether they're with a male or female. Me personally, I try to surround myself with women who always treat me the same. It shouldn't matter whether she and I haven't seen or talked to each other in weeks. We should be able to pick up where we last left off and go on from there. For me that's what a true friendship is all about. It's a relationship that has been built upon maturity, stability, and acceptance of each other. Neither one of us should be tripping. "How come you haven't called me?" There are character variations and emotional levels that lend themselves to the kinds of friendships that you form with another female. A mature friendship withstands the highs and the lows—it's genuine. That being said, let's pause here for a minute.

Whether you know it or not, there are going to be people who will come into your life temporarily. They are only meant to be a part of your life for a particular moment—a season. It could be a month, a year or longer. But however long (or short), people enter our lives on cue. New friendships can come by way of God to help enrich our lives and nourish our spirit. Or, friendships can occur by way of the enemy as part of his plan of destruction. I'll elaborate on this further in chapter eleven.

As much as you and I long to be accepted and likeable by another female, we mustn't accept every new acquaintance at face value. We shouldn't casually think, or assume an extended hand in friendship will be received the way we thought it might be. We can't be so disconnected from ourselves (spiritually) to

SO, WHO DO YOU THINK YOU ARE

the point another female is allowed to manipulate us simply because there's the human need for acceptance. Trying to belong or fit in where you or I are not appreciated can prove detrimental to our well being, both mentally and spiritually. Do you realize the time, energy and work that go into most friendships/relationships become investments that are worth re-evaluating from time to time? Why? It's simple. People have a tendency to outgrow each other. Where you start out with a girlfriend may not be where you'll end up together. Female thoughts, feelings and attitudes can change at the drop of a hat. And, I say this in love. One day things are going along great. The next day it's like you're talking to a stranger. Another thing too, one female might discover she no longer feels committed to the friendship as strongly as you do. I think a true friendship can best be described as a relationship founded on trust, honesty and a genuine love and admiration for another person, strengthened by total acceptance. You can rely on that female to hold you accountable for your actions. This friend can tell you the truth (even when you don't want to hear it), and you know that you know girlfriend has your back! This friendship is also the one that surpasses all of the others.

God could place certain individuals in your life, to assist you in bringing a vision or dream to pass because they have the inside connection (knows somebody that knows somebody) in helping you to take the next crucial step towards manifestation. This person could have the resources (finances, investors, real estate property, etc.) in accomplishing what has to be done in order to bring the dream to fruition. You could also meet a female sent to provide an encouraging word or to comfort you following the death of loved one. The list goes on and on. But however long (or short) the friendship, learn to recognize divine connections.

We're human. We're females. It's part of our nature to hold on to old pictures of boyfriends. Many of us have a hard time throwing out flowers long after they've wilted in a vase because someone close to our heart gave them to us. We may keep the ticket stub from the movie theatre so we'll remember our first date with a special guy. We girls like holding on to things and people. Then again, maybe I should just speak for myself.

I can easily admit I'm very sentimental. Over the years I have accumulated a large assortment of cards given to me by family members, co-workers and friends. I've even dried petals from flowers that were sent to me. I have various kinds of pretty ribbons once wrapped around a special gift. I used to keep pictures taken of me and old boyfriends, but years ago when I attended a women's conference, the speaker said something profound. "How are you going to find a husband if you still have pictures of your last boyfriend tucked inside a shoebox under your bed? That relationship has ended. It is part of your past. Go home, tear those pictures up and toss them in the trash!" When I returned home later that day, that's exactly what I did. I pulled my box of mementos down from the bedroom closet. Then I sat on the side of my bed ripping those old pictures to shreds. Afterwards I gathered up the torn fragments and threw them in the kitchen trash. But it didn't stop there. I also got rid of stuffed animals, jewelry and a few pieces of clothing that old boyfriends had given me. I cleared the past out of my apartment, taking it a step further by walking to the outside dumpster. Do you want to know something? It felt good throwing those things away! Actually, I found it to be exhilarating!

Girlfriend, nothing happens by chance. I didn't *just happen* to attend the women's conference on that Saturday morning. I was supposed to be there. I needed to hear the message in order for me to move forward. It was during a time when the words of that speaker help set me free! I'm realizing more and more sometimes people come into our lives just to open our eyes to a truth. The thing is, seldom do we see them coming. I think maybe its God's way of coming to the rescue of His daughters to keep them on the path predestined for them to travel. All good things come from God. If you've met a female who shares time, energy, and confidentialities with you—a true best friend, she was God-sent to assist along your journey. This female has whatever you might need for any season. Love her. Appreciate her. Treasure her. Value your girlfriend.

Now as good as all of that may sound, don't be naïve. You mustn't overlook the enemy's tactics to try to distract you with the opposite of where God is trying to take you to. There could also be females who walk into your life sent by the devil himself. This particular person is sent to bring division, havoc and discord into your life. That's why it's vital that you ask God to give you a spirit of discernment so you can steer clear of individuals who generate chaos, confusion, and negative energy. I refer to this group of females as thorns. They've been sent to disrupt the positive flow in your life. Generally speaking, quite often it won't matter if this person is female, male, family member, church folk, or a co-worker. The motive will be the same—steal, kill and ultimately lead you to destruction! The enemy has intentionally sent this person or persons into your presence to try to get you off track (confuse), set you back (strife), and distract (change your focus) as a means of preventing you from reaching your God ordained destiny.

We were born with love to give. Therefore, we all want to be loved, but at what price? Ask the woman in the mirror what she thinks about so-n-so. Does she experience a sense of uneasiness whenever he or she comes around? Does she believe this person will add enrichment to your life? Does the woman in the mirror think you're wasting too much of your time and energy because you want this person to like you, in spite of the fact you can see they're using you? Take the woman in the mirror into your confidence. After all, she was the true friend you met as a child when you first gazed upon a mirror at the young girl's face staring back at you. She's been there every step of the way.

Everybody wants to be liked by others. People want to be accepted for who they are on the inside, not just for what others can see with the physical eye. Case in point, I'm learning acts of kindness do not solidify the sincerity of ones motives or actions. We can only go by what we're able to see. The true agenda of an individual rests hidden within the walls of their heart. However, eventually a person's heart does reveal the true character of that man or woman. Over the years I've met a number of females who were regarded by others as being pretty nice. But as it turns out, these dolls were pretty selfish, pretty self-centered, pretty mean spirited, and pretty conceited. Before you ask, I'm not friends with any of these women. They were using acts of kindness so long as it benefited them. Once my eyes were opened, I began putting some distance between me and them.

Ecclesiastes 3:1 and 3: 6 reads:

"There is a time for everything, and a season for every activity under heaven. A time to search and a time to give up." (NIV)

How appropriate!

Chapter Seven

The Things We Do For Love (Male Relationships)

> Do not be unequally yoked with unbelievers [do not make mismated alliances with them or come under a different yoke with them, inconsistent with your faith]. For what partnership have right living *and* right standing with God with iniquity *and* lawlessness? Or how can light have fellowship with darkness?
>
> II Corinthians 6:14 (AMP)

When I first sat down at my computer to begin writing this chapter, I thought it should be fairly easy. Then I had another thought. Since civilization began with one man, why not start by writing about God's first creation—a man named Adam. I liked this concept—begin at the beginning.

In Genesis 1:27 it reads:

> "So God created man in His own image, in the image and likeness of God He created him; male and female He created them." (AMP)

This is my own perception, but I imagine God is so beautiful, mere words cannot describe it. He's a majestic God. That leads me to believe when He formed his first man from the dust of the ground, God created an equally beautiful human—in

His likeness. As I lingered over my thoughts about God and Adam, another man came to mind, Jesus Christ (The Messiah). Surely He too must be a man of radiant beauty. Perhaps so much so, it's one of the reasons why the Roman soldiers hatred of Jesus drove them to savagely whip, beat, punch, rip out His flesh and disfigure His face! The Bible says by the time Jesus was nailed to the Cross at Calvary, He was barely recognizable! If any of you were able to see Mel Gibson's movie, *'Passion of Christ'* when it premiered in theatres, Mel Gibson's adaptation portrayed this very thing. I have seen a lot of movies about Jesus, but I had never seen the portrayal of the savage beating the Bible speaks of. Please understand this is my personal interpretation based upon my private time reading the Bible. And, while Adam may have been beautifully created from the ground of the earth, it wasn't until God breathed into his nostrils that Adam became a living being.

Genesis 2:7 reads:

"God formed man out of dirt from the ground and blew into his nostrils the breath of life. The Man came alive—a living soul!" (THE MESSAGE)

I believe God took His time to design His first man creation to look and have the character of his Creator (Father). Not long afterwards Adam was given an assignment by God. He was to name every animal, bird, tree, flower, plant, fruit, and vegetable that existed in the Garden of Eden. Have you ever considered God didn't want Adam to become lazy or too complacent that he would've become ungrateful for everything God lavished upon him in the Garden? I'm just asking. Whenever I read God's Word, my mind becomes flooded with questions. I tend to ponder over what I read in the Bible, don't you? Personally speaking, not every chapter and verse in the Bible is easy to comprehend when I read the King James Version. That's why I invested in other Bible translations of God's Word. While I'm reading, I want clarity—revelation. I crave a greater understanding. Sorry, I got off track here for a minute. Let's get back to Adam.

SO, WHO DO YOU THINK YOU ARE

Day after day Adam communed with God in the Garden. He had no awareness of being naked before His Father. Adam was happy in his natural element. He walked about the Garden unrestricted in mind, heart and spirit. Adam went about the Garden in complete freedom. He wasn't inhibited by negative thinking, nor was Adam ashamed of being naked (transparent) before God. In other words, God's first man had nothing to hide. Most of us have probably read the Book of Genesis. We've read the verse where God didn't want Adam to be alone in the Garden of Eden. God envisioned a perfect creature for his perfect man. He put Adam into a deep sleep supernaturally opening his side removing one of Adam's ribs. God sealed Adam's side with new flesh. He then began sculpting and modifying another creation. This beautiful creature would be compatible for Adam. God's new creature was fearfully and wonderfully crafted. He looked upon His beautiful creation as another Adam (man).

Genesis 5:2 reads:

"He created the male and female and blessed them and named them [both] Adam [Man] at the time they were created." (AMP)

God awakened Adam from his deep sleep presenting him with the perfect companion, friend, lover, confidant, conversationalist, helper and wife. The female Adam had been created *just for him*. Having spiritually discerned what God had done while he'd been asleep, Adam responded. "This creature is bone of my bones and flesh of my flesh. She shall be called woman because she was taken out of man!" (Genesis 2:23) God joined Adam and the woman together using one flesh. This might explain why it's so easy for females to become emotionally attached to the opposite sex, especially once we physically engage. "When is he gonna call?" Suddenly we can't think about anything else except that man, practically 24/7. There is a connection between sex (physical attraction) and emotional attachment. Even if the man is only interested in one night of sex, we respond from a feeling of attraction, freely giving ourselves away knowing he has no intention in ever seeing us again! Nevertheless, the following morning, we get up emotionally attached. Now let's get back to the Garden. Adam named God's female creation Eve (Mother of the Earth) after God gave her to be Adam's wife. Did you notice any similarity to what took place in the Garden and now? Natural fathers also give their daughter's hand in marriage to their future husband.

Meanwhile, God provided Adam with everything he needed to know concerning the Garden of Eden. God gave explicit instructions for Adam to follow. He forbade Adam not to eat the fruit from the tree of knowledge about good and evil and blessing and curses located in the center of the Garden. (Genesis 2:15-17) But we all know that directive went in one ear, and out the other. The devil entered the Garden seizing an opportunity to place division between God and man. He cleverly disguised himself as a serpent. Which by the way when I read this again, I got a mental picture of the serpent walking upright. I say this because the serpent didn't crawl on his belly until he was cursed by God. (Genesis 3:14) You want to know something else? It's quite possible the animals that lived in the Garden spoke a universal language that both Adam and Eve understood. Think about it. Eve didn't know she was carrying on a conversation with Lucifer disguised as a snake. That causes me to pause. Eve wasn't startled by dialog coming from the serpent in the Garden because I think she was accustomed to the animals talking.

In the meantime, Eve entertained what she heard the devil saying. After processing *his suggestion* to taste the fruit of the tree, she then reached for the appealing fruit hanging from the tree of life. Having tasted the fruit, Eve encouraged Adam to do the same. Instantly their (natural) eyes were opened. They were able to distinguish good and evil. The devil acted quickly in an attempt to pervert their minds and hearts. Shame fell upon Adam and Eve. They realized they were standing in paradise Eden in the flesh—naked. Almost immediately, Adam and Eve sought refuge in the Garden to hide their nakedness. God's first man and woman became imperfect creatures the day sin entered the Garden of Eden. Within those few passing moments godly perfection would forever be lost outside the Garden.

SO, WHO DO YOU THINK YOU ARE

Adam and Eve experienced two new human emotions. They were filled with fear and shame. God had not imparted fear in them, yet they hid themselves (frightened) behind the tall trees in the Garden. As usual, God strolled through the cool breezes in Garden paradise in search of His children. He looked for them, but Adam and Eve were ashamed for God to see them naked. "*Adam, where are you?*" God inquired. With reluctance, Adam finally made himself visible, peering out from behind a tree. "I heard you walking in the garden. I was afraid for you to see me naked. So I hid from you." The Bible states God is all-knowing, therefore, I believe He already knew what had taken place in the Garden of Eden between the man, the woman, and the serpent. "*Who told Adam he was naked?*" God demanded. Adam didn't hesitate. "The woman gave me fruit from the forbidden tree. After I tasted it, my eyes revealed that we were naked." (Genesis 3:10-12)

Okay. This is where I stop telling the story. The minute Adam placed all of the blame on Eve without taking some of the responsibility for what happened, future relationships between males and females would struggle due to a lack of communication.

Till this day, the devil intervenes in relationships as a means to keep men and women at odds with each other. It may be the new millennium, but too many relationships still suffer a breakdown in communication between the sexes. I don't like saying this, but a large majority of men have difficulty stepping up to the place of responsibility in their relationships. Look what the devil started! He cleverly plotted to deceive God's first woman. Eve believed a taste of that luscious fruit would be alright. She totally disregarded God's instruction (His Word) not to eat from that tree! Instead of Adam taking authority (being the head) over his wife by obeying God's Word, he willingly participated. Adam cowardly hid behind bushes placing all of the blame on the woman when God confronted him following his actions. "It's the woman's fault!" Talk about not owning up! Adam enjoyed tasting the forbidden fruit too!

Once he and Eve ate from the tree of life, their hearts filled with a rash of emotions—feelings. I often wonder when reading Genesis wasn't it Adam's place as the man of the Garden to keep the lines of communication open with the woman? Adam didn't have to accept Eve's suggestion that he eat from the forbidden tree too. Then again, it was the only tree in the entire Garden that Adam hadn't tasted of its fruit. Is it possible curiosity got the better of him when he saw the taste was good to the woman? There were other trees that bore exotic and delicious fruits Adam had eaten before Eve showed up. The devil knew exactly what he was doing by using Eve to lure Adam to fall into the sin of death. "God doesn't want you to eat this fruit because then you'll become like him," the serpent hissed. (Genesis 3: 2-6) They were already gods, made in God's perfect form and likeness! The devil was jealous, filled with hatred for God's man and woman. "You'll know what God knows about good and evil once you eat of this tree," he went on to tell Eve. The devil twisted God's Word. I've often wondered when reading Genesis, what difference did it make which creature the devil manipulated in persuading the other to eat from the forbidden tree. Weren't the results still going to be the same? The instant either Adam or Eve ate of the tree, sin and death was going to enter the world God had created. Perhaps the devil lied to Eve because she appeared to be the more vulnerable creature of the two. Which brings me to the point of this chapter—male relationships.

Men and women are different. Boys and girls are different. Plain and simple—different! Case in point. The male species doesn't observe things the same way we do. Most men don't internalize situations like women do. We don't rationalize things the same way. Male and females don't adapt to change the same way. And, we definitely don't think the same way. Girlfriend, male + female = different! You know it! Sure, the sexes compliment each other in the sense that we were genetically created to fulfill a physical need for each other, as well as populate the earth. But outside of that, males and females are different! Now, let me stop before what I've said so far gets misinterpreted for male-bashing. Truly that's not what I'm doing.

SO, WHO DO YOU THINK YOU ARE

Female-male relationships are being challenged more now than ever before. Marriages are dissolving (divorcing) much too soon because neither party is willing to dig in their heels to fight to make it work. Or, one party is willing to try harder, but the other one rejects the idea of trying to keep the marriage together. I've learned in marriage a lack of communication and/or miscommunication is a separation waiting to happen. Personally, I hated (yes hated) whenever I was put in the position to wonder whether my second husband understood exactly what I was talking about because he seldom asked questions. As a matter of fact, he contributed very little response or feedback during many of our conversations. But to keep it real, there were plenty of times when I wasn't crystal clear about what he said either. I'd say one thing. My husband would come at me with the complete opposite of what I was talking about. Let me be blunt. I'm not about to come off like all of the problems in my second marriage were totally his fault. It wouldn't be the truth. I can easily admit I messed up too—a lot!

Now girlfriend, I realize you may not appreciate this chapter, but do yourself a favor, read it anyhow. The way I see it, how can we help each other grow stronger (spiritually/mentally) if we shy away from being openly honest with each other? I'm honest enough (free from people bondage) to say right here— right now. I have goofed up in my relationships with good men, as well as not-so-good-men. Truth be told, I'm not the easiest person to live with. There! I said it! I have a few on-going issues that my Father and I are *still* working out. Prime example: I believe everything should have a place. It doesn't matter if it's my work place, or my home. Everything should be in order and have a specific place where it belongs. When things are not in their rightful place, I CAN GO BALLISTIC! My ex-husband never quite got on board with that concept. Regrettably, men don't come with manuals. However, if your man came with a how-to manual, please write a book! Females everywhere will want to read it!

So, what do you say we learn a thing or two, or three about male/female relationships, according to the Word of God? First I want to start off by saying any relationship that has resulted in separation or disappointment need not be categorized as the 'end of the world'. That's paramount before we go any further. Frankly speaking, I suspect if you and I were to look more closely at ourselves, it's highly probable the disappointment we feel isn't as much at fault with the other person as much as we might *think*. Girlfriend, you and I may not want to admit this, but usually something on the inside has gone unaddressed, which leads to an uprising in our relationships. Often time females bring disappointment on themselves by making unwise decisions when it comes to the opposite sex. I think whenever a female places certain emphasis or expectations upon a man but will not consider it open for discussion she's setting herself up for disappointment. Why is it, we girls automatically assume men understand our needs wants, likes and dislikes? It doesn't work like that! On the other hand, regardless how high we might set the bar, many females enter into relationships believing that man will meet *all* of their needs, and *fulfill* their every want. Girlfriend, it just doesn't work like that! Unfortunately, when these men fall short of our expectations, that's when negative thoughts, feelings, attitudes and behaviors begin creeping into the relationship. Before long, we find ourselves wallowing in disappointment because the relationship is no longer quite what we thought it was going to be. We had all these unrealistic fantasies going into the relationship. Now we're walking around bottled up with disappointment in the same man we fell madly in love with!

But the truth is, if you step back and take a deep breath, you'll see you are more disappointed within yourself for having let the relationship get to a point of fault-finding. I tend to believe there are precautionary measures females can take to avoid being disappointed. If they're open and honest about pet-peeves, or old emotional wounds that will easily trigger an argument quicker than lighting a match (cause they haven't been delivered in those areas), it gives that man the option to stay or leave before the friendship becomes too serious. However, most of us choose to keep the not-so-perfect stuff under wraps and spring it on them later. And when we do, Mr. Man starts showing his *true self*. Then we find the relationship is starting to elevate to a level of chaos because two personalities came together under false pretenses.

Let's look a little closer at questions that probably shouldn't be omitted during conversations in newly formed relationships. Is this a friendship that could develop into a solid—stable relationship? Do I want to invest a lot of time and energy into this friendship that is showing signs of lacking any real substance? Does this friendship project signs of longevity? After spending a considerable amount of time with this man, I can see he's just not that into me. Is it time to let this friendship go?

You'd do good to remind yourself, if the friendship/relationship signals potential problems lay just over the horizon, the enemy won't be too far behind. He'll wait until the opportunity seems appropriate to initiate his game plan solely with the intent to kill, steal, or destroy that relationship! (John 10:10) Now mind you, the enemy also gets plenty of help from us when these relationships start to sour. He's not the culprit for everything that goes wrong, but the enemy will definitely drop by to carryout his mission of utter failure and defeat. The enemy knows should we allow a spirit of failure to invade our thought process it will only be a matter of time before the heart will follow. Once the mind starts influencing the heart, that relationship is headed for disaster!

Disappointment is one of the leading problems in relationships with males. Suddenly Mr. Wonderful ain't so wonderful anymore. And guess what? He's probably thinking you're not exactly what he bargained for either! Don't kid yourself. Men have high expectations too! The vast male population expects their significant other (wives/girlfriends) to be all that and a bag of chips! But since I'm not writing this book for them let's keep the conversation flowing between us girls— okay?

It won't matter how spiritual you are, or how much faith you profess to have. If you're drifting in a sea of disappointment, how long do you think it will take misery to jump aboard to come along for the ride? Learning to recognize what's really happening in a relationship provides you with an opportunity to defuse possibilities for splitzville. After all, it's what you don't know that will always leave you wide open for enemy attacks. If you fully understand what God's Word says about male-female relationships, you have a better shot at coming against the enemy when he starts lurking around. Like it or not, most relationships females find themselves involved in are normally the direct result of two things: (1) How they see themselves; and (2) What they think about themselves. The 'how' and the 'what' are two very important components that play out in our relationships. How and what can be the deciding factors in the success of a good, productive, balanced, and sound friendship/relationship.

Let me introduce you to Sandy. Lately Sandy has been feeling unappreciated by her husband Jack of 15 years. One evening while unloading the dishwasher, she notices the trash cans are still sitting next to the garage. With a long drawn out sigh Sandy turns from the window closing the curtains. "Hon, you mind rolling the trash cans to the curb? Trash gets picked up tomorrow. Remember?" Meanwhile, Sandy is thinking she'd really like to tell Jack. "Look! Why must I always remind you that trash gets picked up every Tuesday and Friday! I'm sick-n-tired of telling you every week!"

Whoa! Sandy calm down! Where is all this coming from? Could it be that your daddy couldn't remember to take the trash out either? Years later are you haunted by the overbearing loud sound of your mother's voice giving your daddy a tongue lashing whenever he forgot to do something? As a young girl did you promise yourself you'd never talk rudely to your husband when you grew up? Ugh? Well, strangely enough after 15 years of marriage, instead of informing hubby about this pet-peeve, you kept silent as he sat parked in his man-chair conveniently arranged in front of the big screen TV listening to you drag the trash cans to the curb week after week.

Deep down inside Sandy has harbored years of resentment, and she's about to explode! This leads me to question. What does Sandy think she's accomplishing by keeping quiet? Peace? I'm all for keeping the peace, but there's a big difference between maintaining the peace and shucking responsibilities. Sandy hasn't helped either one of them by not bringing this issue to the forefront. What she's done is unconsciously festered resentment toward this unsuspecting man. I've been there with the trash thingy. I'd get really mad with my husband because he just wasn't getting it! He was never quite sure which two days the trash got picked up. *"Every Monday and Thursday, like clock work!"* Sorry I had a flashback!

Unhealthy attitudes and mindsets prove themselves to be taxing spiritually as well as mentally. I think harboring ill feelings toward others gets in the way and stifles our spirit. Any type or source of negativity prohibits you from believing change is possible. Negative energy takes root inside the heart and the subconscious. Over time if not confronted and dealt with, it can breed resentment, disrespect, fret, despair, disillusionment, and so on. A combination of those ill feelings ultimately will destroy a relationship. I don't care how sanctified the woman says she is. Whether the relationship is with God, your husband, fiancé or a boyfriend, negative junk residing on the inside of you will rip your relationship apart! Sooner or later past wounds, unresolved issues, or ill feelings can best be conquered by a genuine act of faith to overcome them. You can't hope you'll get over them. You can't wish you could get over them. If the enemy has his way, he'll make sure you don't *ever* get over them. He'll have you peering through blurry eyes, staring at failure and defeat in your relationships. But through spiritual eyes of faith you'll see yourself clearly as the conqueror God says you are. (Romans 8:37) And, while being a conqueror has a ring of encouragement, you should understand there will be relationships that are not, salvageable, and cannot be saved. I'll be talking about that a little further in the chapter.

Meanwhile, we girls must learn to let go of past hurts and disappointments. We've got to stop covering old wounds with band-aids. This is easier to say than it is to actually do. But in a weird sort of way, doesn't holding on to past hurts give us the right to be angry? Isn't it justifiable to *still* be upset about something a man did, or didn't do? Said, or didn't say? Not really. Think about it. Where has justifiable anger gotten any of us lately? Personally, clinging to old hurt only made me miserable. Naturally, back in da' day (before I was saved), I didn't see anything wrong with clinging to hurt with both hands holding on tight. No one could've told me, I didn't have the right to be angry or harbor un-forgiveness. I wasn't born again, so how could I know anything about the power of God's Word? I was angry! How dare that man treat me that way? But in spite of it all, I was moving on without him, or so I thought. Actually, the only going forward was taking place in my disillusioned mind! I was in serious deception mode. How could I possibly be moving forward if I was harping on what so-n-so had done to me? Yet, I believed I was moving pass the hurt and anger. That's not to say I didn't accomplish a few things following these break-ups, but I shudder to think how many God-appointed opportunities I probably missed because I couldn't release that man through forgiveness. By not confronting the past, I had no idea I couldn't freely (spiritually/mentally) move toward the future. I'd later discover this was a character flaw. It was something I had to *learn* about Miss. Farrell.

And, speaking of learning, nowhere in this book do I want to come off like I did any repair work on my own. Indeed not! It took the saving grace of God, and His loving mercy to deliver me from always looking back and holding on! It's the grace of God that has kept me mentally and spiritually from sinking further into darkness and deception. Thank, you Lord! The reconstruction of my character is a personal, ongoing process each and every day. Girlfriend, I have not yet arrived! I'm involved in a no-holds barred daily deliverance relationship with my Heavenly Father. I don't kid myself. There are still some issues He's dealing with me about. As my Creator, God's well aware of what needs purging, shaping, deprogramming, and stripped away to make this sometimes unruly flesh become more like Him.

SO, WHO DO YOU THINK YOU ARE

I think it's safe to mention here, whenever any female looks back on her life feeling like it hasn't exactly been a bed of roses, maybe she should remind herself about Lot's wife. Instead of her anticipating the better, more rewarding life God promised lay ahead, she turned looking over her shoulder at what had once been. The Bible tells us Lot's wife never had the opportunity to experience all the wonderful things God said awaited her in the promise land. Me personally, I don't want to miss one thing God has promised in His Word that is available to me as a child of the Kingdom. I want all of Him. I want every blessing that has my name engraved on them. The days of looking back, wondering what I coulda-shoulda-woulda done in my marriage have long since ended—thank God! After all, looking back wasn't going to change one thing. What was done was done.

Philippians 3:13 reads:

"Brothers, I do not consider myself yet to have taken hold of it. But one thing I do: forgetting what is behind and straining toward what is ahead." (NIV)

Can I take a minute to address my readers who are single? Do you have a desire to be married? That's great! But have you *really* thought long and hard about what you say you *really want* in your marriage? Let's establish a few facts—okay? (1) It's alright to be single. (2) Reminiscing is only good when it involves happy memories. (3) Looking back, wishing Mr. Shouldamarriedme, instead of whatshername will only lead to missing out on perhaps an even greater relationship God has lined up for you. (4) You owe it to yourself to forgive Mr. Shouldamarried me. (5) That man doesn't know you're still pining over the break-up. (6) Mr. Shouldamarriedme has moved on with his life. (7) So should you!

When you dwell on the past, you waste precious time that could easily be devoted to something more meaningful. Do you know Boaz could be crossing your path everyday? But how will you recognize (discern) him if you're looking back at what might've been? Stop walking around day after day driven by unforgiveness that is only fueling self-pity and releasing lots of frustration. This attitude isn't doing anything for you spiritually or mentally. You'd be surprised to know harboring unforgiveness can also affect your physical body. Clinging to the past keeps you bound, holding your heart captive. But you're not without help. Jesus can heal you from the crown of your head, down to the soles of your feet! All too often many females have no concept they've come under the enemy's attack spiritually or mentally. When you look at your reflection in the bathroom mirror, and the woman staring back at you has little or no light behind her eyes, that's a sign there's an inner disturbance brewing. You're gazing into the lifeless eyes of a spiritually grieved female. More than likely, the hurt and disappointment she's been suppressing has left negative images in her mind. The eyes of the woman staring from the bathroom mirror probably doesn't have even the tiniest ray of hope (light), because she cannot escape the past. The woman in the mirror is wounded—broken.

Proverbs 18:14 reads:

"The strong spirit of a man sustains him in bodily pain *or* trouble, but a weak *and* broken spirit who can raise up *or* bear?" (AMP)

A bruised spirit breeds negative emotions (meanness, anger, distrust, inferiority, and hatred), which can lead to unrest within a person's soul. If untreated, feelings of this magnitude silently produce discord, strife, envy, disrespect, blame, hostility, resentment and doubt. Now I want you to ask yourself. How can any relationship with a man be expected to survive with so much inner turmoil stirring in the midst of it? I used to stare into the dark, lost eyes of the woman in my bathroom mirror. She was hurting! She was downright miserable! As a result, there were times my second ex-husband became the unsuspecting recipient of embedded memories from past relationships. I fooled myself into thinking I had resolved certain issues, but I hadn't. It wasn't until I began to seriously ask myself. Where was the resentment towards this man coming from? Why was I being motivated to think and feel the way I did? I have to be honest. Because of past relationships gone wrong, I didn't realize insecurity was serving as a release to go toe-to-toe with my ex-husband. I'm not proud of this, but sometimes I would look for ways to start petty arguments just so I could work off my frustrations. And, after every argument, I'd be disappointed with myself for allowing frustration to be used to attack him when he hadn't done anything to deserve it. It wasn't fair to him, nor was it right! I've since apologized, and asked his forgiveness for my actions.

I recall as a girl about age ten, making a promise to myself that I wasn't going to let a man tell me what to do. Sometimes I was witness to my father talking to my mother like she was one of us kids. But I wasn't having it when I grew up! Needless to say, when I married the first time in my early 20's, my mind was well made up. Submit? Are you kidding? Wasn't trying to consider it—at all! My husband wasn't going to be the boss of me! The point I'm trying to make here is this. Just from observing my parent's marriage, I already had a preconceived idea for my future as a wife. I was a ten year old kid. How could I possibly know those thoughts (seeds) planted within my mind, verbalized through my mouth (declaration) would one day bring back what I'd spoken out as a child? Those insubordinate, stubborn seeds lay undetected for years quietly growing to full maturity. The words once mouthed over and over as a child literally came back to haunt me as an adult. That being said, by the time I married for the second time in my 40's, I had mellowed out quite considerably. I was prepared to let this man wear the pants. I wanted him to keep me covered as head over his household. At this stage of my life I was born again. I knew what God's Word had to say about the union of marriage.

Ephesians 5:23-24 reads:

"A husband is the head of his wife as Christ is the head and the Savior of the church, which is his own body. Wives should always put their husbands first, as the church puts Christ first." (CEV)

During the last five years of living single following my second divorce, I've learned we girls must make every effort not to bring old baggage along from the past into future relationships. The new man in your life doesn't deserve to keep reliving an unpleasant break-up that occurred long before the two of you met. Whenever you go after him (attack) motivated by frustration or repressed anger because he's not anything like Mr. Backinmypast, you only hurt yourself by avoiding the real problem—you! Girlfriend, take a look in the mirror and get it together! Pray! Ask God to deliver you from the past!

Please note: I honestly believe good, reliable, responsible, mature, caring and loving men are still plentiful. Not *all* men are married! No, they're not *all* incarcerated! Not *all* of them are sleeping with other men! The devil is a liar! Still, as a single woman desiring to be married be forewarned. If you insist on ignoring unresolved issues, you run the risk of sitting home alone every weekend. It's one thing to sit home as a choice, but it's another to be sitting home alone because you're too complicated to get along with a man. Begin confronting the woman in the mirror, or you might not be joining the dating circuit anytime soon. Address your issues! And, I say this in love. But today's society is increasingly becoming a society of single households. God did not create mankind to live alone. (Genesis 2:18)

Men, women, boys and girls have attributes that are necessary for the other in keeping proper balance between the two sexes. Males have their role in a relationship. We have ours. God fashioned the male and female species to compliment and complete the other. We were mindfully created to be fruitful (blessed) and multiply (reproduce) in the earth.

Genesis 1:27-28 reads:

"So God created man in His own image, in the image *and* likeness of God He created him; male and female He created them. And God blessed them and said to them, Be fruitful, multiply, and fill the earth, and subdue it [using all its vast resources in the service of God and man]." (AMP)

On the other hand, females must learn to respect another female who has made a conscientious decision to live alone and not involve herself in a male relationship. Personally, at this stage of my life, I choose to live alone. I'm very comfortable in knowing who I am. Thanks to the goodness of God, I'm financially able to stand on my own. I'm not saying I don't experience a financial scrape now-n-then, but for the most part, I'm doing rather well. Plus, I've dreamed of becoming an author for so long, it wouldn't be fair to a man to be in a relationship with me at this time. Writing has become a top priority. Not only that, I want to be available to go wherever God says go at a moments notice. I want to be able to catch a plane, hop a bus, or get a train at the last minute to fulfill speaking engagements. I want to be available to do whatever God would have me to do without having to explain why I'm doing it, or how long it might take for me to complete my assignment. At this season of my life, I only want to be responsible for one person—me. Dating is currently not on my agenda. However, if God has other plans (fall in love and marry again), it will be His Will. God promised if I believe (by faith) all things are possible unto me, He'd fulfill my heart's desire—writing. But I'm also realistic. I understand there are certain males who sometimes let their macho egos get the best of them if the woman has a career she thoroughly enjoys. Intimidation can breed strange fruit in a relationship. Anybody know what I'm talking about?

My life as a single woman is very peaceful. I prefer to keep it that way without any boyfriend drama. Let's be honest. Even while we're dating these men, they still want and/or expect us to do most things that only should be carried out by a wife. I'm quite content to enjoy life to the fullest in God. If it's His Will for me to rejoin the dating circuit, He'll let me know. So far, God hasn't said a word! Single ladies I want to encourage you. *"Enjoy the wonderful life God has given you! There isn't anything you can't do for yourself. Don't ever forget you are fearfully and wonderfully made! God created you with everything you need to take care of yourself. Having a man can be a good thing, but only if having this man in your life is producing a relationship that is flourishing and maturing in the ways of God. Girlfriend, please do not sell yourself short or compromise your value, and self-worth just so you can have a man. It's not difficult to drive a nail into a wall. With practice, you'll become a pro at hanging pictures! You are equipped. You are never alone. God is always there and He loves you for real!"*

Now I'd like to speak to divorced/separated ladies. Did your relationship get off to a great start only to loose its luster along the way? Have all kinds of crazy thoughts been popping up in your head? If only he had given you another chance, what you woulda done different? If only you coulda held on a while longer what might've made the difference? Maybe you shoulda thought about it a little longer before you let him walk out the door? Do yourself a favor. Shut that kind of thinking down! Dwelling on woulda, coulda, shoulda will mess you up! Girlfriend, I have two words for you. **MOVE ON!** And, I say this in love. Let yesterday, last week, last month or last year remain in the past! Allow today to become your future! Please don't be offended or misunderstand why I'm speaking in this tone. I'm not being insensitive to your plight. From one divorced female to another, I certainly can understand you're probably upset, dazed and maybe even a little confused. You've probably asked yourself a thousand times why the marriage didn't last. Lord knows I must've asked myself that very same question over and over again. Therefore, I have a lot of empathy for how another woman is feeling when she and her man have gone (or going) through a permanent separation. I have no doubt suggesting that you move forward might sound distant and cold. But when you've done everything within your power to hold a relationship together, and it still falls apart, don't deny yourself other opportunities for happiness. Don't waste another minute living with false hope. When a husband informs his wife 'it's over', that usually means the marriage is over. So, I ask you. Why continue depleting yourself (mentally and/or spiritually) anymore than you already have? Get up! Move one foot in front of the other! I think the best thing any divorced, or soon-to-be divorced female can do for herself is retain her dignity. Fears can be calmed and stabilized by taking in the Word of God. Turning to the Bible instead of dwelling on the circumstance supplies the willpower for rebooting self-confidence. While you may feel injured, you will learn through God's Word how to rely upon His great strength, instead of trying to function on our own. If you will allow your mind to flow in the habit of believing God is able to restore a broken heart through faith, then God's Word can better readjust a tormented mindset. Your spirit-man replenishes itself by way of the renewing power of God's marvelous healing Word. Did you notice anything? I just pointed out five very good reasons why the past should be left behind. If you really want to experience brighter days—better days now that your marriage has ended, it's imperative for you to discipline yourself to let go of yesterday, and really leave it there. You also need to find it within your heart to forgive this man for hurting you. It's not that you're doing it for him, you must do this for you. Forgiveness is the first step to being healed in your heart, and restored whole in your spirit.

The enemy seeks out females (on purpose) hoping to interject the terrible double D's of division and discord into their male relationships. But even if he should succeed in causing division in your marriage, life doesn't stop because your man is gone. Show the enemy you might've been knocked down, but you're not going to stay down! Take your life back! Kick the devil upside his head! Your life isn't over just because your husband is no longer a willing participant! The devil is a liar! He wants you to believe without that man you're nothing—that you can't make it without him—he was the greatest thing to come along since sliced bread, and so on. Lies! Lies! Lies! Girlfriend, I don't care whether the relationship ended in divorce, a broken engagement, or a steady boyfriend suddenly decided he wants to date other females. Life must go on! As a matter of fact, this could very well be the best opportunity to begin anew—fresh! Are there goals or dreams you kept postponing throughout the relationship? Well, instead of thinking life is over without this man why not focus on letting God heal your brokenness? Concentrate on building up your faith to believe God has a divine pathway that leads to you becoming completely restored! Believe God is about to show up and show out in ways you've never imagined or experienced before!

Here comes a 'but' clause. But you have to put *all* of your trust in Him, especially if you feel you were victimized in this relationship. I'm proof that God will, and can put you back together again! He can take what seemingly appears chaotic, and create tranquility. God can turn your life around for the greater good. (Genesis 50:20) The truth is, God may not bring another man for you to marry, because He's about to open a door that's going to launch you into your ordained purpose and destiny. I honestly can relate with any female who doesn't see something positive evolving out of a divorce. You're hurting. I get that! But please, be encouraged! Dry your eyes! Hold your head up! Pray for comfort, deliverance and spiritual mending. As a suggestion, find Scriptures that coincide with what you're feeling. Write them down so you can begin to declare (aloud) them over your situation. And, while you're going through this healing and restoration process, ask God to give you His kind of peace that will surpass your comprehension. (Philippians 4:7)

Colossians 3:15 reads:

"Let the peace of Christ rule in your hearts, since as members of one body you were called to peace. And be thankful." (NIV)

Instead of allowing woulda-shoulda-coulda to torment and have dominion over your mind, pray for God's strength in the difficult days ahead because you're going to need all the strength you can muster, especially in the quiet hours. I know you may not accept what I'm about to say, but your life could actually turn out to be more fulfilling than you thought possible without this man.

I'd like to share something with you. Within a few short months following my divorce, (a couple of things occurred beforehand), I watched my circumstances do a three hundred sixty degree turn! Glory to God for His marvelous works! Praise the Lord, I've been moving forward ever since! That's not a boast on me. That's a boast on the goodness of God! I'm much too grateful for how far He's brought me. Girlfriend, there's nothing for me to look back to! The enemy thought he had me. And I'll admit he did, for about two minutes! The enemy was hoping I'd wallow in self-pity. He was taking bets with his cohorts, betting I'd sit around the house day in/day out fixated on what might've been. The devil was counting on me driving myself nuts over what could've been. But instead of buying into his hissing lies, I began reading God's Word. I gave God praise (in advance) for a brighter future, even though I was hurting. By faith I believed my situation would pass and I'd be the better for having gone through the experience.

If you wondered whether I became angry when my husband announced his decision to move out of the house, I did. I'm not going to tell you in his absence I didn't cry myself to sleep a lot of nights. I did. I missed him. I hadn't wanted our marriage to end. However, in spite of my heavy heart I had sense enough to know I couldn't wallow in a woe-is-me state of mind for very long. Every night I read the Bible. I watched a lot of Christian TV. I also listened to inspiring and encouraging Christian CD's. I took steps to do whatever was necessary to keep building up my faith. I desperately needed to believe God was going to do wonderful things in my future as a single woman. I thanked Him in advance for preparing the way in spite of the dumb stuff that was going on around me. The Holy Spirit also reminded me. "You're a world over-comer! Trust in the Lord with all of your heart, and lean not to your own understanding!"

As the daughter of Almighty God, I would definitely recover following this divorce. With that truth echoing in my spirit, the next morning I opened the front door of my house as far back on the hinges as the door would permit. Then I reached for the kitchen broom. I swept anger, depression, hurt, guilt and confusion out the door, down the porch steps, to the sidewalk, and into the street where they belonged! They had overstayed their visit! On that Saturday morning I decided to take a stand. Those lingering negative spirits had to go because my God is faithful to His Word. He promised to never leave me, nor forsake me. The various passages of Scripture I read each night gave way to a marvelous light of hope. I honestly believed with all of my heart the days ahead were going to be much better than the days of old.

But, here comes another 'but' clause. But we have an obligation to be faithful to God as well. We *must* do our part. We must make a commitment to healing. If you read my first book, then you know I strongly believe there is nothing too hard for our Heavenly Father. Neither is there anything we can't do (by faith) through our Lord and Savior, Jesus Christ. Now, hear me loud and clear with what I'm about to say. When we get involved in relationships with men that end up doing spiritual, mental and physical harm to us, God doesn't stop loving us because we leave these men, or don't stop them from leaving us. In fact, I'd go as far as to say, once a female makes a quality decision to get out of an abusive verbal and/or physical relationship (God didn't bring together in the first place), there's an outpouring of His love upon that female even more because of the agonizing hurt and pain she's had to endure. Much like our natural daddies, our Heavenly Daddy wants to protect us from going through pain and heartache. God shields a broken daughter, whether her pain is visible or she's experiencing a private pain that no one sees.

Would your natural father condemn you for finally disconnecting yourself from a relationship that has been dragging you down, and the kids along with you? Well, God won't either. Girlfriend, do you really believe that an abusive relationship is part of God's plan for you? Don't you realize the more a man is beating on you, or calls you out of your name, your true identity fades away, and you're no longer walking as the female who God predestined you to be? She is still there underneath the pain and sorrow. It's our Creator's Will for each of His daughters to lead healthy and prosperous lives.

III John 2 reads:

"Beloved, I wish above all things that thou mayest prosper and be in health, even as thy soul prospereth." (KJV)

Unfortunately, we're the ones who mess things up along the way. God knows everything. He sees everything. God already knew you and I were going to date the wrong men. He knew we would fall in love with men who didn't want or appreciate us. He knew we were going to engage in pre-marital sex with guys who were slick enough to con us into bed. He knew some of us would find ourselves pregnant having to give birth to children out of wedlock. God knew His daughters would marry men who didn't meet His approval or receive His blessing because this wasn't the man He had intended for His daughter to marry. That's why we older women really ought to be mindful of younger females. They're watching us. These young females observe the ways in which godly women conduct themselves in friendships/relationships with the opposite sex. I think as godly women our interaction in a male relationship(s) should demonstrate how much we love and value ourselves. I'd like to use the following illustrations of male/female relationships. They no doubt will closely resemble someone we either know, or they'll be a reflection of ourselves.

Couple # 1: Meet John and Bria. The two of them frequently exchanged pleasantries and bashful smiles at church. Within a short span of time Bria secretly fell in love with John. And what young lady wouldn't? John is single. He's handsome. And, as far as appearances go, appears to be a very nice young man. John sings in the church choir. He ushers. He faithfully attends church—a godly young man. Bria was thrilled when John finally asked her out on a date for dinner and a movie. John has been exceptionally nice while they've been dating. He's shown himself to be very considerate and quite charming. Eleven months later into their courtship John popped the question. Bria pinched herself. She couldn't believe John was asking her to be his wife. Naturally, Bria accepted his proposal of marriage. Her prayers had been answered. It had been her heart's desire to marry a godly man—someone who people would respect. Bria wanted her husband to be a man people looked up to, in and outside the church. She asked God to send her a godly man who would truly love her because Bria thought of other females as being prettier than she rarely saw herself. Out of all of the other attractive single women at church, John had chosen her to be his wife. That night over a candlelit dinner, a very surprised Bria couldn't stop pinching (figuratively speaking) herself when John placed a modest diamond engagement ring on her finger. Bria felt like the luckiest woman in the world. John was going to be her husband!

Three months into wedded bliss, Bria and John got into a rather heated conversation. Bria suggested they move out of John's apartment when the lease expired in four months. She openly expressed a desire to buy a house so they could start a family. John on the other hand, retorted stating he was content to remain living in his apartment. Nevertheless, Bria continued voicing her concerns. She hadn't felt John's apartment was her home too. Bria has always been an outspoken female. While she and John were courting he discussed wanting someone who wasn't afraid to speak up for herself. A show of self-confidence had been one of the things that attracted him to Bria. She was well educated and intelligent. Bria knew what she wanted out of life. Unlike the women he'd previously dated, Bria didn't require high maintenance, which kept more money in his wallet. Bria almost immediately liked John from the first time she spied him sitting across the aisle with his parents one Sunday morning. His father had recently been promoted at his job causing John's family to relocate. Bria was proud that John had recently graduated from law school and gotten hired by a local firm in the position of an associate attorney earning a six figure income.

Up until now, John hadn't objected to Bria freely speaking her mind. But, the idea of moving out of his spacious two-bedroom apartment wasn't going over too well with him. Lately, he was growing tired of his place being the only topic Bria wanted them to talk about. Meanwhile on this particular evening, as the discussion of buying a house continued, their voices started to climb. Both Bria and John's adrenaline elevated. She refused to back down. As far as Bria was concerned, John's behavior was unfair. Why wouldn't he want to buy a house they both could call home?

Following their honeymoon, from the first day Bria moved in, John hadn't made her feel very welcomed in *his apartment*. Every piece of furniture had to be kept exactly the way John had it arranged. Any ideas or suggestions Bria offered for making a change around the apartment was instantly refuted. In the back of Bria's mind, as she sat listening to his reasoning why they should stay, she began thinking John was acting childish. She wanted him to seriously consider buying a house! Besides, it wasn't like they couldn't afford a home of their own. He was an attorney. She was an elementary school teacher. Finances were not a problem. Bria was hoping they might have a baby in the next year. Trying to raise a baby within the perimeters of an apartment with little room for growth had not been the way she envisioned their marriage.

Bria sat next to John fuming. She couldn't understand why John was being so stubborn. Suddenly out of nowhere, John caught Bria totally by surprise. Without any warning John turned slapping her across the face with the back of his hand. Then just as quickly he reacted drawing Bria into his arms, begging her to forgive him. She was so shocked by John's actions, Bria couldn't speak. With tears streaming down her face, John pulled his wife close to his chest. "Baby, I'm so sorry! I'm sorry, Bria!" he whispered. Bria deeply loved this man. She thought she knew everything there was to know about him before they married. Up until now, John had never shown any violent tendencies.

Bria's mind flashed back to the months leading up to John's proposal, and the afternoon of their wedding. Early on while they were dating, she thanked God for bringing John into her life. Even though the side of her face was stinging from the backhanded force behind John's large hand, Bria believed John speaking softly into her ear. "Sorry baby. I'll never do that again. Bria, I love you too much to ever put my hands on you. Please forgive me!"

Well, a little over five years has passed since that incident. During which, Bria has become a master at smiling through one disappointment, only to quickly be followed by another let down. It turns out John isn't the caring man she once thought him to be. Whenever Bria is in the presence of family, friends or church folks, she says very little and smiles. She responds to those who still ask how's married life, with the words they seem to want to hear. "Things are going good for John and me."

Within five short years, Bria has taught herself how to camouflage a broken heart. She hides any evidence of being physically abused. The enemy whispers incredulous untruths when he sees Bria at her most vulnerable state. "It would be embarrassing if anyone ever finds out that the godly man people see in public—the good loving, God-fearing son in-law, husband, father, and church deacon is really an imposter. What will you do when people find out your marriage is based on a lie? A lie you swallowed the first time John hit you!" he whispers. The louder the enemy has whispered, the more Bria has grown afraid of what others might say about her marriage to John. She decided it was better to remain silent even if it meant she lived in constant fear for her and her two young children. Regrettably, after almost six years of living in a turbulent marriage, Bria has lost her identity. Because she lives in a perpetual state of fear, Bria no longer speaks out against anything John might say. She never knows what will set him off, so Bria has learned when to be mute and invisible within the walls of their home. She now lacks the self-confidence and assurance she once prided herself on before marrying John.

Unbeknownst to Bria, she began deceiving herself two years into the marriage. She told herself John would stop beating her when he learned she was expecting their first child. Bria was right. During the nine months of her pregnancy John behaved like the man she fell in love with. Twice a week he showered her with gifts. Not long following their baby girl's birth, John's physical and verbal anger reared their ugly heads. Only this time the abuse returned with more intensity. Thirteen months later when they welcomed the birth of their second child the fighting abruptly stopped. Bria prayed day and night that whatever this generational stronghold was over John, it had finally been broken.

At the hospital she looked upon John's face when he held their second baby. Behind his eyes she saw the love John had for his newborn son. In spite of the violence, Bria still loved John with all of her heart. But what she hated about him was his uncontrollable temper. In the months preceding the birth of their second child, John hadn't so much as raised a fist or his voice to Bria. Peace had returned to their home. Bria believed her prayers had been answered.

Two weeks before Christmas while Bria was feeding the children dinner, John came home that evening agitated from work. Before she could inquire who, or what had upset him, John flew into a violent rage. He grabbed Bria forcing her to stop what she was doing by pulling her away from the kitchen table, dragging her up the stairs to their bedroom as Bria struggled and fought to free herself from her husband's hold. John opened the closet doors shoving Bria inside with no means of escape past the clothes hanging there. John repeatedly struck Bria viciously assaulting her. The next morning an emotionally, physically bruised and battered Bria could barely get out of bed to care for the children. Over the Christmas holiday she alienated herself from family and friends. Bria invented excuses to keep anyone from seeing any evidence of John's abuse. She stayed within the privacy of her home until the bruises were less visible. It was almost a month later before her bruises healed.

Like any good mother, Bria is devoted to raising her young daughter and son to have values. She's doing the best she can to be a mother that her children will love and respect. Yet, John has no problem letting his children witness the physical or verbal abuse against their mother—his wife, the woman he vowed to cherish and protect. Every day Bria lives in the big suburban house she dreamed they'd buy one day. She lives inside this beautiful home spiritually broken, lonely, and disconnected from her family. Because of her shame, Bria has distanced herself from her closest friends. Through it all she has tried to hold onto her faith in God. Still, Bria questions how a loving God could watch this man viciously beat her time and time again. Alone, in her silent fears she wonders if God cares whether John might possibly kill her. But Bria's greatest fear, apart from death is that their young children would be helpless to watch him do it.

Couple #2: Meet Mr. Goodlooking and Karen: On their very first date, Mr. Goodlooking established he wasn't a one-woman-at-a-time kind of guy. He explained as a single man, he has avoided tying himself down to one woman because he's

SO, WHO DO YOU THINK YOU ARE

waiting for someone special to come along. Karen was well aware he had previously dated a few of the single women in the office. She also knew those dates hadn't gone very well. What Karen didn't bother to ask any of those women was why hadn't their dates developed into anything beyond a first date. Unbeknownst to Karen, it didn't take the women in the office long to discover Mr. Goodlooking wasn't worth a second date. But Karen was so elated Mr. Goodlooking had finally asked her out on a date, she disregarded the other women in the office. Meanwhile, on their first dinner date to an upscale restaurant, seated across a candle-lit table, Karen sat dazzled by Mr. Goodlooking's cute, kissable lips and sparkling white movie star smile. Most of what he was telling Karen about himself went in one of her pierced ears and out the other. Overall, the date went fairly well. Mr. Goodlooking asked to see her again.

It's been three months of dating, and Karen is now beginning to wonder why she has to go on keeping their relationship a secret however, she hasn't bothered to press the issue with Mr. Goodlooking. Instead, she has resolved herself to accepting the explanation that he thought the other women in the office might treat Karen differently because she was going out with him. What? Pleeze! Unfortunately, Karen fell for that lame explanation.

Seven months later Mr. Goodlooking dropped a bomb on Karen. He told her about another woman he had asked out on a date. But he was quick to add just because he asked this woman out, didn't mean he wanted to stop seeing her. Karen was satisfied and didn't voice any objections. She quietly looked back at him through eyes blinded by love. In her heart, Karen believed her relationship with Mr. Goodlooking was worth the investment of her time and energy, because you never know, she could be the one! Mr. Goodlooking knows his plan to keep Karen sold on the idea that he wants to be sure their relationship is serious before he takes her home to meet his parents, has been successful thus far. Beneath his façade Mr. Goodlooking is confident that in the ten months they've been going out, there isn't anything Karen won't do to keep him happy. In the meantime, Karen has fantasies of being *the one*. She is thoroughly convinced that sooner or later Mr. Goodlooking will stop wanting to date other women. She believes he'll wake up to realize that a good woman has been standing in front of him all along. And when he finally does get tired of playing the field, Karen plans to be right there waiting.

As their relationship is approaching a year, Karen suddenly found herself sitting home alone for the second consecutive weekend. While sitting on the long sofa staring at the walls, Karen's mind started toying with her emotions. She recalled a conversation she once had with her mother when she was a teenager. "Young men need to sow their wild oats before they settle down. It's best to let them date as much as they can before you consider marrying them." Then Karen's mind shifted to a time when there was no Mr. Goodlooking or anyone else in her life, which wasn't so long ago.

Before Mr. Goodlooking came along Karen was very comfortable with her size. She knew she'd never wear a size two, but she accepted that fact. She was a full-figure woman and Karen loved every inch of her body. However, after hearing the kind of woman Mr. Goodlooking preferred dating, Karen practically started starving herself because she was afraid he'd stop dating her if she didn't lose some weight. Now, whenever they go out to dinner, instead of Karen enjoying an appetizing meal from the menu, she shrinks back. "I'll have the house salad with no dressing," she says returning the unopened menu to the waiter. Then she watches Mr. Goodlooking chow down on his delicious looking hot meal.

Within twelve months Karen has spent more money than she dare tell any of her girlfriends, especially knowing not one of them thinks Mr. Goodlooking is worthy of her. Prior to Karen spending money for only the best hair weaves, she always preferred wearing her natural hair in sassy short styles. But after she began dating Mr. Goodlooking, he informed Karen that he liked his women to have long, silky straight hair. The fully loaded fancy foreign car Karen let Mr. Goodlooking con her into buying (he drives it more than she does), is starting to put a strain on the checkbook. Without realizing what she's been doing, Karen has tapped out a large sum of her retirement savings to keep Mr. Goodlooking interested. They flew to the Cayman Islands twice (at her expense) because he expressed a desire to go there for vacation when he got *his finances* in better shape. But who could blame Karen for spoiling this gorgeous hunk of a man? She's soooooooooooooo happy to finally have someone like Mr. Goodlooking in her life! Every time they're in public, Karen notices stares from other women who are probably just pea-green with envy! She also sees the way her co-workers start gawking whenever Mr. Goodlooking drops by her desk. Karen supposes those women are probably sorry they didn't date him a couple of more times before writing him off

Karen turned her thoughts back to the phone sitting next to her. It hadn't rang once since she came in from work on Friday. It was Sunday evening and Mr. Goodlooking hasn't so much as called to say hello in three days. A sigh of disappointment escaped passed her lips. In the past, the men Karen found interesting didn't give her a second glance. Because of her weight, coupled with age, Karen had just about given up any hope of ever finding someone who could look past those things. She dreamed of finding a man who loved her for the beautiful person who lives on the inside. Karen longs to be married. Three of Karen's closest friends are now married with babies. When Mr. Goodlooking asked her out, Karen leaped at the chance to be seen with a man in public. After all, dates seemed to occur less often once she turned 30.

Karen is one year shy of turning 40. She has not heard the words "I love you", and it's been a year of exclusively dating Mr. Goodlooking.

Still, Karen remains hopeful a marriage proposal isn't far away. She is determined to do whatever is necessary to keep Mr. Goodlooking, even if it means walking around too blind to see what's really happening in their relationship. Karen has made herself believe if she were to stop seeing this man the second she's out of the picture, Mr. Goodlooking will marry someone else. Karen feels she has waited a long time for the attention she received from Mr. Goodlooking. He may not be the most trustworthy man in the world, but it sure beats not having a man!

Regrettably, a year later after making plans to spend a week with *her man* at a romantic Caribbean couples resort, (at her expense) in celebration of her fortieth birthday, Karen finally saw Mr. Goodlooking for who he really was. One of Karen's co-workers pulled her aside to show her the morning newspaper. There it was in black and white in the section listing the names of people who had filed for marriage licenses: *Candace Grover and Mr. Goodlooking.*

SO, WHO DO YOU THINK YOU ARE

Karen couldn't believe what she was seeing. With much pain, Karen thanked her co-worker for bringing it to her attention.

For two weeks Karen pretended to be uninformed about Mr. Goodlooking's future plans to get married. On the morning of their flight to the Caribbean, Karen arrived at the airport in plenty of time to carry out her plan. She sat watching other travelers rushing about to catch their planes while waiting for Mr. Goodlooking to join her. An hour later there he was looking good as ever smiling, waving to Karen. She stood to her feet taking a deep breath. Karen never dreamed it would come to this. She'd given this man everything and he in turn had betrayed her in the worst kind of way. "Hi Baby!" he said kissing Karen's cheek. She took another deep breath. "Hi," she replied barely returning his smile. "What's wrong?" Mr. Goodlooking inquired noticing Karen's agitated expression. Karen stepped closer to him so no one else would overhear what she was about to say. "What's wrong? You'd go on this vacation with me knowing you're planning to marry another woman! How dare you use me for two years! I thought you loved me! I've been a gullible fool!" Mr. Goodlooking stood at a lost for words. "But but, I..." he began to say. "There's nothing you can say!" Karen quipped. "How long were you going to keep stringing me along? When did you plan on telling me that you were getting married? I want you to get away from me before I do something I might regret! I'm going on vacation alone where I can think! I need to clear my head. For two years my life has been about you! I need to get my life back on track, the way it was before I let a snake like you in it!" Karen leaned in closer speaking into his ear. "But more importantly, while I'm laying on the beach soaking up the sun, I'm going to forget I ever knew you! I hope you have a nice life, because in case you didn't know it, what goes around comes around!" Karen smiled at Mr. Goodlooking before walking away heading for the line where other passengers had begun boarding the plane.

Couple #3: Meet high school sweethearts, Daisy and James: Daisy met and fell in love with James in their freshman year of high school. James is the only man Daisy has ever loved. She and James were happily married two weeks following their high school graduation. Even though she was young in years, Daisy took their wedding vows very seriously. Over the years she and James have built a strong marriage upon the love and trust they have for each other. Their marriage is based on the values and morals instilled in them from youth. James is a hard working family man. He's an elder at church. He's well respected in the neighborhood where they live.

One afternoon James and Daisy were sitting alone in their family room. The children had gone off to do whatever it is teenagers do on a Saturday afternoon. Today would be a day Daisy wouldn't soon forget. Nothing could've prepared her for what was about to happen as she sat across the family room from her husband. There had been no visible signs that James was no longer happy in their marriage.

James stood up slowly from his favorite chair drawing a deep breath. For weeks he'd been rehearsing in his mind how best to approach his wife. Today seemed to be the perfect day since the kids weren't around. He went to stand in front of the large window. James folded his arms watching the neighbor's boys playing across the street. "Daisy—I don't want to be married anymore," he blurted. "The kids are practically grown," James quickly continued, just in case Daisy may have forgotten how old their three children were.

SO, WHO DO YOU THINK YOU ARE

"You can keep the house. The only thing I want is to be free."

But that wasn't the whole truth. Daisy was far too intelligent than to buy into 'the children are almost grown' rationale. She silently wiped a single tear that had fallen, relying on her inner strength to try to keep a civil tongue in her head. Daisy briefly closed her eyes, praying she wouldn't pick up the table lamp and throw it across the room at her husband. "James," she spoke calmly. "We've been married 36 years. I've known you for even longer. The kids are practically grown? How'd you come to that conclusion? James, they're far from being practically grown. Our children are twelve, sixteen, and seventeen! Now you're trying to tell me they're almost adults? Ugh? Did you say I can have the house?" Daisy raised her body from sitting on the sofa. "Gee, how generous of you!" She moved closer to where James stood with his back to her at the window. Daisy folded her arms across her chest using body language to speak for her, demanding James make eye contact. He turned from the window lowering his eyes, then finally raising them again to meet Daisy's angry stare. James swallowed. "There's another woman…" James looked away confessing he'd been seeing this woman for over two years, and they had a 14 month old baby daughter.

Suddenly Daisy felt sick to her stomach. James has been the one and only man she's ever loved. At age 13, from the minute she first saw the cute boy helping his family move into the house next door where she lived with her family, Daisy immediately developed a school girl crush. James has been her everything. Daisy stood paralyzed in front of the window wondering how long James had been unhappy with her. She imagined her life would never be the same without him. Dreams she had as a younger woman were put aside. Making her husband happy had been her number one priority. James didn't want her working when the children came along. That's when she got behind James supporting him in his career because she believed his dreams were more important than anything she might dream for herself.

After thirty-six years, how would she be able to face people? What would people at church say when the news began circulating that James had left her for another woman? How could she face family and friends once everyone found out James had not only been unfaithful in their marriage, but he and this woman shared a baby together? The shame! The humiliation! How was she going to get over such a disgrace? What about their children? Had he even thought what kind of an effect the news of another woman and a divorce was going to do to them?

Daisy vacated the family room without saying another word, deeply disturbed by her husband's announcement. "God, why would you allow this to happen?" Daisy thought aloud climbing the stairs to escape the presence of James. She closed the bedroom door behind her, hurrying to the side of their bed, dropping to her knees. Daisy buried her face in the bedspread sobbing. She'd been a good wife. She thought she and James were best friends—soul mates till death separated them. Whenever he encountered problems on his job, she was his sounding board. Daisy encouraged him to follow his dream knowing how much it meant for James to operate his own accounting firm. It was because of her, James had the faith and courage to quit his job at a reputable brokerage firm. How could James forget the sacrifices she'd made for him? Didn't thirty-six years count for something? She has been his lover, companion, and confidant. How could James betray her like this? Daisy shook her head as tears steamed down her cheeks. She knelt along side of the bed clasping her hands together. "Dear God! Help me!" she cried out in a low whisper inside the empty room. "I don't know if I can handle this! My heart is breaking! I love this man! I can forgive his infidelity, if he changes his mind and stays with me! Help me, Lord! Help me find strength for my children! Give me the strength to hold my head up high and not feel humiliated!"

Daisy wept openly on bended knees. One thought after another penetrated her mind. James has a baby with another woman kept ringing in her ears. Then Daisy's imagination took over. Women at church will have a good time laughing and gossiping behind her back. She knew of two women in particular who would say she got exactly what she deserved! Daisy had overheard a disheartening conversation one Sunday following church service between her fellow Christian sisters. The two women were in the ladies room unaware she was standing within earshot behind the closed stall door. "Daisy thinks she's too good to socialize with us because her husband is an elder and sits on the church board. Ever since she's been coming here, she's always acted like she and her family are better than everybody else. Even her kids are snooty!" The two women giggled stepping outside the bathroom leaving Daisy behind the closed door inside the stall. She wondered had she really presented herself as anti-sociable all these years. And if so, Daisy thought those two women were going to enjoy watching her world fall apart. Daisy could only imagine what they would be whispering behind her back to the other women at church. "Serves her right with her stuck up self!" The very idea about people at church talking about her family made Daisy's stomach churn. She slowly shuffled to her feet hurrying from the bedroom to the adjacent master bathroom.

Within a matter of minutes Daisy's marriage had gone from trust and security to betrayal and humiliation, but she was determined to hold her head up. She prayed asking God to help her get through the days ahead, not for herself, but for her children. She wanted to be strong for them. Daisy silently observed her husband removing some of his clothes from the bedroom closet and dresser drawers. James said nothing, but he could feel his wife's eyes watching his every move. "How long before you come back to get the rest of your things?" Daisy asked as she went to sit on the edge of the bed. "If you're leaving me for another woman, there's no need to drag this out. I'd like for you to have all of your things out by this weekend. If the kids and I are going to be living here without you, I'd rather we get used to the idea as soon as possible." Daisy continued. James turned from the open closet staring at his wife. "I know you probably won't believe me, but I really am sorry for hurting you. I never wanted this to happen, Daisy." She glared at him from across the room. Daisy stood up from the bed struggling to keep from crying. "James, I want you out of here before the children come home. If I need to get in touch with you, I'll call your office." As she approached the bedroom door to leave James alone to resume packing Daisy hesitated turning, looking over her shoulder. "Thirty-six years and this is what I get? Why James? Never mind! With God on my side, the kids and I will be fine. As a matter of fact, we might be even better off without you, than we were with you here."

"I want you to file for divorce as quickly as possible. I trust you won't be contesting my request to have sole custody of our children. I'll contact a realtor tomorrow to put the house on the market. After you and I sell the house, we can split the final sale so I can buy another house for me and the kids. We can discuss more specifics later. In the meantime, I'm calling a lawyer." Daisy then left the bedroom satisfied that the actions of her husband weren't going to shatter her world. She smiled to herself walking down the hall away from the bedroom, feeling stronger already.

Couple # 4 Meet Kyle and Rhonda: Kyle is every woman's idea of the dream-mate. He's a loving, thoughtful, tender, caring, affectionate, and hard working provider for his family. Kyle is the head of his household. He prays for his wife Rhonda every day, keeping her covered. Kyle's number one priority is seeing that his wife is genuinely happy. From the moment Rhonda accepted his proposal of marriage, Kyle never wanted to put her in a position that made her feel insecure in their marriage.

Over the years Kyle has frequently showered Rhonda with gifs just because. He doesn't wait until it's her birthday, Mother's Day, Christmas, or any other special calendar day. For Kyle everyday is special being married to Rhonda. The gifts are simply expressions of his devotion to her. Kyle affectionately and openly displays his committed love, whether they're alone or out in public. Their children never have to question if he loves their mother. From the first time Kyle saw Rhonda walking across the college campus grounds, he knew she was the one for him. All throughout their two years of courtship during college Kyle made it his business to learn as much as possible about Rhonda.

As their friendship developed into a serious relationship, Rhonda informed Kyle upfront she was not sleeping with a man who wasn't her husband. Kyle agreed, thereby making a commitment to abstain from sex during their courtship. Kyle was what Rhonda had been looking for in a boyfriend. She was relieved to know there wouldn't be any pressure from Kyle. She loved Kyle because he respected her wishes. He never tried to make her feel guilty for not wanting to engage in pre-marital sex. They began attending church off campus with a couple of friends. They got into a habit of studying the Bible together in preparation of their future union as man and wife. Kyle expressed wanting their home to be a Christian home. When the children came along, he wanted them to know and love God as much as he and Rhonda did.

Over time, their love has grown even stronger. Kyle and Rhonda's relationship is the envy of other men and women. There are some who find it hard to believe that he and Rhonda are *really happy* in their marriage. Rhonda is Kyle's best friend. They understand intricate details about each other no one will ever know. On their wedding day, the young college grads pledged a commitment to their marriage, and to each other. Kyle and Rhonda are soul mates—till death do them part. Early on, they recognized a divine connection existed between them. There's nothing more I can tell you about Kyle and Rhonda, except to say. "Way to go, girl!"

These four couples are fiction. I used them to illustrate the varying scenarios that commonly exist in male-female relationships. Are you aware sometimes fiction doesn't stray too far from truth? Perhaps you know someone like Bria. Do you know anyone like Karen? What about Daisy? Do you know a woman who has a terrific marriage like Rhonda does? More than likely, we all know, or have known females like the ones I described in this chapter. It's highly probable someone reading this book may closely resemble one of the characters in these illustrations. No female (including me), is immune from finding herself involved in a relationship such as the ones I highlighted.

Oh! So you think you're too smart to get involved in an abusive relationship like Bria found herself in? You say you're far more intelligent than Karen to fall for the charm of a strikingly handsome man who is only interested in taking advantage of your good nature and your bank account? So, you think you would know whether your husband was having an affair outside of your marriage?

Girlfriend, do you honestly *think* you're above letting yourself become entangled in a relationship like the women I wrote about? Oh really? I pray you wouldn't! But I'm here to tell you, **we all wanna be loved**! What female hasn't wanted to believe her man isn't real with his feelings or isn't telling her the truth? What female hasn't wanted to believe her marriage will last forever? But more importantly, do you know any female who hasn't wanted to believe she'll always have true love with her man? Sorry to say this, but female hormones have a way of leading a lot of us straight to the road called trouble. Let's face it. Feelings are indicators, as well as motivators. They can either assist in certain situations, or they can hinder the situation. Emotions do one or two things: (1) produce a positive outcome, or (2) create an unproductive result.

One thing is certain. Whether a female's relationship lasts seven weeks, seven months, or seventy years, I haven't met one yet who doesn't give 100% of herself to a man when she truly likes and/or loves a man. Females in general invest a lot of time emotionally and just as much highly charged energy into their friendships/relationships, expecting a full return on their love. However, usually once the relationship comes up short after pouring everything (spiritually, mentally, physically, and sometimes financially) into these relationships many females are left feeling frustrated in their man and in themselves. That's about the time dreadful self-incriminating questions start adding insult to injury. "Is there more I could have done?" "What did I do to make him want to leave me for somebody else?"

If I haven't learned anything since my divorce, I've learned this. I shouldn't count on or expect another human being to make me happy! Seeking and finding happiness is a task one must conquer. Actually it's unfair to place that kind of pressure on a husband, a boyfriend, or even a female friend. How high you set the bar to achieve happiness rests solely upon your shoulders. You and I have a choice. We can either choose to go through life miserable, blaming everybody else for the lousy way we feel, or we can choose to find joy and happiness in spite of it. You can make your own self happy starting with the kind of environment you create for yourself. Taking ownership and responsibility for whatever does, or doesn't happen in your life is a sign of maturity. I'm a firm believer it's God's Will for each of His daughters to enjoy their lives to the fullest! But the final decision has to be yours. Jesus came into this world so that you could have joy in your life, as well as live it in abundance.

John 15:11 reads:

"These things have I (Jesus) spoken unto you, that my joy might remain in you, and that your joy might be full." (KJV)

Most females should understand that their feelings determine a large part of who they are—their personality. I think feelings and emotions serve as sensor tools to assist in helping us better know and understand our true selves. Depending on which way these feelings are flowing on any given particular day, at any given particular moment, they can also stop you from fulfilling the purpose and plan ordained for your life. Simply put. It means you and I mustn't become comfortable in *how we feel* a large majority of the time. Female emotions are fickle. Yes, I said it! Okay? Com'on girls! You know it's true! We meet a terrific guy and can be on top of the world. Then as time passes we can do a flip on Mister Terrific. "Please do not call me again!" I know because I've been there! I've done that!

Normally feelings don't give notice when they're about to do a hormonal shake-up. Emotions just do their thing. But they are not who we are. It's how we allow them to shape our personality that can create unnecessary chaos, especially when dealing with the opposite sex. You and I may not always respond rationally to certain situations, but the more we're willing to learn what makes us tick as an individual, and where these negative feelings derive from, we can then better learn how to take control over them and not allow feelings to have control over us. A female's emotions should be taken into consideration when making choices in selecting the kind of man she wants to let into her life. Maybe you should read over one of those four illustrations again mentioned before in this chapter.

I don't want to burst your bubble, but a new friendship with a male may not develop into anything more than being his friend. Like a sister-friendship. Could you handle it? Could you accept he doesn't want anything more from you than being your friend? Girlfriend, not every man that crosses your path is meant to be a boyfriend, or the man you'll marry.

At 50-something, I've had my fair share of giving love and being loved, along with experiencing heartache at losing love. Shortly after my divorce in 2007, I learned a very valuable lesson. I suspect somewhere deep down inside I knew all along that I hadn't bothered to ask enough questions during our courtship. The truth is there were several occurrences that took place which should've made me take the time to explore them further. Instead, I chose to ignore them. And, in all respect, my ex-husband didn't ask many questions either. But putting red warning flags aside, he and I entered marriage in love. We were deliriously excited about our new union as man and wife. We were going to grow older together. Unfortunately, within a few short months while we were *still learning* about each other, we hit a snag. Character traits began revealing their true selves. There were things that could've easily been discussed, had we taken the time to ask more questions while dating.

Before I came along, my husband lived alone throughout most of his adult life. To say suddenly finding himself having to share his space with a female was a big adjustment, would be an understatement. His home was in Atlanta, which meant I had to relocate. The very idea of picking up everything I owned was as scary for me as it was exciting. Still, I was happy. God had sent me a terrific man! I was in love! But those excited, giggly school girl feelings were soon evaporating. Almost from the instant I stepped inside *his apartment* in Atlanta, it hit me. This was his home—his environment. A wave of homesickness for my apartment back in Delaware rushed over me. Suddenly I needed a piece of furniture, a picture, anything that was familiar to me. "*Hey! Unlock the moving truck! I need to get a few things out—now!*" I heard myself saying before my husband and his brother exited the living room in search of lunch.

Since I had no job I was left home during the day while hubby went off to work. Being left alone I'd get in my car driving around (got lost a lot!) trying to learn how to get from point A to point B. It didn't take long to master my way around Decatur, Georgia. After getting up going to work for over thirty years, I never thought I'd say this, but within a matter of weeks I grew bored staying home. I didn't know what to do with myself. Then one afternoon I got this brilliant idea! Why not make a few changes around our apartment? Anyone who knows me knows I enjoy decorating. I personally think a home should reflect the person, or persons who live there. As a new bride, I wanted my husband to come home to an apartment he could be proud of. Great idea! The following morning after sending hubby off with a kiss, I sprang into action! The plan was to get everything done before he came home from work. I wanted to surprise him!

The morning started with scrubbing baseboards, washing down walls, and disposing what looked like junk. I even moved the living room furniture around. I cleaned every nook-n-cranny of that apartment. My transformation from a bachelor's apartment into a home for two was shaping up very nicely. By the time I completed my assignment later that afternoon, the apartment not only had the appearance of a cozy home for two, it felt more like home to me. I couldn't wait for hubby to come home from work so he could see it! Well, when he arrived home from work, hubby took one long (I'm talking long!) hard look around the living room. It didn't take a rocket scientist to see he wasn't impressed by all my hard work. "What did you do?" He closed the door behind him. The man was in shock! "Who told you to change things in here?" Hubby was not a happy camper! He didn't appreciate the initiative I had taken to clean up the apartment to make him a home.

What I mistook for cluttered mess, and more junk than I'd ever seen in my life, had actually been a systematic way for him to find things. "Who asked you to change my stuff around!" he repeated. That question reminded me of something. We never discussed how I'd fit into his home. Within that moment of thought, his question told me all I needed to know, however late it might've been. My great idea to clean up had turned out not to be that great so far as he was concerned. Instead of looking at the apartment as a fresh new beginning for him and me, he saw change as intrusive. The disturbance of *his things* signaled B-I-G trouble. But then again, I thought the apartment was now *our home*. All I had wanted to do was please him by organizing the place. I tried creating the kind of atmosphere I was accustomed to having in a home. After all, wasn't I going to be living there too? I only did what any woman would've done—right? I added a few feminine touches to his bachelor's pad. Major mistake!

"I don't know where anything is! I had all *my stuff* just the way I wanted it!" he exclaimed. Hubby was really upset! After taking a couple of deep breaths he continued to rant and rave. I thought it was best if I tuned him out as I slowly looked around the spotlessly clean living room. The apartment probably hadn't been that clean since he moved in! I wanted our home to look inviting when you opened the door. As he huffed and puffed, I was becoming a little salty and started thinking, "*This place was a wreck! It looked like a bomb went off in here!*" Told you I was getting salty! "*I don't know how you could find anything with this place looking the way it did! I've never seen so much paper and junk!*" Hubby threw his hands up in the air (frustrated) and stormed out of the living room.

"Farrell!" I heard his voice climbing. Oh! Oh! I was in even bigger trouble! I rushed from the living room to the short hallway that separated the bedroom from the bathroom. "You should've asked me if you could put curtains in here!" Now I ask you. What woman doesn't hang curtains up to a window? Especially a bedroom window! Was this man serious? What made him think I wanted to sleep in a room with only shades covering the windows? Pleeze! Those two bedroom windows didn't block out enough privacy for me. By this time his hollering was really starting to make me wonder if I had married a crazy man.

Long story short, that day was only the beginning of disagreements and a lot of misunderstandings that were soon to follow. If only I had asked more questions. Are you sloppy? Do you want me to cook, or would you prefer to do most of the cooking? What can, and can't I do when I move into your apartment? Will you have a problem if I move something around? These questions may seem small and irrelevant, but I quickly found out they had been necessary prior to this marriage. Unlike my first husband who was all too eager to let me express myself keeping house, this man was totally different. I *assumed* he'd want me to do *wifey* things when I moved in.

I shared this part of my history because I'm pretty sure I'm not the first woman (nor the last) who thought she could change her man. Most females think they can change their men into who they want them to be. I soon learned with my ex-husband raising my voice didn't work. If anything, he tuned me out even more, which leads me to this question. How many of you reading this book honestly believed your husband, or your boyfriend was heaven sent? I sure did! I entered that marriage completely convinced God had answered my prayers. My second husband was a God-fearing, born again Christian man. How could he not be *the one* I'd been praying for? Please don't misunderstand. I'm not making light of my marriage. The union (matrimony) between a man and a woman is serious. The vows the two of them exchange between each other are more than mere words. Those vows pronounce more than just man and wife after you recite them. The exchange of words in a vow evolves into a covenant the two of you agree to keep before God and all of them folks you invited to the wedding as witnesses. However, what I've finally come to realize is this. A marriage must include God everyday, 24/7. He should be all up in it! Unfortunately, when God is no longer welcomed to participate, or He's being ignored altogether, there is bound to be discord in the home. The Bible tells us a house of division will result in confusion and a lot of arguments.

SO, WHO DO YOU THINK YOU ARE

Mark 3:25 reads:

"If a house is divided against itself, that house cannot stand." (NIV)

Instead of the two of us uniting (as one) consulting God for direction and guidance, we acted out of the flesh by turning on each other. When my ex-husband and I began doing things under our own accord, the relationship quickly soured. And you want to know something else? Our relationship was irrelevant to the fact that we religiously busted the church doors wide open every Wednesday and Sunday. Oh sure hubby and I had the appearance of the picture perfect couple, but God hadn't been a part of our marriage for months. We were going to church looking one way, but behaving totally different behind closed doors. Attending church didn't help resolve the issues we left brewing back home. As we sat in church shoulder to shoulder, smiling and looking ever so much in love to the people around us, both our minds were preoccupied instead of focusing on what the pastor was saying.

My husband and I participated in church ministries. We smiled. We linked hands when it came time to walk up to the offering basket. Then we'd smile some more. But as soon as church was over, we could just as easily turn back to Mr. and Mrs. Jekyll before we reached the parking lot! Still, God remained left out of the majority of our conversations and most of our decision making. The only communication that did exist between us developed into selfish single-minded tones and overtures. Within three short years the 'D' word began escaping pass our lips freely—more frequently. The Bible says out of the heart flow the issues of life.

Proverbs 4:23 reads:

"Keep *and* guard your heart with all vigilance *and* above all that you guard, for out of it flow the springs of life." (AMP)

That Scripture is Gospel truth! Within our hearts lay planted a seed of divorce. I knew we'd have what we were saying, but when hurt and discord entered the relationship, we lost all sense of right and wrong. Perhaps had I been more in tune with myself (knowing who I was), after being single for over thirteen years I would've given more serious thought and consideration before becoming involved in this relationship. I was out of touch with dating—serious dating anyhow. Prior to meeting my husband, there had been a couple of boyfriends during my thirteen years of singleness. With the exception of one relationship, there hadn't been any serious involvements.

I was approaching my 40's when my ex-husband and I met. I had experienced loneliness from time to time, but what single female doesn't? That being said, during my marriage I quickly learned that we can occupy the same space with someone every day and still be lonely. Single living shouldn't make a female react out of desperation. I say this now because I realize the fear of being alone played a huge part in my decision to remarry. I'll admit this was not an easy thing for me to come to grips with, but truth be told, it had been such a long time since a man showed any interest in me since Mr. Alreadymarried. Once that relationship ended I put my heart on lock down. Meeting my husband revealed how much I had missed the company of a man. I missed the interaction that happens between a man and a woman. I'm not referring to sex. Too often we girls get companionship and sex twisted! What I missed was hearing a man's voice on the other end of the phone who wasn't one of my brothers calling. I missed having a man ask to take me out to dinner, or go see a movie together. I missed a man pulling the chair out for me at a restaurant. I missed a man complimenting me, telling me how good I smelled, or how nice I looked in what I was wearing.

I think females (young or old) should check themselves, especially if there's been a time lapse since their last date. We need not be afraid to ask the woman in the mirror, "Am I being overly zealous? Am I too anxious?" I think being over the age of thirty can lead some females to find themselves entangled in relationships with men that do them more harm than good. That's not to say a female can't find a decent, good man. What I'm saying is more times than not, reacting out of desperation leads to getting involved with the wrong men. A lot of females settle into relationships that do nothing for them spiritually or mentally. Who you are on the inside doesn't flourish. Your spirit man becomes stifled—silenced. Too many females throw caution to the wind thinking in the back of their minds they can change a man. They ignore all the red flags. They open their heart to men they have no business being with, or even worse, engaging in a sexual relationship with a man who has no intentions of marrying them. Other females marry men who fail to bring anything financially to the relationship, but will gladly spend her last dollar. These men have no conscience when it comes to letting a woman 'foot the bill' for practically everything. One man after another, are allowed to enter homes where young children are exposed to all sorts of perverted, delusional and misconstrued melodrama. These children probably see and hear things far beyond their years, which ultimately could result in them growing up confused about male-female relationships. So the cycle repeats itself with daughters and grand daughters.

As much as you and I desire to be loved and express our love by giving of ourselves, we need to be aware counterfeit love does dwell among us. You must discern to who you deem worthy of receiving your priceless gift of love. I don't have to tell you how fragile a female's heart is. The heart of a female can easily be led astray, sometimes betrayed, but more importantly, easily broken. Therefore girlfriend, proceed with caution. Guard your heart. Be not only mindful, but very careful when deciding to attach your heart to another. That's not to say men haven't had their hearts broken too. However, the difference between the sexes is men seem to rebound from heartache much quicker than we do. A lot of females mourn over the break-up of a relationship, especially if she fell head over heels in love. If that's the case, we should give ourselves an amount of time to recover from a love gone bad before we start thinking about hooking up with another man. Then again, maybe I should just speak for myself. Ugh?

Girlfriend, if your friendship/relationship starts to lose its integrity, be cognizant of the situation. Don't lower your standards. Don't risk compromising *your* integrity for the sake of having a man who doesn't qualify to have you, or edify your spirit! If this relationship is taking its toll on you mentally and grieving your spirit, chances are **he ain't the one!** Get to stepping or send him stepping! Don't you know you're much too valuable to tolerate the actions of a man, who can't see you're worthy of being treasured like the jewel you are? And I say this in love. The thing is, the enemy is always somewhere observing females. He lurks about watching for any potential friction stirring in our relationships so he can begin planting untruths in our minds. The Bible says the enemy is the accuser of the brethren. (Revelations 12:10) Once the enemy knows he's got your attention, he turns up the heat whispering lies and innuendos. "Who's going to want you at your age? You should've kept that man! Do you really think God cares whether you're happy?" The bottom line. We all wanna be loved. No two ways about it. Females have a desire to experience real love with a man. However, I think a female over a certain age, especially a female who practices celibacy, probably should ask herself an important question. "Do I want to risk being with this man to the degree that it might cost me my salvation?"

Whenever I see or hear of a couple's marriage that has lasted 30, 40, 50, years or longer, I marvel at the longevity of their love and commitment to each other. I can't help but wonder why is it that the vast majority of females can be a part of a life-long relationship with another female, who loves and accepts them just the way they are, but find it difficult to experience a lasting, loving friendship/relationship with a man, leads me to ask. "Why on earth do we girls tend to settle for less in our male relationships than we do in our female relationships?"

Chapter Eight

Snared By the Words of Our Mouths

> For by your words you will be justified *and* acquitted, and by your words you will be condemned *and* sentenced.
>
> Matthew 12:37 (AMP)

The Bible states we are snared by the negative, idle and unproductive words that proceed out of our mouths.

Proverbs 6:2 reads:

"You are snared with the words of your lips, you are caught by the speech of your mouth." (AMP)

Why is it that so many females have a hard time relating the mouth to the mind? They both primarily function along the same lines. Negative speaking has as much power as stinking thinking to snare us too! Don't you know that negative thoughts pave the way to uttering unproductive words with unconscious ease? Agreeing with our mind day after day telling ourselves that we'll never get out of debt, eventually will be spoken out of our mouth, confirming what we *think* we believe to be true.

The enemy uses the mind to paint negative images upon a female's heart to distort her true identity. Nasty untruths are planted inside the heart aimed at tearing a female down mentally, as well as spiritually. Then as if that isn't enough, the mouth comes into agreement by giving voice to those untruths. "Why can't I be smart like other women?" "I wish I was attractive!" "Why do good things always happen for other people, and never for me?" "I wish I had friends, but nobody likes me." "Why do I always end up with men who mistreat me? Maybe I don't deserve to be happy." "I guess this is about as good as it's ever going to get." Sound familiar? I've spoken out one or two of those questions before.

When it comes to changing negative behavior, you must strengthen your spirit-man by feeding it on the Word. First you should understand how vitally important it is to speak *life* into, and over yourself. Negative conditions are not going to change if the mind cannot be elevated, or stimulated to rise above them. The Virgin Mary would not have conceived Jesus had she not lined her mind up with her heart to believe the angel was speaking the truth on behalf of God. Mary believed (by faith) in God. However, Mary did ask a legitimate question. "How can this be since I am a virgin?" The angel assured Mary she had found grace and favor with God as His chosen vessel. He went on to explain the Holy Spirit would come upon her and the Most High would take possession of her womb. The angel reiterated to Mary with God nothing is impossible. No word from God is without power, nor is it unable to be fulfilled—never forget that. Mary believed the birth of the Savior of the world was coming through her. And how did she respond? "Let it be according to what you have said." (Luke 1:26-38)

Can we be honest? Wouldn't you agree most of us allow ourselves to get upset over some thing, or some one fairly easy? Would you agree many of us tend to react irresponsibly to situations and circumstances from time to time? Let's face it! The hormones can sometimes go beserk! Then again, I'll just speak for my own hormones. Maybe you don't have any problems when your hormones zig when they probably should've zagged. But girlfriend, when I get upset, especially over a situation that could've easily have been avoided, my emotions are all over the place! I don't know if I'm coming or going! Even when I'm asleep my mind doesn't slow down or turn off. My eyes might be closed, but the mind is fully awake trying to figure out how to fix the problem. Now, you're probably wondering, how would I know my mind is still in overdrive if I'm sleeping? Well, I know because when God wakes me up the next morning my body is tired. I feel like I ran a marathon race during the night. I'm irritable and sluggish—but mostly irritable! The instant my feet hit the carpet my mind picks up right where it left off from the night before. Normally whenever I have trouble turning off my mind from imagining the worse, it serves as an indicator I definitely need to pray. I'm in need of renewing my mind in the Word of God, believing He will help me out of another fine mess I've gotten myself into. Usually, by the time my commuter bus reaches downtown my thoughts have pretty much subsided. I'm no longer stressing out wondering what to do. Gradually as the morning moves along, my mind returns to other things—pleasant things like buying a couple of pairs of new shoes!

Girlfriend, you and I must determine within ourselves (by faith) to believe God is able to change us, by calling what we desire to see manifest in the natural out of the spiritual realm.

Romans 4:17 reads:

"As it is written: "I have made you a father of many nations." He is our father in the sight of our God, in whom he believed—the God who gives life to the dead and calls things that are not as though they were." (NIV)

Possessing real faith requires acting upon whatever the person has faith to believe is possible. Faith squarely places the responsibility on the person to do something in the natural while believing God is working on their behalf in the spirit realm. Every female reading this book has been given a measure of faith to believe. Without taking action to pursue inner change, it will remain a distant thought. You have to adopt relentless faith to bring about manifestation. That's the kind of faith that will have people looking back at you thinking she must be crazy! Faith involves feeding your spirit with God's Word *on purpose*. I think the status of ones level of faith plays a much larger part in character transformation than many females realize or understand.

There are no two ways about it. A negative mindset projects a negative self image, which weighs heavily upon the spirit. Fear and doubt affect your speech. What comes out of your mouth will ignite and dictate your circumstance. A poor self image not only contaminates your spirit, it touches everyone you come in contact with. The way and/or ways you think about yourself and life has everything to do with where you are right now. Sorry to say this, but humans linger over negative thoughts. They usually keep thinking about them until what they're thinking comes out of their mouth. That can only be a good thing if those thoughts are centered on faith. However, if those thoughts are birthed (spoken) out of fear, that's not good. The Bible says out of the abundance of the heart the mouth will speak.

Matthew 12:34 reads:

"You offspring of vipers! How can you speak good things when you are evil (wicked)? For out of the fullness (the overflow, the superabundance) of the heart the mouth speaks." (AMP)

If a female is always thinking she's unworthy, guess what? Her demeanor probably reflects that thought. If she's constantly thinking everybody else has good fortune, but she never ever has anything good happen for her, guess what? More than likely everybody around her does appear to be a winner, and she's a loser. If a female constantly heard how pretty she was, but received little else byway of encouragement, guess what? That's probably about all she has going for her—her looks.

Do you see where I'm going with this? How and what females think of themselves is just as detrimental as what they say! It's imperative that you consistently read God's Word to help keep the mind (thoughts) in line (agreement) with what God says. One has to make a conscientious effort to **want to** repair years of negative, nonproductive attitudes, thoughts, feelings, misconceptions, lies, and so on. Girlfriend, **you have to want to**

change! Until you reach a conscientious decision for change, you won't change. But be encouraged. With God all things are possible! The Holy Spirit (God) will help you to become the woman you're esteeming to be. Through God's Word you can be spiritually transformed into the female He created you to be! Still, the enemy is going to try to fill your head with a lot of nonsense to disbelieve the truth. Let's not kid ourselves. The enemy could care less about us praying because he knows when the **want to** ain't working, it gives him more ammunition for shutting us down. But the devil is a liar! He purposely plants negative suggestions into your thought process hoping you'll take the bait. The enemy hates females! Therefore, you and I have to accept God's Word as truth—the only truth!

God's Word is fully capable of restoring the mind, spirit and soul. This is why you should nourish your spirit everyday. If you neglect to feed your spirit, you run the risk of not being able to recognize (discern) one devilish lie from another. I think one of the best things any female can do for herself is ask God to strengthen and increase her **want to**. The enemy is on a mission of ruin! He's out to steal your identity, kill your spirit and destroy any possibility of you ever possessing righteousness. He doesn't care anything about you, and will use any unsuspecting person to help him accomplish his mission. The devil doesn't want to see a born again Believer leading a healthy (spiritual/mental) peaceful and prospering lifestyle. He'd rather see females walking around in circles missing every God-ordained opportunity just so they can feel like a failure. It's to his advantage (not yours) to have you thinking thoughts of being unworthy to receive the promises of God's goodness.

I think the enemy pursues defenseless females who don't like themselves. He zeroes in on those females who for whatever reason find fault with their physical appearance. They become easy prey. Let me ask you something. Have you noticed how the numbers continue to climb with females having cosmetic plastic surgery? If a female doesn't like herself, odds are she doesn't love herself. This kind of wayward thinking only gives the enemy an upper hand in wreaking havoc with her mind. He will plant all sorts of suggestive thoughts, ideas and images in the mind of a female to keep her bound, hoping she might possibly isolate herself from others. After all, if she doesn't like the person she is, why should anyone else? This type of female will usually build a wall around herself to keep anyone from getting too close.

There are far more females than you may realize who view themselves as undeserving of being liked or loved so they avoid making friends. It keeps her safe from being hurt, quite possibly because someone from her past hurt her deeply, and the wound has gone unhealed. Unfortunately, the longer she goes without confronting negative behavior, or at least try to understand why she behaves the way she does, she will sabotage her own fate. But I'm here to tell that female it doesn't have to be that way. You're a child of God! You can be free! You can walk in victory! You can take control over your mind, your spirit, your soul, and even your body! Every thought and idle word spoken that is contrary to God's Word will become null and void!

Philippians 1:6 reads:

"Being confident of this, that he who began a good work in you will carry it on to completion until the day of Christ Jesus." (NIV)

That's good news! Every no good, rotten accusation the enemy (the accuser) whispers in your ear is a lie! Every vicious attack he's ever carried out against you can be overturned! Hallelujah! Girlfriend, the enemy doesn't have one ounce of power over us, unless we relinquish that power to him.

Isaiah 54:17 reads:

"No weapon formed against you will prevail, and you will refute every tongue that accuses you. This is the heritage of the servants of the Lord, and this is their vindication from me, declares the Lord." (NIV)

That's what the devil doesn't want females to discover about themselves by reading God's Word. He knows once she becomes a diligent student of the Word, she will grasp just how powerless the enemy really is against a daughter of God! In order to stand up to the plots and schemes of the enemy, you and I need to fully comprehend who we *really* are. Girlfriend read the Word! Romans 8:37 says you are more than conquerors! A female's state of mind has a lot to do with the make up of her character and integrity. Please understand your destiny is predicated on how and what you think about you!

I'd like to tell you a story about a woman named Claire. She was born with an extraordinary gift for drawing. Claire has never been married and doesn't have any children. In Claire's youthful days she believed in a dream. Now at age 45, for as far back as Claire can remember, she envisioned herself pursuing a career as an illustrator of children's books. When Claire was seventeen, she began attending a prominent art school. This was Claire's first time living away from home, but she eagerly anticipated the opportunity to prove to her parents she could be responsible living on her own. Claire was a friendly, likeable young woman. She quickly made new friends. Within hardly anytime she adapted to her new surroundings on the large college campus, seldom longing for home. For a first year college freshman living on her own, things were going pretty good for Claire.

The following spring, Claire's parents phoned her dorm requesting that she come home during spring break. A few weeks later Claire was met by her father upon her arrival at the train station back home. On the short drive from the station to home, Claire's father regrettably explained that after working for the same company over 40 years, he was being laid off. Finances would immediately have to be cut back. They might not be able to afford to continue sending her to school. Claire rode in the passenger seat next to her father quietly listening, holding back the tears stinging her eyes. Just the idea of having to leave school grieved Claire.

Two weeks later Claire returned to the campus telling no one of her family's plight. She inquired about financial assistance. Claire applied for various part time openings at the nearby mall. Meanwhile, she continued attending classes as if nothing were any different. She refused to think about the possibility of having to quit school. Instead Claire believed with all of her heart her father would find another job in plenty of time before the next semester. Unfortunately, at the end of the following month Claire was summoned to report to the registration office with grim news. Her application for financial assistance had been denied. Her mother's yearly income disqualified Claire, even though her father's job had been terminated. Still, Claire was determined to remain in school.

At night she lay in bed thinking how close she'd come to accomplishing her goals and fulfilling her dream. Claire worked two part time jobs at the mall in between classes, but it wasn't enough to pay her tuition. With much regret and overwhelming sadness, Claire was forced to dropout of college. She returned home to live with her parents and two younger siblings. The happy, confident young woman, who only fourteen short months ago had gone off to college, was not the same person who came home. Claire now thought of herself as a failure.

Upon returning home Claire managed to get a job working at one of the banks downtown. A year later she was promoted from bank teller to a bank officer. Within a matter of months Claire's new position allotted her with enough money to get an apartment. She used wisdom in purchasing a nice used car. Claire wore big smiles around family and friends. She pretended she hadn't been affected by having to leave college. No one would've suspected her heart was shattered the morning her father arrived on campus to drive her home. With each personal item her father carried out of Clare's dorm room, placing inside the family car, Claire watched in silence. As far as she was concerned, everything she'd ever hoped to accomplish with her talent for drawing had ended the moment she began packing for home. Claire's dream died that April morning. Life no longer looked promising.

Well, that was twenty-three years ago. During that frame of time Claire lost the desire for painting and drawing. It grew to be much too painful to think about what might've been if her father had not lost his job. Claire's easel, along with other art materials from college lay hidden away inside a hall closet. The dream to become a book illustrator was hidden in seclusion against the closet wall, camouflaged by winter coats and jackets. Unbeknownst to Claire, she hadn't failed, but the enemy took advantage of a young woman's crushed spirit. He convinced her, the dream was lost forever. Therefore, she might as well forget about it. Claire believed his lying whispers. Over time she persuaded herself it was too late to consider going back to college. After all, who'd want to hire someone her age over a younger more talented artist?

Sadly, the enemy seized an opportunity to turn Claire's mind against her. The enemy saw his work was done and moved on to try to destroy someone else's destiny. In the meantime, Claire's thoughts switched gears. She found herself longing to find true love. Most everyone she knew was married. Even her two younger siblings were now married with children. Claire was starting to question if there might be something wrong with her. She was a fairly attractive, intelligent 45 year old woman. Why couldn't she meet a nice man, fall in love and get married like everybody else? Why didn't she get asked out more frequently on dates? And, why was it when she did have a date, she seldom received another call asking to see her again? Wasn't it enough that life had cheated her out of her dream? Was life going to deny her of finding love too? One question after another flooded Claire's mind. She felt like a cloud of unfairness was hanging over her head. It didn't seem to matter how much she prayed or read the Bible, did God even care that she was lonely? Like so many of us, Claire listened more to the lying voices in her head rather than believe God had the power and ability to show Himself strong in her life.

Well, you've heard Claire's story. Now I'd like to tell you about Natalie. She was the little girl in the neighborhood all the kids teased because of her large size. All throughout Natalie's developmental years she endured cruel name calling from her peers. Girls her age shunned her, but Natalie had tough skin. She learned very early it was better to ignore the other kids.

Natalie walked head held high, and to the beat of a different drum. But what her peers didn't know about Natalie was that despite their hurtful comments about her large body frame, how they saw her wasn't how Natalie saw herself.

All throughout her child-rearing years Natalie's mother spoke of the beauty she saw inside Natalie. She taught her young daughter to like and to love herself. At age 17, Natalie prepared to leave home for college. During the transition from living away from home Natalie made a decision to monitor what she ate, how often she ate, and how much she ate. With discipline, Natalie trimmed down from a size 18 to a size 12. It had been a challenge, but Natalie began taking her health more seriously. She became one of the most popular students on campus. Natalie happily graduated from college four years later, a spiritually determined, self-confident young woman.

Thirty years later Natalie achieved success in every area of her life. She's an executive at a major media company, has purchased her own home, and drives the car of her dreams. Natalie travels the globe to countries she once only dreamed about as a little girl. On occasion the enemy would try to undermine the words of encouragement spoken by her mother. She might've been a tender, innocent and vulnerable young girl, but the devil failed at making her think, or feel less than the person she believed her mother said she was. As Natalie approached puberty the enemy tried attacking her self-esteem. But, he was unsuccessful because of the foundation that was laid (instilled) during the years she most needed to like and love herself. Her mind had been programmed to think good thoughts. Natalie's youthful character blossomed into a woman secure in understanding who she was on the inside.

Both Claire and Natalie are fiction. I used these illustrations to further explain how important it is for every female reading this book to appreciate all of the wonderful qualities and characteristics God lovingly and graciously bestowed within them. Wouldn't you agree there are too many Claires in the earth? The enemy must no longer be allowed to get away with distracting the truth. A large population of young girls and teenagers coming behind us are being held captive by inferior images they have of themselves. The devil has gotten away with accusatory untruths long enough! As Christian women, we have to take a stand. We need to be God's witnesses here in the earth.

Isaiah 43:10 reads:

> "You are my witnesses, says the Lord, and My servant whom I have chosen, that you may know Me, believe me, *and* remain steadfast to Me, *and* understand that I am He. Before Me there was no God formed, neither shall there be after me." (AMP)

If we *know* God loves us, our younger females need to know that He loves them too! If we *know* God desires only His best for His daughters, they need to know it too! More times than not, a lot of females have come face-to-face with untruths staring them right in the eye. For example: Someone thinking she can never rise above slanderous gossip or malicious accusations is a lie! Jesus endured far worse. He understands firsthand about slithering tongues. Jesus had lies spoken against His character everywhere He traveled.

Young females should look at themselves and begin giving themselves affirmation about who they are. Most times encouraging yourself works. It is all in the perception. How you perceive yourself matters most. Each of us has been created in the image of God! A young female thinking she'll never be as pretty as the female she sees on the covers of magazines is being deceived by what appears to be the perfect image of what a female *should* look like. Realistically, these young females should see those photo magazine covers for what they really are—airbrushed!

If young females are being taught to concentrate on having money (at any means) because the more she has, the happier she'll be in life, that's teaching them to be unrealistic and irresponsible. As a result of being misguided, she won't grasp God is her Jehovah Jireh—her provider. Chances are she probably won't understand even if she does have *all* the money in the world, it still won't solve *all* of her problems. What she should understand and needs to be taught is the fact that possessing a lot of money could create problems for her, especially if she is unprepared to handle financial responsibilities. I could go on and on, but God's Word couldn't be any plainer. As children of God, young girls and young women have more going for them than they realize.

If you and I are going to be of any assistance to females younger than ourselves encouraging them to grow strong in the Lord, and have a mind of high self-esteem, we've got to conquer our own negative thoughts and poor self images. We too must reject the devil's lies over God's truth—the incorruptible Word! God says you're a treasure! That means you are valuable! (Exodus 19:5) **BELIEVE IT!** God says let the weak say they are strong! (I Corinthians 12:10) **TRUST THAT!** God says you've been redeemed from the hands (insults, accusations, lies) of the enemy! (Psalms 106:10) **BY FAITH—BELIEVE IT! TRUST IT! KNOW IT!** Self-condemnation will destroy a life mentally as well as spiritually. In the Book of Romans we're told there is no condemnation for the female who is in Christ. (Romans 8:1)

Don't you see? That's the entire strategy of the enemy wrapped in a nutshell? Condemnation immediately fell upon Eve in the Garden of Eden. The enemy purposely set out to destroy Eve's trusting and loving relationship with God. And, he's been tormenting females ever since. Nevertheless, you are not without resources or power! God has imparted every female with the ability, the authority, and the power to crush the enemy under her pretty pedicure feet! The Bible says "*life and death are in the power of the tongue.*" Power is right on the tip of our tongue! But here comes a 'but' clause. But words are first formed within the mind before they're ever spoken. Meaning, you and I have been given the power to say (verbalize), or to remain silent about what we're thinking—good (life) or bad (death). The thing is we don't have to agree with every crazy, nonproductive, negative thought the enemy plants in our mind by speaking it out. According to Proverbs 18:21, you have the power to change for the better! I also want to share another Scripture which also serves as a reminder that you possess spiritual power. Proverbs 23:7 says *"as a man (woman) thinks, so shall he (she) be."*

Undeniably, there's a correlation between the mind and the tongue. Life and death does indeed rest upon how a female chooses to respond to thoughts while bringing her tongue under control. A large number of the younger female millennium generation will go through life unaware of their true identity. In this instance I'm not referring to family-related identities. I'm talking about a higher identity—their spiritual identities. I think many of them are longing to understand who they are, and why they're here. Some have probably questioned does God really exist? And if He does, where is He whenever she needs Him?

Where is God when suddenly she's faced with a pregnancy at 14 years of age, afraid, and feeling like she has nowhere to turn? Where is God when a young newlywed catches her husband on the internet watching erotic pornographic images, or finds him surfing sexual chat rooms late at night when he thinks she's sleeping? Where is God when a young single mother of three children under the ages of four has thirty days to vacate their apartment because she lost her job and can no longer afford to pay rent? **WHERE IS GOD?**

He's right there! God is waiting for His mature daughters to step up to the plate! He's waiting for me and you to become vocal witnesses to these young lost and confused females. He's waiting for us as born-again Believers to boldly proclaim His Word. He's waiting for the Christian women who aren't afraid to tell young girls and young women how the Word of God has the power to heal them everywhere they hurt. He's waiting for me and you to unselfishly share experiences before, and after we accepted Jesus Christ as our personal Lord and Savior.

Will you dare to be the one to step up and speak out? Will you allow God to work in you and through you to minister the truth to a young female in a crisis? Can the woman in the mirror count on you to take your dutiful position as a child of God? Are you ready to prove to the enemy that you know who you are, and to whom you belong? Will you boldly exhibit that you're neither afraid, nor are you ashamed to pass along such worthy information to the next female generation?

I cannot ignore one other thing that probably should also be noted. Females need to learn how to forgive and let go. Girlfriend, forgive the people who may have hurt you in the past. Let them go! Let the hurt go! Let yourself go! Move forward! Get on with your great, blessed life! It's time to really enjoy life and stop letting the past control today! Don't you realize harboring un-forgiveness is also a snare? If your heart is fueled by hostility and un-forgiveness this is another type of infirmity.

Start conversing with the woman in your bathroom mirror. Express the depth of love, respect and appreciation you have for her. Tell this female over and over again how much God loves her until she looks back at you from the mirror wearing a big grin because she believes it to be true!

One of the things in life I've learned is people aren't responsible for encouraging me the way I should be able to encourage myself. What am I saying? Girlfriend, learn to do whatever is necessary to motivate you! Stir your own self up! Prophesy over your own life! You were born with the ability to speak into existence whatsoever you desire to see manifest! **OPEN YOUR MOUTH—SAY SOMETHING!** The snares of my thoughts gave way to a negative, verbal lifestyle. If I thought something, I said it. "*Oh, you make me* sick!" Not long afterwards I had a terrible headache, or my stomach felt queasy. Girlfriend, please do not let what you're thinking fall out of your mouth and risk altering your preordained destiny! Learn to think before giving voice to negative thoughts and images conjured up by the enemy. Stop allowing the snares of your mouth to shape your future!

Chapter Nine

Count It All Joy

Count it all joy when you're feeling a difficult time while understanding your faith is being tested.

I Timothy 2:14 (AMP)

I wasn't sure how I was going to write this chapter. Then my thoughts and fingers started flying over the computer keyboard. The death of my mother—my best friend, in the summer of 2008, is still very fresh in my mind. I remember exactly where I was when the hospital called on the afternoon she died. Sure, I've managed to go on living without her. Yet, I struggle from time to time, because it hasn't been easy living without her. Oddly enough in these last four years, I find myself waiting for her to put the key in the door yelling, "*Wilma! I'm home!*" That was one of the many ways she and I affectionately greeted each other. My usual quick response would be, "*it's about time, Fred! Where you been?*" No. I'm not in denial. I know my mother has gone on to be with the Lord, but I do experience bouts of unrealism every now and then. To this day my heart aches to hear my mother's voice—her laughter. God knows I miss her so much!

When I open the front door of my home, the first place my eyes gravitate to inside the living room is the framed picture of mommy wearing that big wonderful smile of hers. No matter how many times I walk pass the end table, glancing at that picture brings me comfort. I treasure this photo more than others because it was one of the last pictures taken of her. Traces of silver gray hair outline mommy's pretty, chestnut brown round face. Her dark brown eyes appear to stare directly into mine. Her eyes are happy. "*Miss you, mommy.*" I whisper as I pass by the end table. Since her death I often wonder if and when this painful ache in my heart will end. But sometimes just as quickly as that thought comes to mind, I question if my heart were to suddenly stop aching, does that mean I'll no longer think about mommy? Will I stop missing her altogether? Perhaps it's selfish, but I never want a day to go by when my thoughts don't include memories of her. In retrospect, I can admit, a large part of me still hasn't completely let her go. However, I'm thankful to the Holy Spirit for bringing the Bible Scripture James 1:2, to my memory. While reading it, my eyes captured verses three and four as well. Allow me to share these verses of Scripture with you.

James 1:2-4 reads:

"Consider it pure joy, my brothers, when ever you face trials of many kinds, because you know that the testing of your faith develops perseverance. Perseverance must finish its work so that you may be mature and complete, not lacking anything." (NIV)

These words are a reminder that even during some of the most turbulent and unpleasant times in my life when I'm faced with difficult situations, I need to hold onto my faith and keep my chin up. I need to trust God, and continue walking by faith, believing *everything* will indeed be alright. I can only speak for myself. But under stressful conditions I usually don't remember these Scriptures in the Book of James. Past experiences have left me feeling the complete opposite of joy. While under adverse conditions more times than not the flesh immediately begins to wage war against my spirit. However, as a Believer, I'm well aware of what the Word of God says when under attack. Still, I'm human. Therefore my flesh rebels or retaliates on occasion.

SO, WHO DO YOU THINK YOU ARE

I certainly didn't count it all joy when at age 42, my younger brother Dezret passed away in his sleep. From what my family and I were told, his only complaint had been he wasn't feeling well when he and a friend went out to dinner earlier in the evening. Unable to finish eating his meal, Dezret thought it best they leave. There were no outward signs he'd die later that night. The initial shock of his death hurt my family and me very deeply. It hurt because he hadn't finished living out his dreams. I thought how unfair! My grief turned to anger, but I kept it hidden. I carried it in silence. Whenever someone spoke of Dezret, I equated the anger rising up inside of me with grief. Months later I came to realize the anger stemmed from not being able to look upon his face one last time. I felt I'd been cheated somehow not being able to see him—to tell my brother how much I loved him. I couldn't even kiss him goodbye. There hadn't been a proper farewell, and this troubled me.

I didn't want to count it all joy when at age 41, I miscarried my third baby. I didn't want to count it all joy while my marriage dissolved right before my eyes. I couldn't count it all joy when my siblings and I were informed there was nothing the doctors could medically do for our mother, except make her as comfortable as possible while we stood in shocked disbelief gathered around her hospital bed. Count it all joy? Are you kidding?

These particular Bible Scriptures aren't easy to digest, especially when someone is experiencing a severe brokenness in their heart. Although, as a Believer, I fully comprehend God knows all things, and no matter how grave the situation, He's still in control. I think many of you will agree that life takes us through all kinds of gut-wrenching challenges which often result in struggling to trust in faith. We tend to question God's ways even though we know nothing in our lives catches God by surprise. He knew long before I did that my marriage would only last seven years. God knew the minute Dezret came into this earth in the year of 1961, he would celebrate his 42nd birthday in May 2004, be the best man for one of his dear and close friends at his wedding that June, sing happy 1st birthday to our nephew

Andrew come July, then go home to be with the Lord in September. Our God is all-knowing; Omniscient! He has infinite knowledge of every fiber of our very lives and being. God knows the end from the beginning. He knows what is, and what is yet to manifest in the lives of His children. He is our Jehovah-Elohim, our Lord and Creator.

Another way I interpreted James 1:2, was to recognize my human frailties. It's quite possible God may have given James this written instruction for that very reason, so that humans wouldn't forget they are fragile beings. Regardless how traumatic a situation or circumstance might be, it's God's desire that you and I push pass the human nature of our pain, lest we risk sinking into such a state of despair, it could destroy us spiritually mentally, or even physically. God has assured (promised) He'll make everything better if we rest ourselves in the joy of His love. (Palms. 16:11)

James 1:2 is also an instruction to seek joy in spite of how low we are feeling. Those Scriptures reaffirm that by faith, not only will you and I get through the heartache, and pain, we'll come out even stronger for having pushed past the experience. I can honestly say that in the four years that mommy has been gone I've drawn closer to God because I *had to*. The only way I was going to survive—if I was going to continue walking by faith, leading a full and satisfied life without mommy, I HAD TO draw closer to the one person equipped to help me in moving forward. None of my family or friends actually knew I was trying to find a sense of understanding why had she gotten sick unto death? Why couldn't mommy have awakened from the coma and be completely healed? Why did she have to die? Those questions bombarded my mind. I could feel anger filling my heart once again.

I can now better understand my mother's heartache following my brother's death. There's no doubt in my mind losing her firstborn son at a young age, and so un-expectantly shook my mother to the very core of her soul. To others she may have appeared to have handled his loss well. But I lived with her. Mommy wasn't quite the same. Dezret's death broke her heart.

SO, WHO DO YOU THINK YOU ARE

Regrettably, due to the circumstances surrounding his death, as a mother she hadn't been allowed to look upon his face—to tell him how much she loved him—to give her son a final kiss of goodbye. I think it haunted mommy that the last time she saw her son alive was at her grandson's first birthday party. It was her last happy memory of her firstborn son. I imagine mommy pondered over 'if only' she had known what lay ahead, there are things she would've done differently on that day. There are things she would've said to Dezret. Now, there are a few 'if only' that have haunted me too. In the days, weeks and months that followed Dezret's death, mommy managed to stand strong. She had to go on living in spite of how she might've been feeling.

From time to time I'd notice a shadow of sadness cast over her face for no apparent reason. It's during those private, silent moments I believe mommy was thinking about her son, especially if a holiday was approaching. Mommy's demeanor changed. I'd come in from work to find her already dressed in PJ's and lying in bed. "*You okay?*" I'd inquire. She offered half of a smile, nodding her head. But for the remainder of the evening she said very little, if anything at all. It was obvious to me, her spirit weighed heavy.

Another holiday would come and go without the presence of Dezret's participation. He left a void as a brother, an uncle, and a son. Understandably, emptiness echoed inside my mother's heart over the loss of her son. Once Dezret went home to be with the Lord, I made it my mission to spoil mommy as much, as often as I possibly could. I wanted to try to fill that empty space in her heart. On occasion out of nowhere, I'd hear mommy say. "A parent shouldn't have to bury a child. Children are supposed to bury their parents." The reference of parent and child was clear to me who she was talking about. Now, I too feel a void—an uncontrollable emptiness that manages to find its way into my heart. Nevertheless, God gave His children instructions to count it all joy. Therefore, I'm learning this is what I *must* do.

Farrell Ellis

Life has a way of dishing out all sorts of losses, whether the loss is that of a loved one, being terminated from a job after X-number of years of being employed, a foreclosure on your home due to the declining economic pitfall, a spouse announcing he wants a divorce and the list could go on and on. But according to James 1:2, we should count it all joy. Reading that Scripture, almost seems like a contradiction. However, there's evidence all throughout God's Word it's anything but that. There are probably countless other Believers who had to push passed life's trials and disappointments again and again. When the hour came to go it alone once family and friends had left to return to their own lives, I *had* no choice except to take God at His Word. If the healing process was going to start, I needed to believe my exhausted body and weary mind could be restored.

Well, it's been four years since mommy went home to be with Lord. I take a dose of healing medicine (God's Word) every morning and evening. There's no doubt in my mind that it's the love of God that has sustained me since July of 2008. But, I don't kid myself. I still have quite a ways to go. I am not there yet. I'd be a liar, if I were to tell you anything different. Yes, the days have grown brighter, but on the tough days, it's not easy to force myself to push pass the pain. So how am I able to do this? Sometimes I listen to one Gospel CD after another, which allows me to praise and worship God in song and dance. Other times I read Scriptures aloud for encouragement until I feel my spirit stirring, increasing in strength. I also watch funny movies to turn my sadness to laughter. The important thing is I've learned to do whatever is necessary, regardless of the way I'm feeling or what currently may be happening in my life. I'm learning to *count it all joy*!

As a born-again Believer, I have to know that I know I'm never alone. That's the bottom line. Even though the enemy might try to convince me otherwise, I tell him what I think about him and his lies. I keep it moving! My Father has promised He'll always be with me no matter where I am, or in spite of what I might be going through. In the Book of John, Jesus experienced the loss of a loved one (Lazarus), but despite His sorrow, Jesus pushed past the pain. He trusted in His Father to do what He said He would do. The story of Lazarus' death demonstrates how wondrous and powerful God really is! Through Jesus, He showed Believers as well as non-believers He alone is able to restore life to dead situations that were believed didn't have any life left in them. Jesus commanded His friend Lazarus to get up from the grave. From there, Jesus traveled from town to town fulfilling the prophetic divine design and purpose of God.

You and I are here on assignments orchestrated by God. He wants all of His daughters to fulfill the plans and purposes He specifically predestined for each of us. There isn't a more perfect mentor for you and I to emulate in our Christian walk than Jesus. He knows what it means to lose a home. Upon Jesus return to Nazareth where he'd resided as a young boy, Jesus found Himself unwelcomed. (Luke 4:24; John 4:44) Jesus understands that children (you and I) are likely to be influenced by self incriminating thoughts, ideas and feelings that lead to faint hearts.

I John 3:20 reads:

"Whenever our hearts in [tormenting] self-accusation make us feel guilty *and* condemn us. [For we are in God's hands.] For He is above *and* greater than our consciences (our hearts), and He knows (perceives and understands) everything [nothing is hidden from Him]." (AMP)

There is not a single emotion, or feeling Jesus doesn't understand. He understands how it feels to be unfairly judged by others. He understands how hurtful it is to have slanderous accusations made against ones integrity and character. He understands that malicious gossip and rumors can leave a person friendless, left to die (spiritually) a slow death. (Luke 23:10-11) By taking on the sins of this world, Jesus (who knew no sin), experienced every imaginable kind of human emotion, sickness, disease, and temptation. Girlfriend, when you feel ashamed for things you've done in the past, or feel like you're the only one going through a rough problem, or might be feeling confused and alone, you can go to Jesus. With much compassion He truly understands. Jesus was ridiculed by people who refused to accept

Him for who He was—the Messiah. He endured humiliation at the unmerciful hands of Roman soldiers. (Matthew 27:27-31; Mark 15:16-20; John 19:2-3.

If you're trying to bring restoration back to your life under your own accord, you won't be able to do it all by yourself. You're going to need Jesus! Cry out to Him! He understands! Jesus loves you! He shares your pain! Jesus can heal you everywhere you hurt! The Bible says Jesus wept out of a broken heart over the death of His dear friend Lazarus. That means Jesus understands what it feels like to have a heart overcome by sorrow. (John 11:35)

Females can't go through life with their heads buried in the sand. There are going to be unforeseen challenges that will occur in your life. Some will come with a warning. Others will not. If you feel like you're at a place where you think you can't make it another day after being disappointed, keep standing! Stand firm (unshakeable) upon the truth of God's Word! Keep trusting Him! In other words, just **KEEP IT MOVING!** It doesn't mean you've hit rock bottom! What you're going through is a test of your faith. Pass the test! Girlfriend, get up! Put one foot in front of the other! **MOVE!** Shake off disappointment! The enemy has a trap set. Beware! Stay away from the trap! Pray! Ask God to strengthen you. The enemy not only wants you to think negative, he wants you to *feel* just as bad so you'll start to believe your chances are slim in overcoming this temporary situation. But the devil is a liar! With God, *anything is possible*! Nothing is too hard or difficult for our Heavenly Father!

Luke 1:37 reads:

"For with God nothing is ever impossible *and* no word from God shall be without power *or* impossible of fulfillment." (AMP)

If you've lost a loved one, with God's help, your broken heart will mend. He promised to give you beauty for ashes and a garment of praise for a spirit of heaviness. (Isaiah 61:3) With God, each day does get brighter. God's strength and grace will spiritually energize you. Believe (by faith) you can go on living, even in the absence of your loved one. God's grace is sufficient. Therefore, please be encouraged. Count it all joy! Thank God for the precious memories left behind by your loved ones.

II Corinthians 12:9 reads:

> "But He said to me, My grace (My favor and loving-kindness and mercy) is enough for you [sufficient against any danger and enables you to bear the trouble manfully]; for My strength *and* power are made perfect (fulfilled and completed) *and* show themselves most effective in [your] weaknesses *and* infirmities, that the strength and power of Christ (the Messiah) may rest (yes, may pitch a tent over and dwell) upon me!" (AMP)

Perhaps you were suddenly laid off from your job due to the economic crisis happening around this country. Now you find yourself forced to apply for unemployment benefits, and any other charitable supplement until you can start working again. Girlfriend, this too shall pass! Do not let the enemy (or his cohorts) tell you another job won't be available for you! Nothing is too hard for God! When one door closes, He can swing open another one! It's quite possible your next job will be a substantial increase, as well as offer future career opportunities. Count it all joy! By faith, believe God is able to shine light into what appears to be a dark place. This was a hard life-lesson to grasp, but I've learned that sometimes being disappointed isn't the worse thing that could happen. On the contrary, quite often feelings of disappointment force a person to make a quality decision. They might never have done anything had it not been for the disappointment.

Depending on the level of a female's disappointment, she will either prepare for spiritual battle to take her life back, or she'll succumb to the pressure and forfeit her kingdom inheritance because she refused to fight. One or the other is apt to occur. Often times when a female comes under attack, the enemy has come to deliberately shake-up her faith, especially if she's been operating out of a strong heart of faith. It's during such times when she must ask herself, "am I going to take this lying down, or am I going to get up and fight?"

Know this! Adversity is meant to knock you down and keep you down! The enemy recognizes for the most part females are emotional, fragile creatures. Look how quick he zeroed in on Eve in the Garden! The enemy seized an opportunity to pervert God's Word. And while we may be living in the millennium era, he's still using perversion as his number one tactic for corrupting the minds of females all across the country. "Did God *really* say?" (Genesis 3:1)

There are some females who have been equipped spiritually and emotionally to carry a lot pressure on their shoulders. I'm not one of them. Even though I've been regarded by other females as a strong woman, I appreciate the compliment, but prayer sustains me. Prayer is the only way I've been able to cope with the storms in my life. "*Lord, please help me! Lord, I need you! Lord, if you don't help me, no one else will!*" I'm not always in a place where I can position myself on my knees. But understanding who I am as God's child, I know that I know He hears me whether the prayer is lengthy or short. "*Lord, help me!*" I can always rely on Him in for strength my weakness. The Bible says. "Let the weak say they are strong." (Joel 3:19) (Emphasis added) The more I confess God's Word, the more the Word comes alive within my heart. That's what faith is. Repeatedly confessing what the person believes is possible.

Deuteronomy 31:6 reads:

"Be strong, courageous, and firm; fear not nor be in terror before them, for it is the Lord your God Who goes with you; He will not fail you or forsake you." (AMP)

This chapter may have gotten off the topic for a smidgen, but I wanted to share my testimony. I'm learning to embrace (count it all joy) every aspect of my life, whether it's good, or not-so-good. I'm also doing better at controlling my emotions by not over reacting when certain situations crop up. Glory to God! All I have to do is continue walking by faith, trusting God at His infallible Word! His Word will not return void. This is what I believe and therefore I speak! *"My word will not return unto me void! It shall go to the place to where I sent it, and produce what I'm calling into existence!"* (Isaiah 55:11) (Emphasis added)

According to Hebrews 11:1, faith is the substance of things hoped for—something to look forward to—expectancy. I believe when you make a declaration (by faith) your words are lining up with God's Word. Why? Because faith is now! Putting your faith to work by believing what you decree will ultimately manifest itself. Learn to hold with both hands onto your confession, believing it's just a matter of time (God's timing) before you will see the results of calling those things that you can't visibly see (yet) as though you're already experiencing what you declared. For example: You can't declare you're rich, if you have a poor-woman's mentality. So, confess you're rich out of your mouth, and retain what you're saying in your spirit, and believe for your bank account to increase!

Girlfriend, believe (by faith) your broken heart is being fully restored. It doesn't mean you're not physically hurting. It just means you're being persuaded your heart is already healed. Giving utterance to the faith that resides within your heart can transform what is currently happening. Soon the heartache and pain will be a distant memory. As a matter of fact, I can now think about my brother without swelling up with anger. He's been gone nine years, but my love for him remains just as strong as when Dezret was alive. I reminisce about him, and smile. Dezret left behind a lot of loving memories. There are times I find myself laughing, thinking back on something he either said, or did. Dez could have my family and me laughing till we cried! God delivered me from the anger of losing Dezret. Thinking about him, or talking about him doesn't hurt anymore—thank you, Jesus! I miss him, but it no longer hurts to keep his memory alive within my heart. And, however long it might take, I know day after day my heart will ache less and less for my mother. If God did it once, He can certainly do it again.

I said all of that to say this. Regardless to whatever you may be up against, begin (by faith) to count it all joy! Stand firm against the lies of the enemy. He's going to try to discourage you from getting up when life knocks you down. Send him a message that says you know who you are, and to whom you belong! Get up! Get to strutting! If there's no one around to offer encouragement, girlfriend encourage yourself! Don't ever give up living the precious and wonderful life God so lovingly bestowed upon you! I'd like to say three words of inspiration to every female reading this chapter. **GOD IS ABLE**! If it wasn't true, I couldn't have written this book. By faith, believe you've already got the victory to overcome a temporary state of spiritual paralysis of the mind!

Now, before I end this chapter, I'd like to toss a few 'what ifs' at you for a minute. What if you've lost a loved one...what if you're being harassed and threatened by creditors...what if your man is acting up in the relationship...what if your finances are a mess...what if you're not sure God is listening when you pray...what if...what if...what if? What if I share some Scriptures with you? In doing this, I pray your mind will be renewed and your eyes enlightened. Allow these Scriptures to minister to your spirit as well as massage your heart. Can I suggest reading them aloud? Why? Because hearing God's Word being released out of your mouth replenishes the spirit with Jesus joy!

> And be not grieved *and* depressed, for the joy of the Lord is your strength *and* stronghold. (Nehemiah 8:10) (AMP)

> You will show me the path of life; in Your presence is fullness of joy, at Your righthand there are pleasures forevermore (Psalm 16:11) (AMP)

> Weeping may endure for a night, but joy cometh in the morning. (Psalm 30:5) (KJV)

SO, WHO DO YOU THINK YOU ARE

Then will I go to the altar of God, to God, my joy and my delight. (Psalm 43:4) (NIV)

They that sow in tears shall reap in joy. (Psalm 126:5) (KJV)

May your saints shout for joy! (Psalm 132:9) (NIV)

For to the person who pleases Him God gives wisdom and knowledge and joy. (Ecclesiastes 2:26) (AMP)

The meek also shall increase *their* joy in the Lord. (Isaiah 29:19) (KJV)

Everlasting joy will crown their heads. Gladness and joy will overtake them, and sorrow and sighing will flee away. (Isaiah 51:11) (NIV)

For I will turn their mourning into joy, and will comfort them, and make them rejoice from their sorrow. (Jeremiah 31:13) (KJV)

These things have I spoken unto you, that my joy might remain in you, and *that* your joy might be full. (John 15:11) (KJV)

Not only is this so, but we also rejoice in God through our Lord Jesus Christ, in through we have now received reconciliation. (Romans 5:11) (NIV)

The Kingdom of God is not meat and drink; but righteousness, and peace and joy in the Holy Ghost. (Romans 14:17) (KJV)

May the God of hope fill you with all joy and peace as you trust in him, so that you may overflow with hope by the power of the Holy Spirit. (Romans 15:13) (NIV)

God's Spirit makes us loving, happy, peaceful, patient, kind, good, faithful, gentle, and self-controlled. (Galatians 5:22) (CEV)

Ye rejoice with joy unspeakable and full of glory. (I Peter 1:8) (KJV)

Chapter Ten

Only You Can Be the Best At Being Who You Are

> Ye are of God, little children, and have overcome them; because greater is He that is in you, than he that is in the world.
>
> I John 4:4 (KJV)

Who you are spiritually (the real you), is reflected by your character, your integrity, and your self-value. The sooner females grab hold of the fact that God has created them (in His image), to be *who He created them to be,* the better off they will be for accepting this truth. I do not believe human beings are supposed to recreate (physical alterations) what God has already created. There's no need to reinvent the wheel. Now don't misunderstand. I don't have a problem with physical surgeries that are necessary due to an accident of some sort, or medically because a female may have a large breast size that is starting to pose a health issue. But of late, it seems society is urging females (they're getting younger) to go through extreme unnecessary measures for the sake of misdirected perceptions of what beauty is, and what it isn't.

Then again, this is me talking...how I see it, especially after viewing an evening news broadcast that reported the death of an 18 year old girl who died from complications during a cosmetic lypo-suction procedure. I was disheartened to hear the news anchor reporting this had been a birthday gift from the girl's mother. I couldn't begin to imagine the woman's grief over the loss of her only child. Behind the news anchor was an attractive photograph of the deceased teenager. Judging from her picture, this girl couldn't have weighed more than 115 pounds, if that. Why did she think her thighs were too large? Better yet. Why would a mother agree to let her teenage daughter undergo this kind of risky surgical procedure?

A vast majority of females (me included), place a lot of emphasis on their outer man. Yet, seldom is much attention given to their inner-man. However, with time the outer man of any female is going to start to sag a little bit here and even more there. Some females start to wrinkle prematurely in certain areas. There are parts of a female's body that will show signs of aging before they reach forty. On an even larger scale of the female spectrum, have you noticed aging is accepted less and less by women over thirty? Do females fully comprehend growing older is inevitable? Why are so many of them rejecting God's design for human nature? Do you know someone over the age of thirty who has become somewhat obsessed with finding the means and ways to avoid growing older? Is she a Christian? Is she a non-Christian? Deception doesn't discriminate!

The beauty/fashion industry is solely dependent upon the vanity of females. After all, it's what keeps them operating such lucrative companies. Seemingly everywhere I turn it appears like it is taboo for a female to grow old. But the devil is a liar! A female should accept the aging process not only because it is part of God's plan, but this is the way of God for all mankind. Whether we like it or not, aging is part of God's divine order. It's far from being portrayed as some sort of curse! The devil will stop at nothing to deceive us! Personally, I view physical maturity as a blessing. If I live to see another birthday and my health is good, that's truly a blessing from God! Every female should celebrate her birthday with vigor! Each morning when God opens your eyes and you feel physically fit, and wake up in your right mind, that's a blessing! Not to be blunt, but perhaps the next time you wake up from a cat nap or a full nights sleep, think on this. Somebody somewhere didn't! This ought to be reason enough to give God praise when your pretty pedicure feet touch the floor! Don't be afraid to embrace the aging process. Instead, look at it this way. It's by the grace of God that you're even still here!

If someone were to ask me (chances are they won't), I'd have to say in today's fast-paced microwave society seems that now more than ever, females try to be someone other than who they are. I think a lot of females are having deceptive fantasies. They're being deceived to believe with the right make-up, hair and clothes they can look just like their favorite singer or movie star. That simply is not the whole truth. No matter how hard you and I might try, we are not going to look like them. Why? Because those beautiful faces and statuesque bodies are handled by other people! I don't wanna bust your bubble, but your favorite celebrity is actually a product of the beauty industry's ingenuous way to create an illusion. If you were to remove all that make-up, take out the hair weaves and extensions, those same females could pass you on the street, and you wouldn't recognize Miss. Celeb. Bottom line, they are still ordinary females underneath all the hair and make-up. They have problems too. They deal with insecurities. They're challenged by inferiority complexes, and so on.

I think beauty is like most anything else—fleeting. The fashion world, the music industry, the movie moguls, magazine publishers, and advertisers are in the business of promoting glamorous fantasy. And you know what? The fantasy-deception has been working for centuries! Until recently, airbrushing photographs of models and celebrities was a well guarded secret. I recall as a teenager, I purchased a lot of fashion magazines to keep me abreast of trends with clothing as well as hair and beauty tips. Each month the face of another beautiful model graced the cover. "*Wow! She's sooooooooooooo pretty! Wish I looked like her!*" Little did I know in my teen years I was cracking open the door for an opportunity to allow the enemy to suggest negative thoughts of being un-attractive. Had it not been for the reassurance of my mother that there wasn't anything wrong with the way I looked, I very easily could've fallen into that trap. Thanks mommy!

Don't you know there isn't anything a well-known female who's known to have had surgical nips-n-tucks performed on her body we can't have done to ours? Talk about changing times! Ten plus years ago medical insurers would not cover cosmetic surgeries or alterations for the average working woman. Now, many of those same insurers do. The average 9-to-5 working female has the means to get a face lift, tummy tuck, lypo-suction, facial surgery, breast implants, laser this, and laser that if she has a desire to change something about her physical appearance. The enemy is especially seeking out females who aren't pleased with themselves for one reason or another. And, once he finds a candidate he has a field day filling this female's head with all sorts of negative ideas, thoughts and images of herself.

May I ask you something? Yes, it's personal. But humor me for a minute. When you look at your reflection in a full-length mirror, are you *really seeing* you for who you are? Do your eyes play tricks on you? Does your brain immediately compute another image different from the image in the mirror? Those are very important questions. Why? Because a spirit of deception can discreetly take up residence within your mind without your knowledge, and remain there until you evict it out. The enemy is always going to use his single most destructive device against you. He will use your mind against you as part of his scheme to discourage you from seeing the true beauty God has lavished in you, and upon you. Don't ever forget! The devil hates females!

I'm in my late fifties. Ask anyone of my girlfriends and they'll tell you, you won't find me bad-mouthing my age. I'm staring 60 in the face, and proud of it! Glory to God! I'm very grateful to be alive! I'm appreciative for another day to be in the land of the living! I'm growing older, so what? I pray the older I get, the more I mature spiritually, and grow in wisdom.

SO, WHO DO YOU THINK YOU ARE

In this chapter it's my attempt to convey a simple message. **BE THE VERY BEST AT BEING WHO YOU ARE!** I'm pretty sure that statement isn't anything profound, or something you haven't heard before. However, I wanted to point out as a reminder just how detrimental it is for a female's overall well-being that she be the absolute best person God has created her to be. When you gaze into the eyes of that female peering back at you from the bathroom mirror, she is someone you should know inside out—frontwards and backwards—through and through. As the woman in the mirror returns a lingering stare, you may notice her eyes reveal everything about you. Let's be honest. Girlfriend, sometimes a spirit of ugliness (bad attitude) makes its way into our hearts. But for now we're not going to go there. Let's keep our focus on the woman in the mirror.

While you're standing in front of the bathroom mirror, open up your heart by allowing that woman to become an advisor, a confidant, a therapist, and your best friend. You can trust those eyes looking back at you. They will not lie. If you're not afraid to learn some truths about yourself, no matter how unflattering those truths might be, the woman in the mirror will speak from a concerned heart. The Bible says our eyes are the light into our souls.

Luke 11:34 reads:

"Your eyes are the lamp for your body. When your eyes are good, you have all the light you need. But when your eyes are bad, everything is dark." (CEV)

I like to think the one guarantee you and I have whenever we stare into the eyes of our own reflection in a mirror is this. The positive ways in which we think, or the self-confidence we feel towards ourselves would continuously rise from the depths of our soul, spiritually connecting us to our Heavenly Father. Personally I don't think it's healthy to long to be *just like someone* else. Idolizing another female to the point of wanting to look and transform your character to be *just like hers* jeopardizes your identity. Example: My friend Debbie may look wonderful wearing cherry red lipstick, but it doesn't mean that shade of red will be attractive on me, especially when I factor in the difference in our skin tones. I can remember as a child hearing my mother say, "If your friend jumps off the bridge, are you going to jump in too?" Mommy was a stickler about her kids not doing what we saw other kids do. My three siblings and I had it drilled in our heads at an early age to follow our own minds. We were taught not to rely on what another child (outside the home), said, or thought. "Learn to think for yourself!" That was mommy's motto. All throughout our child rearing, those words helped shape us individually, well able to stand on our own two feet without becoming solely dependent upon someone else.

I'm not a mother, which translates to me not being a grandmother. However, I'd like to salute all the women who are mothers and grandmothers! Thanks to my sister Renee and her husband David, I've been blessed to be an auntie to a wonderful little boy named Andrew! I'm also an auntie to Jeannette's adult daughter, Fredreca and Jeannette's granddaughter, Alexis byway of our life-long friendship. I thoroughly enjoy the role of being an auntie because it provides me with opportunities for spoiling these beautiful children! I said all of that to say this. Lately, in my observance of pre-teen girls I pass on the street or see at church, I can't help but notice they seem to share a common denominator. These girls are influenced by their female peers, regardless whether what they see them doing is right or wrong. So it raises a question. If these young girls aren't being taught how to love, respect and appreciate their God-given uniqueness, aren't they more prone to accept an immature word from one of their peers more so than an older female, including their own mother? Grandmother?

This millennium generation consists of a large number of female children who were born when their mother was 15 or 16. Now their 15 or 16 year old daughter has children of her own, making the mother a grandmother well under the age of 40. Unfortunately, if this mother doesn't understand or recognize her significance in the earth, how then can she exhort any kind of awareness upon her daughter? Sad to say, but this high-tech, tex'n generation of girls, teenagers and young adult women are prime targets for the woes of this fallen world. But it doesn't have to be that way! Mothers and grandmothers have got to step up to the plate!

Shortly after writing my first book, I discovered another gift that lay dormant. God unveiled a voice for public speaking. He's given me a heart to go before other females, with a platform (through my writing) to be used for His glory. I want to shout from the rooftops! *"You are special to God! He loves you!"* It has become a heart's desire to encourage females everywhere they don't have to go through life feeling lost or alone. You have a Father who will fight for you when no one else will. You have a loving Father who won't turn His back on you regardless of your messes. You have a protective Father who will shield you in times of trouble, and open your eyes to the deceptions of this world. It's my prayer that God will continue to work in me and through me for His Will and purpose in helping to spread the Gospel to His daughters, especially young females—stay tuned!

Proverbs 30:11-14 reads:

"*There is* a generation that curseth their father, *and* doth not bless their mother. *There is* a generation that are pure in their own eyes, *and* yet is not washed from their filthiness. *There is* a generation, O how lofty are their eyes! *and* their eyelids are lifted up. *There is* a generation, whose teeth are as swords, *and* their jaw teeth *as* knives, to devour the poor from off the earth, and the needy from among men." (KJV)

Knowing who we are and to whom we belong starts by finding our identity in the Word of God. We must learn who we are as Believers according to God's Word. However, I also think it's equally as important that you and I discover (on purpose) the hidden value and godly impartations residing on the inside of us. Then and only then will we possess the necessary abilities and/or skills required for transferring this vitally life-altering important information to the next generation. I'd love to see noticeable change taking place throughout this generation of young females instead of what I've been witness to thus far. I realize it can't happen until you and I make conscientious, well intentioned efforts to fully comprehend who we are. If we neglect to learn and study the Word of God, whatever we say will fall on deaf ears. The Bible says one must study to show themselves approved.

II Timothy 2:15 reads:

"Do your best to present yourself to God as one approved, a workman who does not need to be ashamed and who correctly handles the word of truth." (NIV)

The uninformed cannot lead the uninformed. It's just that simple. I can no more sit down with a teenager to discuss sex outside of marriage constitutes sinning against her own body, if I'm having grownup consenting sex with a man who isn't my husband, because I'm misinformed about God's Word. How can I expect a young girl to govern her mouth, if what she hears coming out of mine is ungodly and boisterous due to my lack of knowledge? I certainly can't inspire or encourage a young woman to stand firm in her faith and uncompromising when it comes to following her dreams if she's seen me stop pursuing dreams of my own because I don't understand Bible faith principles. Do you see where I'm going with this?

Christian women with daughters, granddaughters, nieces and so on, I challenge you to become mentors outside the walls of your church. You should be a mature woman a young female can approach easily without any fear of rejection or afraid she'll be judged. We don't want to be *so spiritual* they avoid us, or run in the other direction when they see us coming. We have to come down on their level. We must speak candidly during these conversations about ourselves as well as be transparent. If you're a born again believer, walking in right standing with God, daily feeding your spirit on His Word, you're an excellent candidate for mentorship! The time to act is now! Females our junior need to hear about the love of God! Girls, teens and young women are dying spiritually every day! I see them hanging around on street corners getting into mischief, being lead astray by their peers. Many of them live in homes practically forced to raise themselves because their 30-something mother, who was

SO, WHO DO YOU THINK YOU ARE

pregnant at age 16, is too busy trying to recapture her youth! It's a vicious cycle. And, the enemy is doing everything he can to keep it that way! But the devil is a liar!

Earlier today I was reading an article in our local newspaper. Two teenage girls ages 16 and 17 are likely facing prison sentences because of their association with a 22 year old man. Apparently this adult man was able to persuade the girls to accompanying him to a neighborhood convenience store where he committed robbery at gun point. The article indicated if they're convicted of accessory to armed robbery, and who knows what other charges were alleged against them, they will spend a considerable amount of time behind bars. Reading that article was quite disturbing. Sixteen and seventeen year old girls should be thinking about college, not about serving jail time. They should be embarking on promises of bright futures. These girls are examples of so many females who are out there in the world—lost. Clearly they do not understand there is a connection between them and God. They have no idea of the love He has for them.

And while we're on the subject, let's not overlook the females who are preacher's kids (P. K.'s). We can't assume just because her mother or father is the leader(s) of a church she isn't dealing with peer pressure, or struggling to find where she fits in. You and I must no longer ignore the fact that identity theft is an epidemic that has managed to worm its way pass church doors and into the sanctuaries. As mothers, grandmothers, and aunties the time has arrived to stop turning, looking the other way. This isn't just a 'Christian' plight it's the mature female thing to do. I realize there may be some young females indirectly linked to us. She might be the daughter of a friend. Nevertheless, we have a responsibility to exhibit ourselves—be examples of godly women. It's up to you and me to conduct ourselves in a confident and godly demeanor. I have no doubt the younger females coming up behind us will listen when they see how comfortable we are in our own skin (because we know who we are), they can then become more relaxed in theirs.

Titus 2:3-4 reads:

"Guide older women into lives of reverence so they end up as neither gossips nor drunks, but models of goodness. By looking at them, the younger women will know how to love their husbands and children, be virtuous and pure, keep a good house, be good wives. We don't want anyone looking down on God's Message because of their behavior." (The Message)

Please correct me if I'm off-base, but I read that Scripture as a godly instruction for the seasoned (mature) female Believer. This Christian walk isn't *all* about us. It's about serving others and sharing how good God has been in our lives. We can share our stories with the younger generation. We can openly tell them how Jesus took our messed up lives and changed them for the better. As born-again Believers walking by faith, we should be living testimonies—proof that God is faithful to His Word. You and I have an obligation to reach out to this young generation.

Titus 2:7-8 continues:

"But mostly, show them all this by doing it yourself, incorruptible in your teaching, your words solid and sane. Then anyone who is dead set against us, when he finds nothing weird or misguided, might eventually come around." (The Message)

Do you remember what it was like when we were their age? Personally, I wouldn't want to be in their platform shoes, especially in this day and age. And to think, when I was a teenager I felt like I was pressured to fit in. The issues and problems challenging many of these girls can run rings around what I experienced. That's why I feel so strongly about mature women informing this younger generation their lives are not without meaning or substance. They need to know their lives aren't a mistake. They matter —a lot! Girls, teens and young women aren't without meaning and purpose in God's eyes. He has great plans for their lives. However, this too is a fact many adult females have to comprehend as well. Girlfriend, whether you are born again or not (yet), you have greatness in the earth,

SO, WHO DO YOU THINK YOU ARE

according to Isaiah 14:24. God loves you! You were creatively designed to lead a righteous, whole, spirit-filled, rewarding life to fulfill *His* divine purpose and plan as the daughter of Almighty God! You were born with significance, purpose and the potential to birth forth what God planted on the inside of you!

Isaiah 14:26-27 reads:

"This *is* the purpose that is purposed upon the whole earth; and this *is* the hand that is stretched out upon all nations. For the Lord of hosts hath purposed, and who shall disannul *it*? and His hand *is* stretched out, and who shall turn it back?" (KJV)

I can honestly say. I enjoy being me! I don't have to vicariously live through my sister Renee, my best friend Jeannette, my other girlfriends, a TV talk show host, a movie star, a famous singer, an athlete, or a million dollar lottery winner. I very much like and love me for who God says I am— His peculiar treasure! (Exodus 19:5; Deuteronomy 14:2) I bask in the fact that God refers to me as *His peculiar treasure.* It makes me feel special! Do you want to hear something? Without having ever read one word of Scripture, ever since I can remember, I just never quite fit in, but I was always alright with being the odd girl because I didn't know how to do anybody else, except me. Proudly, I am indeed a combination of both— peculiar and a treasure!

Not trying to become a part of the 'in-crowd' that made it that much easier to be my own person. It taught me how to enjoy my own company. From a child I could just as easily play alone with my dolls as well as play with the other little girls who lived on my street. And, thanks to my mother, I've always thought I was special, but not in an arrogant way. She didn't spoil me. Mommy just made me feel valuable. My mother assured me, I could do whatever I dreamed, so long as I put my whole heart into it. And, she was right!

Now that I'm a big girl, I value the peculiar qualities and attributes God has imparted on the inside of me. His creativity is what sets me apart from all of His other female creations. Being a peculiar treasure does not come without reward.

According to I Peter 2:9 you and I have been chosen. We're special to God, who has called us out of darkness into His marvelous light. (Emphasis added) I'm confident enough within myself that I don't have to seek after the approval of others. The way I see it, if what he/she sees, or hears doesn't meet their criteria or standards, I can accept that person likely wasn't part of God's plan in my life. The truth is, I don't have the time (neither the energy) to concern myself with, "*why don't they like me?*" I'm more concerned about God liking/loving me, and where He's leading me. At 50-something, I would hope I've grown up to whereas I am less focused on trying to gain people likeability. Now that may sound a little harsh for some of you, but the Bible clearly states what God has to say about being men-pleasers.

Galatians 1:10 reads:

"Now am I trying to win the favor of men, or of God? Do I seek to please men? If I were still seeking popularity with men, I should not be a bond servant of Christ (the Messiah)." (AMP)

Girlfriend, don't misunderstand what I'm saying. Please see the bigger picture here. I'm not coming down on anyone who is people conscious. After all, ideas, thoughts and opinions of others do, and should matter to a degree. You just have to know where and when to draw the line. The truth is, more often than not, I kind of stick out like a sore thumb just about everywhere I go. And I say this because there's a difference between a casual glance and being gawked at. On the other hand, I don't feel inferior when I enter a crowded room with people who may, or may not notice me. I'm perfectly content not to open my mouth (to be seen) because I'm comfortable in being myself. The women in my elite circle know whenever we go out together I may, or may not participate in every conversation. They know I'm reserved and somewhat quiet. That's why I love this diverse group of women because they never make me feel odd or strange. These ladies can tell you, I rarely ever do anything to draw attention to myself. It would be out of character for me to enter a room talking loud, "*hey gurl!*" That's not who I am. Frankly speaking, I don't believe a lady has to make herself seen for her presence to be known.

While growing up, mommy was quick to spell out what a lady did and did not do! My sister Renee and I laugh now, but it wasn't so funny then. Mommy pulled out her book of the dos and don'ts for ladies. She took raising two female children very seriously. Mommy wanted Renee and me to be smart enough to stand on our own, along with developing lady-like qualities. Ask my sister Renee. She'll confirm what I'm telling you. Even Jeannette got a few do's and don'ts when she visited our house. Mommy was old school. She could've cared less about being my friend while growing up under her roof. As long as my siblings and I were living in her house, we would do what she said! My mother didn't play when it came to one of her kids acting up, or acting out.

When I was a little girl, I didn't know anything about *time* out, but I knew a lot about get the belt! With a child's mind, I associated a butt whipping with meanness. I once told mommy, "*you don't love me!*" Although crocodile sized tears were streaming down my face, it's only fair that I mention that was the first and last time I ever uttered those words ever again. Mommy didn't say a word. She answered with a backhanded rebuttal! But I'm forever thankful to this woman. When it was all said and done, those backhands help prepare me to grow into a well-rounded, confident woman. Both Renee and I made mommy proud. My rebellious days as a youngster later became conversations (sometimes exaggerated), between mommy and me over coffee on a Saturday morning at the kitchen table when we lived together at the condo. She and I would sit there laughing till our sides ached! Naturally mommy denied certain things ever happened, especially how quick she was with the backhand.

The bottom line is this. If females (young or old) are insecure in fully knowing who they are, what does that say about them spiritually? I honestly don't think any female needs to mimic, or covet to be like someone else. Is it possible a desire to be a replica (carbon copy) of another female is another type of coveting? I mean, after all, if a female can lust after a tall, dark and handsome man without spiritual conviction, filling the lust of her eyes, having all kinds of impure thoughts, why can't it apply to another female? If one female wants to be *just like* another female because of the way she looks, or perhaps has something the other one wants (and can't have), then how is this any different? Lust is lust! "*I wish I had a lot of clothes like her.*" "*I wish I was married to her husband. He's so fine.*" Coveting; wanting what we see! Lust of the eye!

Then again, maybe that's too strong of a word. Perhaps, using gentler words be better received when describing a covetous heart. How about idolatry—desire—fantasizing—longing? Actually these are the kinds of feelings we should be exhibiting toward our Heavenly Father. Instead, we latch our feelings and emotions on to everyone else, except Him. We should idolize God for who He is, and lust after His righteousness. Our desire should be to want to please Him at all times as obedient daughters. We should fantasize about being alone with Him in His presence. We should long to be pleasing in His sight. The Bible says that God is a jealous God!

Exodus 20:5 reads:

"Thou shalt not bow down thyself to them, nor serve them; for I the Lord thy God *am* a jealous God, visiting the iniquity of the fathers upon the children unto the third and fourth *generation* of them that hate me." (KJV)

That's enough right there to keep me in check by not desiring to fulfill the lust of my eyes. I'm pretty sure you've all heard the old saying, "be careful what you wish for. You just might get it!" You may think you're not everything you'd like to be, but girlfriend, might I suggest be comfortable with who you are for right now? I'm not thrilled with my hair at the moment, but that'll soon be changing next week when I buy a new wig! Seriously though, I can't be moping and groaning, thinking the rest of me isn't up-to-par because so-n-so's hair is looking tight! Having a bad hair day doesn't mean the rest of me is a disaster waiting to happen. On the contrary, the rest of me is doing just fine, thank you.

I think it's very important for every female to understand that making changes to the outward appearance, while neglecting to transform her mind will be a waste of time and energy. Real change—true change starts inside, and spills over outwardly. Once you tap into your God-given inner beauty, it's only a matter of time before it will shine outwardly. Without question, you and I have seen exceptionally beautiful women on TV, on the big screen in movies, on magazine covers, etc., but have you ever noticed a few of those women seem to share a common bond? TROUBLESOME! Some of the most *beautiful* women have a reputation for raising all kinds of hell! Now I ask you. What's so pretty about being downright ugly?

Personally I think the idea of beauty is twisted. People generally overestimate beauty. Frankly, sometimes what others perceive as beautiful I consider modest—average. You and I have probably watched our share of award shows. I enjoy watching them to see who's wearing what. Usually the beautiful people attend these big productions looking fabulously stunning from head-to-toe on the red carpet. However, while I'm watching these shows, I can't help but to wonder what he or she is *really* like when they're not in front of cameras with dozens of microphones being shoved in their faces. How much of their ego gets blown out of proportion as fans yell and scream their name behind them. Perhaps if we were ever given the chance for a one-on-one conversation with our favorite celeb, we'd be disappointed to learn this person is nothing like we imagined him or her might be. Need I say more?

Ephesians 2:10 sums it up like this:

"For we are God's [own] handiwork (His workmanship), recreated in Christ Jesus, [born anew] that we may do those good works which God predestined (planned beforehand) for us [taking paths which He prepared ahead of time], that we should walk in them [living the good life which He prearranged and made ready for us to live]." (AMP)

Why would you want to be anybody other than yourself? It doesn't matter what kind of childhood you had. It doesn't matter if you've been successful or unsuccessful in your search for a mate. It doesn't matter if the people on your job ignore you. It doesn't matter if you're not the most popular female in church. It doesn't matter if other females are dressed from head-to-toe, but your wardrobe is limited. It doesn't matter! The only thing that does matter is this. **STOP THINKING YOU'RE INSIGNIFICANT!**

Girlfriend, you were created with a lot of loving thought, precision and purpose. God brought your parents together to use as vessels for bringing you into the earth. Your mother and father were chosen on purpose. We don't *choose* our families, but we can certainly give love to the people in it. God wanted you here! The devil is a liar when he tells you, God has forgotten about you! God is definitely interested in what you're doing, and how you're feeling more than you might ever know.

While I was writing this chapter my thoughts turned to a question. What is a virtuous woman? The Scripture can be found in the Book of Proverbs. I've heard women refer to either themselves or another female as a virtuous woman. I've seen this Scripture as a signature line in emails. But the more I pondered over it, the more I wanted a clearer sense of what God is actually saying when He makes reference to a *virtuous woman*.

With this question lingering in the back of my mind, I grabbed the Webster's. The dictionary provided the following definition for the word virtuous: 'having, or characterized by, moral virtue, righteous.' Then my eyes captured the definition of virtue: 'general moral excellence; right action and thinking; goodness or morality.'

Having read both definitions, I couldn't help but wonder do I exhibit these qualities in my speech? Does my behavior reflect a woman of virtue? Does my character unveil qualities of spiritual maturity? Naturally, I strive to be a godly woman in most everything I do and say. It's my prayer that God not let me be a silly (immature) woman, but a woman of wisdom,

SO, WHO DO YOU THINK YOU ARE

spiritually empowered and spiritually discerning for every area of my life. Each day I endeavor to be the very best at being who God has created me to be. Girlfriend, I can't do you. You can't do me. You and I can only do our best to be our uniquely created selves. Don't allow the enemy to try to make you copy, or re-create what God has already done. I think when a female tries to separate herself from the person she really is (on the inside), it's like telling God. "You didn't do a good enough job!"

Chapter Eleven

Embrace Your Life

> The thief comes only in order to steal and kill and destroy. I came that they may have *and* enjoy life, and have it in abundance (to the full, till it overflows)
>
> John 10:10 (AMP)

As I anticipate the date of my birth in a few days, I give God praise! Thank you, Jesus! Each year my birthdays seem to come around rather quickly! Life here in the earth deems more important as another birthday passes. But be that as it may, I pray I'm able to physically and mentally keep on doing what I believe God has called me to do. I believe my contribution to the world is to continue writing books proclaiming the goodness of the Lord, and deliver encouraging messages based on those books to the female population through motivational speaking. So, you think that's dreaming too big—impossible thinking? Not with My God it isn't! I receive (in my heart of faith) the promises of God to be the truth! And more importantly, I believe I am the blessed seed of Abraham! Jesus said. *"Nothing will be impossible for me when I believe!"*

Luke 1:37 reads:

"For with God nothing is ever impossible *and* no word from God shall be without power *or* impossible of fulfillment." (AMP)

In the book of First Samuel, God calls the child Samuel while he is sleeping. The voice sounds vaguely familiar to the young boy. Samuel assumes Eli has called him out of his sleep. Samuel answers, "hear am I." But Eli tells the young boy it was not him. The third time when Samuel hears the voice calling in his sleep, he again responds assuming it must be Eli calling out to him. Eli having perceived in his spirit the voice Samuel heard is from God, instructs the boy to go back to bed. He tells Samuel if the Lord calls him again, he should answer. "Speak Lord, for the servant hears." (I Samuel 3:4-10) There's also a Scripture that can be found in the Book of Isaiah, the sixth chapter; eighth verse. It reads:

"Also I heard the voice of the Lord saying Whom shall I send, and who will go for us? Then said I, here am I; send me." (KJV)

This time when I read those Scriptures the words leaped up from the page of my Bible immediately ministering to my spirit. The Scriptures confirmed what I'd been confessing, praying, and asking God to do in my life for His glory.

Months prior to my book signing the Holy Spirit led me to enlist the talents of Carla and Traci, two dear friends of mine. The women who make up my elite circle of friends know I'm a stickler when it comes to doing things in a decent and orderly fashion with a spirit of excellence. They also know I believe females should sow into the lives and businesses of other Christian sisters, which is why I requested Traci and Carla for assistance. I wanted to give their Events Planner Business, *Elite Expressions* exposure. They are two smart, talented and gifted women. I only had to share my vision for the book signing and they delivered in their own unique creative styles.

Meanwhile, a week or so later following the signing of a contract with Carla and Traci for their services, the enemy saw an opportunity to whisper words of doubt. He had seen I was slightly nervous planning this up-coming event. I started questioning myself. Was my book good enough to compete against noted and established female Christian authors? Would the women at my church stop by the in-house bookstore to purchase a copy? Well, as doubt set in, the enemy's hissing grew louder. I began imagining women wouldn't like the book once they read it. And if they didn't, would they demand I give back their money? But if that wasn't enough negative and faithless thinking, I thought what if the books I'd already sold prior to the book signing were my only sales? The enemy had me going. Then my mind shot into overload. But God is a good God! In spite of my anxieties, He was *still* in control!

Let me quickly tell you what happened. Every negative image and thought the enemy suggested was proven wrong! Lies! Liar! It wasn't happening—glory to God! Women who purchased a copy of *Go Beyond Your Dreams* sent encouraging emails! A couple of women approached me after church services wanting to express how much they enjoyed reading my book. But the one thing I found interesting about my newfound readers was these women shared a common thread. Each of their comments echoed the same sentiment. I'd like to share a few of their comments: "I felt like you and I were having a face-to-face conversation." "Your book has encouraged me to go back to college." "After reading your book I've decided to apply for a mortgage." "I'm going to finally start my own business." "Your book was the nudge I needed to stop procrastinating. I've already started putting some things in motion." "Reading your book gave me hope."

With misty eyed humility, I thanked each of those women for their uplifting comments. However, for every positive response that I have received thus far (2 years later) my response is always the same. "*To God be all the glory!*" After all, writing *Go Beyond Your Dreams! (Live Them!)* was God's book from start to finish. Every word, sentence and paragraph was inspired by Him. That's the only way I can explain writing and completing a full-length manuscript. Had it not been for God's divine intervention, I couldn't have stayed focused long enough to write a 12 chapter book! For the most part, I'm a fairly disciplined and focused woman. But I must admit, I have moments of procrastination just like anybody else! It has taken me two years to write this book because instead of implementing good time management skills, there were some Saturdays I played games on the computer. Yes girlfriend, I too put off doing what I know I need to be doing to make my way prosperous—okay?

The women at my church began buying copies from me, as well as from the bookstore. The hissing lie they wouldn't support me was silenced. There were also internet book sales. In the meantime, I asked God to please make *Go Beyond Your Dreams* a contagious read. In other words, one woman would tell another woman and she'd tell someone else. You know what? God granted my petition! I received phone calls at my job from women who heard I'd written a book. They wanted to purchase a copy not only for themselves, but for a girlfriend too. I could feel my faith level rising. During prayer time I laid another request before God. The Bible says we have not because we ask not. Therefore I'm constantly asking God for one thing after another. I asked if He would please send my book outside the borders of my home state, Delaware. Well, He did that too! Our God is an awesome God (love that song), He hooked me up! I have to share this. I'll do it quickly—promise!

I attended a women's conference in New Jersey along with my good friend Monica. Unbeknownst to me, I sold a copy of my book to a woman who has not only become a good friend and supporter she's also become a part of my elite circle. I'm sure Natalia won't mind if I mention her in this chapter. She was one of the guest speakers at the conference that day. I should've known there was a reason why almost immediately from the second Natalia spoke into the microphone, I was drawn to her. Natalia and I both believe our meeting that day was a divine connection.

Following the conclusion of the conference I wanted Natalia to know how much I enjoyed hearing her message. This was a God set up! First of all, the day before the conference I phoned Monica. "*I'm not sure I want to go tomorrow.*" She listened to my excuse, but Monica refused to let me off the hook. So I *had to go*! And, what did Natalia minister on? The integrity of our words, and fear! It was quite obvious to me after hearing Natalia's message the enemy had not wanted me to come. Considering how I had been feeling lately, it was meant for me to attend this conference. She delivered a powerful message! A God set up! While absorbing everything Natalia was saying, I could feel my spirit awakening from its slumber.

During my conversation with Natalia, I mentioned that I had written my first book. She didn't stammer. "Do you have one with you? I want to sow into your life." I answered. "*They're in the trunk of my car.*" She smiled. "Go get me a book!" I made a mad dash from the sanctuary outside to my car and hurried back inside the church. When I returned to the sanctuary another woman was speaking with Natalia. I quietly moved to where they were talking, slipping a copy of my book atop Natalia's packed belongings. I was about to walk away when Natalia's attention turned back to me. Surprisingly she took hold of both my hands. She began praying, speaking words of prosperity over me. I thanked Natalia with a hug for the words of prayer and the book purchase. Before parting she and I exchanged business cards.

As I went to join Monica, I pretty much assumed it was probably the first and last time I'd see, or talk to Natalia. But if our paths never crossed again, I left the church sanctuary feeling spiritually alive and much stronger mentally. God had given me the privilege to meet an inspiring wonderful woman after His own heart. I was grateful to have made her acquaintance. The conference took place on a Saturday. I must've thanked Monica a dozen times on the drive home for not letting me back out of going. She told me the Holy Spirit led her to insist I attend. A God set up!

On Monday evening when I arrived home from work, I noticed the voice message light blinking on the phone. Natalia had phoned earlier that day leaving a heart stirring message. She finished reading my book. I won't disclose our conversation because that's between us. Integrity—remember? But I will tell you this. By the time our phone call ended, once again God had answered a prayer request. *Go Beyond Your Dreams! (Live Them!)* was about to cross the borders of Delaware! My book was now in the hands of a woman living in New York! Natalia was so impressed by what I'd written she purchased ten additional copies. She wanted to present copies to female family members and friends for Christmas gifts. Look at God! If Natalia never bought another book, if she never picked up the phone to call me, my life still was touched to have met this godly woman! I hope I don't embarrass her, but Natalia is an anointed woman with a timely word in her mouth! Love you, Natalia!

I'm switching the conversation again. Thanks for allowing me to share my testimony. Well, my 50-something birthday is less than a week away. Not only am I excited, I'm really looking forward to it. I look good! I feel good! Thank you, Jesus for divine health and strength! Even so, I know somewhere out there another female is dreading celebrating her 50-something birthday. Girlfriend, I gladly welcome another birthday with open arms! Don't you know it's by God's grace and mercy that you're still here among the living? Embrace it! **HAPPY BIRTHDAY!**

In 2010, I didn't do the girls Caribbean birthday celebration with Monica and Jeannette. Instead, I flew down to the big ATL (Atlanta) to visit Jeanette for eight days. I was as equally excited about spending time with *my gurl* as I would've been if we were going on vacation for a week in the Caribbean. 2010 had been somewhat of a challenging year. But through it all, I managed to weather the highs along with the lows. Without going into a lot of gory details, my finances took a nose dive shortly after hosting my first women's conference (which was a success) in May of 2010—praise God! The Holy Spirit brought back to my memory the message of a minister I had recently watched on one of the Christian television networks. The minister said. "When all hell starts breaking loose, the enemy is attacking you because he sees your faith is bringing you into

SO, WHO DO YOU THINK YOU ARE

God's plan and purpose." It was in that revelation moment I became determined (by faith) I was going to overcome this sudden financial lack attack! If I had plenty of money before the conference, then I was determined to recover what had been snatched away!

My Father hasn't given me a spirit of fear! Glory to God, I'm not a chicken. I am an eagle! The threat of my car possibly being repossessed didn't scare me enough to stop believing my well-able Father God would supply my every financial need. The electric company's bright yellow disconnect envelope in the mailbox wasn't enough to make me doubt God's infallible Word! And, as if that wasn't enough, the enemy turned up the flames even more. I came home from work to find the cable company had turned off the phone, which only allowed me access to dial 911. My internet connection was terminated. The cable satellite would not be sending signals to my TV. "*It is what it is*," I heard myself say as I climbed the stairs to the second floor of my townhouse apartment.

Needless to say, within a day or two I adjusted to not having the phone, cable TV, and the internet at my leisure. However, during this time it became all too clear my pay checks were no longer enough to sustain my financial responsibilities. I glanced over at the black TV screen starting to get mad! "*I'm a King's kid! God, what is going on? How come I have no money? Why is it all of a sudden I'm being harassed by creditors?*" I prayed. I wrote new faith confessions. I read God's Word (aloud). I was soooooooooo angry! The Holy Spirit reminded me as a child of God, I've been redeemed from the hand of the enemy. He began to shed some light on my situation. I believed out of a heart of faith following the conference. I would receive speaking and/or book signing engagements in the near future.

God had given me the vision for the women's conference. I trusted Him for the provision, and acted in faith that the vision would come to pass. This women's conference was instrumental in empowering other females to believe by faith, all things are possible. It was aimed at encouraging these women to trust God at His Word. The enemy didn't like that it had been a success! Meanwhile, my finances slowly began turning a corner. I remember telling the woman in the mirror. "*We really do need a vacation!*" Jeannette was also in need of a vacation. The only thing standing in the way of she and I taking a vacation was the money to pay for it. Then I got an idea! By faith in mid-July, I set a plan in motion. At the end of the month (2 weeks before my birthday visit), the plan was complete. I was pretty sure this was going to be a great surprise for Jeannette.

    Since she and I live in two different states, I hadn't been able to share in her birthdays (she's a December baby), except through cards, gifts sent by mail, and long distance phone calls. For the last four years, Monica, Jeannette and I have had the blessed pleasure of celebrating our birthdays in the Caribbean together. Somehow it seemed important for me to make this August birthday vacation in Atlanta about Jeannette too. The more I considered the idea, the more it appealed to me. Without her knowledge, I arranged for us to stay at the Ritz-Carlton in downtown Atlanta for a Girl's Birthday Weekend Get-A-Way! I created a picture book, complete with a letter inviting her to join me in celebrating both our birthdays! It included some other things too, but I told you the necessary stuff. Then I shipped the surprise package by overnight courier. I wish I could've been there to see Jeannette's face when she opened that envelope, but the two phone calls (work/home) I received pretty much provided all the response I needed. Jeannette was floored by the gesture!

    I shared all of this to say, please embrace this wonderful life God has given you! So what if it doesn't seem like much to anyone else? This is your life! **You gotta love it!** The responsibility for being happy with who you are, begins with you. You are responsible for setting ideas, goals, visions and dreams into place if you have a desire to see them come to fruition. It's up to you to *choose* to feel better about who you are. Every female reading this book needs to learn to love the skin she's in. The bottom line is this. No matter how many times I tell you to *love who God has created you to be*, until you digest those words deep down into your very soul—into your spirit, they will produce no effect. Girlfriend, you are one of God's great masterpieces! EMBRACE YOUR LIFE!

Once you were created, God literally discarded the mold. Your uniqueness was created in God's image. We've all seen, or might even know of a set of identical twins. But if you were to look very closely, there's probably something one twin has that the other twin doesn't. One twin could be two inches taller than the other. No matter how much they may look alike to the natural eye, individuality will still set apart their differences. Every person on planet earth whether they live on domestic soil or in a foreign land has received distinctive markings on their fingers that no other human can recreate, or duplicate. I find God's work in the details of the human body astounding! He thought of everything! Our Heavenly Father is a diverse God. If He weren't, don't you think we'd all be the same color, race and nationality? Wouldn't we all speak one universal language? In short, if everybody in the world looked alike and talked alike, I think that would be rather boring, don't you? Just imagine. A world filled with the same kind of people everywhere you went. BORING! Thank God for making us different! Thank God for giving mankind the intellect to converse in various languages. It keeps life very interesting, don't you think? Our lives are meant to be enjoyed to the fullest. If you and I neglect to carve out a niche for ourselves in this big ole' world, we have no one else to blame, except ourselves. God has equipped every female spiritually and mentally with the necessary tools needed to lead a successful lifestyle. In the Book of Hosea (4:6) the Scripture tells us it's God's Will that no one be destroyed for having a lack of knowledge. I've read that Scripture plenty of times before. But when I read it again, my spirit-man internalized the verse this way: **if we lack understanding in knowing who we are as a daughter of God, then everything our Father so lovingly took the time to impart on the inside of us will fall by the wayside.** Failure to tap into visions and dreams or creative ideas, limits the potential for success. Each individual female has been given a free will. Girlfriend, you and only you possess the 'will' to stop yourself from becoming everything God intended. It's up to you to make *your* way prosperous.

There's not a man, a woman, a boy or girl who could ever make me believe it's God's Will for His children to endure hardship day after day, month after month, year after year. I refuse to buy into that lie. And, neither do I believe it's His Will for you and I to be envious of one another because one female has achieved more while the other female hasn't—yet. However, what I do believe is that it is God's Will for all of His daughters to enjoy the many wonderful benefits, blessings and promises as His children, which brings me to this point. There are too many promises in the Bible not to take God at His Word! All the promises (to the born again believer), are "yes" (I believe God's truth), and "Amen" (so be it, in Jesus' name).

II Corinthians 1:20 reads:

"For no matter how many promises God has made, they are "Yes" in Christ. And so through him the "Amen" is spoken by us to the glory of God." (NIV)

When a female's life is infused with one trial after another, she ends up having to deal with a whole lotta drama. It then becomes difficult for her to trust in the promises of God, especially if the enemy is stirring up mischief within those troubles! Girlfriend, that's part of the devil's scheme to hold you back from receiving God's great and good plan for you. He deliberately tries to make females think they can't do any better. Even worse, he'd have us think we'll never go beyond where we are right now. But you know what I always say. *"The devil is a liar!"*

If it were left up to the enemy, celebrating a birthday in my late 50's would serve as an indicator it's all down hill from here. If I had listened to his lies during my search for a publisher, he would've succeeded in cheating me out of making the acquaintance of a wonderful woman Kathy McClure. I would've missed having an opportunity to break into the literary field. That's why you and I have to cast down the imagination, especially when negative thoughts and images start bombarding our mind. If you don't shut them down, your confidence in God's Word will come under question. I can't lie. There were moments when I thought I was too old to continue believing in a childhood dream of becoming a published author. The enemy once implied just because I carried that dream on the inside of me for over thirty years, didn't mean it was mine to have manifest.

So what did I do? I turned to the woman in my bathroom mirror. When her dark brown eyes locked on my face, she didn't mince words. *"So what! You're a late bloomer! Hang in there! God is no respecter of persons, remember? Don't give up! It will happen all in God's timing...not yours!"* Well, after the tough love chat she gave me, there was only one thing left for me to do. I dug my heels in even deeper! I was determined not to entertain the enemy's negative implication with another thought. No way was my imagination going to gain momentum. I started ignoring the enemy, and kept increasing my faith.

I'm finding with God, delayed certainly doesn't mean denied! Age isn't a disclaimer from fulfilling dreams. But I don't take blessings for granted. I'm very appreciative and grateful for God's loving kindness towards me. I'm also aware of how much the enemy hates me. He will stop at nothing to see my demise. The enemy knows I believe in the truth—the Word of God. He has seen by my actions how strongly I believe by faith all things are available and possible for my life. The enemy doesn't want you or me to walk in our God-ordained destiny.

Can I take a minute to pause here? Generally speaking, most females do not discern when the enemy plays her against another female. I've always considered one female disliking another female as a *gurl-thang*. Now, I can't be 100% certain, but what if it's been a *devil-thang* all along? The Bible points out that we wrestle not against flesh and blood, but against spiritual forces. Prime example: Have you ever met a female for the very first time, and she responds like you just stole her favorite Guccci® pocketbook? Or have you ever visited a place and the second you stepped inside the women started shooting sour looks at you from across the room for no apparent reason, other than you walked inside?

Ephesians 6:12 reads:

"For we are not wrestling with flesh and blood [contending only with physical opponents], but against the despotisms, against the powers, against [the master spirits who are] the world rulers of this present darkness, against the spirit forces of wickedness in the heavenly (supernatural) sphere." (AMP)

That tells me dislike from one female towards another isn't necessarily with the person themselves. It's highly probable there could be spiritual unrest that rises to the surface every time the two of them are in each other's presence. Girlfriend, spirits are real! Spirit knows spirit! I suggest you read the Book of Matthew. Whenever Jesus encountered demon spirits (living inside a body), they recognized Him as the Son of God without Jesus opening His mouth.

I don't argue Bible. I don't dispute Bible. I trust Bible. I believe Bible. Because of the Bible, I live by faith. That's why one should make it a priority to read it for herself. In the future, if you experience a negative encounter with another female, just remember *"you don't wrestle against flesh and blood."* It's not the female's fault. Unbeknownst to her, she's being used by the enemy to get you off balance. Unlike this non-discerning female who has no idea she's given her mind, heart and spirit over to be manipulated by the enemy, it's easy for her to casually approach you spewing nasty venom with little regard for how she makes you feel. That's why she can treat you like you're beneath her. That's why it's not hard for her to talk about you behind your back to other females. That's why she can ignore you by quickly turning away like she didn't see you coming in her direction. She doesn't like you. Unfortunately, she doesn't know why she doesn't like you—she just doesn't! This is not your problem—it's hers! Girlfriend, might I suggest to keep it moving! This ain't about you. It's about your godly spirit! Pray for her!

SO, WHO DO YOU THINK YOU ARE

Females can come up against any number of dirty shenanigans instigated by the enemy and his cohorts. It all began with God's first female Eve in the Garden of Eden. (Genesis 3:4-5) Attacking the female psyche started when the devil sized her up. He was able to manipulate and lie Eve out of God's righteousness, abundant blessings and His favorable goodness. Make no mistake. The devil is still manipulating females in the millennium! He has the conniving ability to cheat females out of their kingdom inheritance as daughters of the Most High God.

Genesis 3:1 reads:

"Now the serpent was more subtle *and* crafty than any living creature of the field which the Lord God had made. And he [Satan] said to the woman, Can it really be that God has said, You shall not eat from every tree of the garden?" (AMP)

He's such a manipulator! The enemy has far too many females believing they are orphans and God doesn't care anything about them! **Has God said?** Look how he cleverly applied that question to non-discerning Eve. And, whether you know it or not, he continues to hiss that very same question in a lot of pierced ears, both young and old. **"Has God said He will give you the desires of your heart? Why is it taking so long for your dream to come true?" "Has God said if you believe the petitions of your heart when you pray, you'll receive them? So why haven't your prayers produced what you believe?" "Do you *really* think God cares anything about you?"**

Girlfriend, if we allow ourselves to become seduced by his lies, we're apt to forfeit our kingdom inheritance. God set aside what rightfully belongs to each of His daughters before the very foundation of this world. Suggestive ideas promoting fear will only put you at a high risk to receive your divine inheritance. Now do you understand why I'm emphasizing the importance to embrace each day the good Lord sends you? Make the decision when your eyes open in the morning that you're going to celebrate life! I don't care what may be going on around you.

By faith, be determined you're not going to give the enemy leverage (rob you) of God's mercy to be a participant in the land of the living. I refuse to allow the enemy to distract me from receiving God's best for my life.

I want to conclude this book by telling you this, "Live your best life now while you have it! Live it fulfilling every vision and every dream God imparted on the inside of you before you were born! Live life loving yourself, knowing who you are in Christ, and knowing to whom you belong!"

Girlfriend, you are a fearless, wonderfully, victorious, peculiar, valuable, treasured, redeemed, blessed and highly favored child of The Lord God Almighty! ***"SO, WHO DO YOU THINK YOU ARE?"***

Chapter Twelve

You Can't Pour New Wine Into Old Wineskin

> "No one cuts up a fine silk scarf to patch old work clothes; you want fabrics that match. And you don't put wine in old, cracked bottles; you get strong, clean bottles for your fresh vintage wine. And no one who has ever tasted fined aged wine prefers unaged wine."
>
> Luke 5:36-39 (The MESSAGE)

As I finished writing the final pages of this book, something occurred to me. How can something be considered new, improved, better, or changed if nothing of any significance takes place during the process to effectively make a difference to distinguish the old from the new?

I think a person must first make a conscientious decision to get out of their own way. In other words, *true change* can only begin once we step aside to allow God to make these changes starting from the inside out. The second component involves *really* letting go of the past. And lastly, we must make the effort not to interfere with how God starts implementing these changes. We have to trust Him to know far more what flaws are in need of being corrected better than we thought we could improve on our own. You and I have to stop resisting change, especially once we recognize doubt and fear are the driving forces behind our unwillingness to seek inner change.

I believe *true inner change* is noticeable as its being released outwardly. I also think those around us will be able to see there is something happening on the inside of us. As the process begins to take root, we'll think different. Our speech pattern will change.

We'll start to feel and behave differently. The Bible speaks of becoming a *new creature* upon accepting Jesus as our personal Lord and Savior. Old things (the past) are passed away. Everything becomes new to the born-again believer.

II Corinthians 5:17 reads:

"Therefore, If any person is [ingrafted] in Christ (the Messiah) he is a new creation (a new creature altogether); the old [previous moral and spiritual condition] has passed away, Behold the fresh *and* new has come!" (AMP)

Can I share another page out of my journal with you? When I accepted Jesus in 1996, I didn't feel any different than I had only minutes before I met the acquaintance of three evangelists. When they knocked on my apartment door, I felt compelled to let them in, which was totally out of character for me. Normally I wouldn't open my door to people I did not know. I remember it was a Saturday afternoon when I stood in the middle of my living room eyes closed, head bowed, linked hand-in-hand with the three strangers. They individually prayed for me. Then the moment came to recite the words of salvation. "My sister, you're now a member of God's family!" the man announced with a big grin. I couldn't tell them this was my second time confessing Jesus as my Lord and Savior for fear they might think I was a heathen. "I hope you'll come to visit our church." I smiled at the two women who accompanied the man. "*I'll think about it*!" Then I practically shoved them out the door!

Because I didn't feel any different, later that evening I got dressed and went to my favorite dance club with my sister Renee. Now mind you, from the minute I stepped inside the club my night started off lousy. I couldn't believe it. Not one guy

SO, WHO DO YOU THINK YOU ARE

approached me for a dance. It was as if an invisible neon sign was hanging around my neck flashing 'stay away', but nobody bothered to tell me! Seemingly every man there was deliberately keeping his distance. But did that stop me from going back to the club the following Saturday? No, it did not! Oddly enough, the same scenario started to play out again. Not one man asked me for a dance. In the Meantime Renee was out on the dance floor kicking it out! I couldn't figure out why was I standing alone watching everybody else enjoying their Saturday night? After all, I looked good! I'm not bragging, but I was dressed head-to-toe club-sharp! As the night passed, I was starting to get just a tad salty! Renee was having all that fun on the dance floor while I was standing off in a corner drinking my favorite wine cooler, forced to dance with myself. The truth is, I was growing more jealous by the second! I'm just keeping it real—okay?

Some time around 1:00 a.m., the Dee-Jay played one of my favorite dance songs. Suddenly out of the corner of my eye I noticed a guy heading in my direction. He asked if I wanted to dance. "*Where you been all night? I bought this new outfit purposely for tonight, and nobody got to see it! Yes! I want to dance!*" That's what I wanted to say, but I flashed him a smile and made a mad dash for the dance floor! Finally! I could shake my groove thang!

Now pay close attention because this is where my night went from weird to bizarre! While I was dancing with Johnny come lately, I happened to glance down at my feet noticing what I thought was black confetti on the floor. As I shook practically every inch of my body to the beat of the loud music, I noticed the legs of my pants felt airy. I shifted my eyes downward, but I couldn't believe what I was seeing! My new black leather pants literally were peeling away at the seams! I paid over a hundred dollars for those pants! They weren't plea-tha! These pants were genuine leather! I blinked a couple of times thinking maybe I'd drank one wine cooler too many, and my eyes were playing tricks on me. So I blinked a few more times. But this was no figment of my imagination. The only thing left for me to do was start dancing away from my partner, hoping he wouldn't notice my pants were falling apart. Well, I managed to dance my way back into a vacant corner. *"Thanks, but I don't like this song!"* I lied, shouting over the loud music. He smiled, nodded and disappeared somewhere on the crowded dance floor. I was almost afraid to look again, but I had to know if the legs of my pants were still shredding. When I finally did lower my eyes, I nearly went into hysterics right then and there! My pants were reduced to a pair of short-shorts! I immediately scurried to the dance floor in a state of panic hoping everybody on the dance floor was too drunk to notice me. I managed to find Renee getting her groove on. *"Renee! We have to leave! Look!"* She was dancing and laughing, having a good ole' time! My situation was serious! I grabbed her by the arm. *"Renee! Look at my clothes! You gotta get my coat! Here's my ticket!"* She stopped dancing long enough to give me the once over with her eyes. "What happened to you?" I was near tears at this point. *"I don't know!"* She snatched the ticket from my fingers rushing off for the coat room. I rushed back to my semi-dark corner trying not to draw attention to myself. As best I could, I shielded my tattered clothing. After another minute or two, I saw Renee coming with my coat. I sighed with relief yanking it from her hand, hurrying to put it on. It appeared that I might be wearing a mini dress or short skirt under the coat. So did we leave? No! Renee and I raced back to the dance floor! *"Party over here!"* To this day, I still do not understand what happened to my pants at the club that night. All I know is I got saved in my living room, continued to carry on like I hadn't, and a week later I experienced what could've been a very embarrassing moment. Fortunately for me, no one on the dance floor seemed to notice my dilemma that night.

After about a month or so of being totally confused, I began questioning whether I *really* was saved this time. I had confessed Jesus and been baptized two years prior to accepting Him again. Yet, I thought this time I'd *feel* something different on the inside of me. But I didn't feel saved—whatever being saved was supposed to feel like. I recall on the morning of my baptism I felt no different when my body emerged from the water than I did before the two deacons dipped me backwards in the baptism pool. But God is a compassionate God. My head was full of bees. So what does He do? He sends in a soldier—Jeannette! Recently she had started attending a church across town. Seemingly every time she and I talked Jeannette would go on and on about this church! Naturally, it wasn't long before she invited me to come go with her. Are you kidding? I wasn't trying to get up early on Sunday. I didn't *really* have to go to church every Sunday, did I? Jeannette continued to ask, and I kept inventing excuses.

In the meantime, over a two month period I hadn't mentioned one word to Jeannette about what I'd done. Knowing what I know now about the schemes of the enemy, it was obvious feelings of shame prevented me from telling her. There wasn't one area of my life I attempted to do different. Nothing about me had changed. I went right on doing my thang. That's not to say whenever Jeannette talked about Jesus and salvation I wasn't listening. On the contrary, I heard her loud and clear, but I just *wasn't ready* to give up living my carnal lifestyle. The enemy planted a misconceiving lie in my mind. "Saved people can't do anything fun. They have to walk the straight and narrow path of righteousness." After a while I started to believe those loud whispers of untruths. The enemy took advantage of my ignorance. At his suggestion, I didn't think there was anything wrong with dancing at the club and drinking. I started thinking a saved person had to be very religious. A saved person had to attend church every time the church doors opened. I thought maybe I wasn't ready to be saved! After all, the enemy had practically convinced me being a born-again Christian could be very, very, very boring! I was beginning to wonder if I'd done the right thing by inviting those evangelists into my home. Maybe I should've given myself more time to *think* about accepting Jesus as my Lord and Savior—again!

Well, the following Saturday night I picked Renee up, and off we went to get our groove on at the club! As usual, the place was packed with party people. Almost from the minute Renee and I entered the club, she was greeted by a few acquaintances and whisked off to the dance floor. Naturally, I didn't want to look dumb standing alone, so I headed for the bar. The bartender recognized me. We exchanged polite smiles followed by the same ole pleasantries. "This one's on me, pretty lady!" he shouted over the music, handing me a tall glass of ice along with my favorite wine cooler. "*Thanks! It's crowded tonight!*" He was about to respond when across the bar another patron shouted over the music to get his attention. I gave the bartender a quick friendly smile before I turned to step down from the bar stool. Out of nowhere this guy hems me in. "*Excuse me!*" The last thing I needed was to spill wine cooler on my club-sharp white outfit! The man glared straight into my eyes. "You look bored!" He said. Now remember, Renee and I had only arrived about ten minutes or so earlier before I went to the bar. How could I appear to be bored already? I'd be lying if I said I wasn't offended by his comment, because I was! "*You wanna dance?*" I asked as a means to mask what I was feeling. The stranger gave me this really weird stare. Then I thought, what's with this guy? Does he want to dance or not! "Go home!" He growled. I tried to pretend he hadn't bothered me, quickly scanning the bar just in case one of the patrons around the bar heard what he said. He turned moving away from the bar, leaving me there with a stupefied look on my face. Once I was sure no one witnessed him talking to me, I shot over to a large unoccupied area that overlooked the crowded dance floor.

    I stood (alone) sipping on my wine cooler watching everyone else having a good time. Needless to say, I was bored the entire night. The stranger who approached me at the bar predicted my mood. Turns out I was bored with a capital 'B'. I decided to get another wine cooler, which oddly tasted more like a lemon lime soda. Around twelve o'clock, I was ready to go home. As the night dragged on, my desire to get out on the dance floor subsided. This was definitely a strange night. I'd never been shy about getting on the floor dancing alone, especially if the Dee-Jay was playing one of my favorite songs. But I stood in the same spot looking over the dance floor watching everybody getting their groove thang on.

SO, WHO DO YOU THINK YOU ARE

Well, if you haven't guessed the ending by now, it's only fair that I finish my story. When I dropped Renee home later that Saturday night (wee hours of Sunday morning), I knew it was the last time I'd set foot inside another dance club. Getting back to my strange encounter with the man at the bar, I searched out the entire club, as well as that huge dance floor looking for mystery man. I couldn't find him anywhere. It was as if he showed up at the bar, said what he had to say, and left.

The following morning I woke up much earlier than usual considering I hadn't been asleep that long from the time when I came in from the club. Waking up before 10:00 o'clock on Sunday was unusual for me. Without hesitation, I reached for the phone sitting atop of the nightstand next to my bed. "*Morning Jeannette. I want to go to church with you this morning.*" Praise God! I've been going to the same church ever since!

When I tell you in the coming weeks God had his work cut out for Him, I'm not being flippant. Even though I was attending church more regularly, I still didn't *feel* any different. However, what I didn't know was that God was quietly making changes on the inside even though I didn't *feel* anything. I began reading God's Word more frequently. I listened with intensity to the messages being preached every week at church. I also enjoyed watching various ministers on Christian television. I don't exactly know when it happened, but I began yearning to understand and know more about God and His powerful ways.

Ephesians 4:22-23 reads:

"Strip yourselves of your former nature [put off and discard your old unrenewed self] which characterized your previous manner of life and becomes corrupt through lusts *and* desires that spring from delusion; And be constantly renewed in the spirit of your mind [having a fresh mental and spiritual attitude], And put on the new nature (the regenerate self) created in God's image, [Godlike] in true righteousness and holiness." (AMP)

Since that time, I have a clearer understanding that Christianity involves progression. There is so much more I continue to learn about the true cause for salvation of ones soul. Being born again goes deeper than confessing Jesus is Lord. Salvation isn't just a safety net that saves our souls from spending eternity in hell. I'm grateful God is a merciful God—a forgiving Father. He knows me better than I know myself. God knew long before I did that it was only a matter of time before my twisted thinking would be straightened out. The more I read the Bible, the more I listened to the Word, the more I digested the teachings concerning righteous living, and what it meant to have faith, the more I found myself believing with God, nothing was impossible—including repairing my messed up mine!

There are a few passages of text within this book that were borrowed from the intimate and personal pages of my journal. Loosing my mother—my best friend triggered all sorts of emotions and feelings that could only be released on paper. Writing down my thoughts helps me to release mental anxiety. As a young girl, I recall going off to myself writing in a notebook I substituted as a diary that I kept hidden in my bedroom.

During the latter year of 2008, I started experiencing a feeling of abandonment. From that negative feeling sprang up confusion and anger. As if they weren't enough, emotionally I was also coping with a lack of self-worth. *"I wanted my mommy!"* How could I go on without her? One question in particular plagued my mind just about every day. *"What was I suppose to do now that she was gone?"* Although I couldn't see it then, over the months to come, I'd understand my mother's death was only the beginning of what was yet to evolve into a renewed spiritual awakening.

This July (2012), is four years since mommy went home to be with the Lord. While finalizing this book in preparation to forward to my publisher Kathy, I can proudly—boldly proclaim, *"God is still a mighty good God in spite of everything I've had to go through!"* The past four years have brought forth changes. I freely shared some of those changes while writing this book hoping I'd be of help to another female who might be at a crossroads in her life, in search of meaning and purpose.

SO, WHO DO YOU THINK YOU ARE

Toward the final days of the calendar year of 2010, the Holy Spirit reminded me something Jesus had spoken to the Disciples during one of His ministerial teachings. Jesus told them. **"Neither do people pour new wine into old wineskins. If they do, the skins will burst; the wine will run out and the wineskins will be ruined. No, they pour new wine into new wineskins and both are preserved." (Matthew 9:17) (NIV)** Praise God! Thank you, Holy Spirit!

That Scripture was a powerful and profound New Year's Revelation for 2011. Did you catch that? I didn't say a New Years Resolution. I said a New Years Revelation! Sitting there in my bedroom during my quiet time, I clearly understood my life was in disarray. It needed a spiritual revival. The negative thoughts, images, and behavior that presided over the last twenty-four months needed to undergo a mental and spiritual reconstruction. My life was in dire need of direction. I began praying, asking God for clarity, along with instruction for putting a successful writing career into motion. I asked God to help me to be in the right place at the right time where divine connections and opportunities could cross my path to help pave the way to motivational speaking engagements, in and outside the borders of Delaware.

If I desired change it was going to require a diligent prayer life. Change also meant making a quality decision to fast (turn my plate over) more often. That's when I decided to start fasting seven days out of each month over the next 12 months. No more cutesy prayers. I needed powerful prayers—God connecting prayers, capable of transitioning me into the woman God created me to be. My relationship with the Father could no longer be on my terms. The time had come to redefine my identity. I realized what I'd been looking for was validation from man, when it turns out what I needed the most was to know that I *really* belonged to God. In other words, my desire for inner change could no longer be about my will, but the Father's Will *for me*.

It was in that moment upon hearing the Holy Spirit that I realized my actions stemmed from an insubordinate heart (old wineskin) attempting to do things my own way. Doing what I *thought* was best for me in light of all I'd been coping with. Meanwhile my spirit was suffering. I hadn't begun to consider, nor did I bother to ask God what He wanted from me—expected of me as His child. Those words of Scripture (Matthew 9:17) spoke loudly to my spirit-man. It was a wow-moment! How had I expected God to open doors of opportunities that no man or woman could shut, if I was constantly refusing His parental right to do whatever He deemed necessary in preparation for the kind of success I was believing (by faith) was possible?

2011 would be the year to change for the better spiritually as well as mentally. I believe the Holy Spirit was informing me that my spiritual slumber had come to an end. It was time to arise and shine! God was pouring new wine; His refreshing Word for spiritual revitalization into an old wineskin filled with doubt and silent fears. Not only was He preparing me for where I was going, but this new wine would sustain me in the rough places. Therefore, inner change was going to involve purging old thoughts, ways and habits. I needed to develop a lifestyle of maturity that would teach me how to take control over my flesh before God could lead me to the next phase of my life—a much more rewarding life—to the full!

In the Book of Nehemiah (8:10), it says **"the Lord is the joy of my strength."** It was only natural that I missed my mother. What kind of daughter would I be if my heart didn't ache for her presence? But in spite of these human emotions and frailties, I needed time to believe (by faith) God could fill the emptiness in my heart. That He and only He could fill the void left by my mother, if only He were given the chance. It was time to let go of the sorrow. More importantly the time had arrived to step out of my own way. It was time to *really* let God be God in my life. It became my desire that my Heavenly Father pour new wine into this earthly vessel. I wanted to be transformed by the renewing of my mind and replenished with new wine—a spiritual revival. I'd reached the point of wanting God's loving mercy and His goodness to consume me from inside out unlike ever before from the crown of my head, to the soles of my size seven and half feet!

Sitting alone in my bedroom that evening I made a life-altering decision to line my will in agreement with God's Will. Scripture says, *"taste and see that the Lord is good!"* (Psalm 34:8) Well, I was thirsty and I very hungry! There's another illustration in the Book of Luke (5:36) where Jesus told His Disciples a Parable. *"No one tears a patch from a new garment and sews it on an old one. If he does, he will have torn the new garment, and the patch from the new will not match the old."* **(NIV)**

While I was praying/asking God to help his confused daughter, I hadn't considered what I was actually asking of Him. I opened my mouth with a prayer (from the heart), but I hadn't discerned God had already began doing what I prayed for—to become the woman He created me to be.

Toward the end of January 2011, seems like the more I got before God in my secret place, the more my spirit-man came alive. By the time February rolled around, I knew I couldn't go back to my former ways as a Christian woman. I believed (by faith), what God was doing on the inside of me would soon launch me to a whole other level—the level of divine productivity. I have no doubt I will succeed in every area of my life because I know, that I know I am a child of God! Whenever I read God's Word, it reinforces my faith. What's even better, there isn't another person on the planet who can make me doubt to whom I belong! Much like the old patch Jesus spoke of in the Book of Luke, if I hadn't agreed (my will) to choose God's Will for change, I might well have gone through another year disconnected from Him, yet continuing to live under my own strength. I would have lacked the wisdom to understand that my faith is limitless. I might've failed to recognize this was the season for a new image to outshine the old one.

I don't claim to have the inside scoop on everything there is to know and understand about the human psyche. I didn't attend medical college. That being said, I have not a clue what drives the human species to do some of the things we do. I'm no scholar when it comes to the human nature of mankind, nor do I want to misrepresent myself, but what I am is an observer. Therefore, I dare not categorize all females are alike. Still, I think too many of us (young or old) are stumbling through life because we lack the knowledge of who we really are. Many females (me included) have allowed circumstances, people, situations, and poor self-images to lead them into possessing a mindset of hopelessness. There are girls, teens and other women struggling in silence with bouts of depression.

Every day females battle with low self-esteem and lack self-confidence. Those are very scary places for any female to be in, regardless of their age. That's why I'm so glad we have a Father who loves us with an inexhaustible kind of love! When God looks upon His daughters He doesn't see what we see. Whenever you and I approach a mirror, we're staring through natural eyes. Whenever we gaze upon the appearance of another person, our eyesight absorbs what is within our sight. The Father sees beyond the physical (flesh) because His eyes capture the beauty of His human creations. God cares very little if we're wearing a designer's original, dressed stylishly from head-to-toe, or wearing jeans, His love far exceeds that. God is more concerned about our well-being. He marvels at His workmanship—His individual beautifully created daughters.

Girlfriend please read your Bible. Study it. Learn from it. Who are you? Why are you here? What is your purpose for being in the earth? God says He knew you before you were in your mother's womb. Therefore, it's His Word that holds the answers to explain your *true DNA*. God loves you so much! He has implemented a great and wonderful plan for your life. You were born with divine purpose! You are a female of great character, great intelligence, great wisdom, great vision, great ideas, great value, great inspiration, and great potential! You are the daughter of Almighty God! You are an heir to His Kingdom and a joint-heir to Jesus Christ! The set-time has arrived to reclaim your inheritance. Seeds of greatness were planted on the inside of you long before conception ever took place between your earthly parents. You were already on God's mind in the spiritual realm. That's why you are here. He predestined an assignment with your name on it to be fulfilled in the earth. You were born to give glory to Him in everything that you do!

Let me give you a challenge. Tomorrow morning as you gaze into the eyes of the female staring back at you from the bathroom mirror, pause for a minute. You will be looking into the eyes of greatness!

I John 4:4 reads:

"Little children, you are of God [you belong to Him] and have [already] defeated *and* overcome them [the agents of the anti-christ], because He Who lives in you is greater (mightier) than he who is in the world." (AMP)

Do something for the woman in the mirror, and yourself. Give her one of your best and biggest smiles. Tell her how much you love and appreciate her. Remember, inner change will only be as effective as the female who decides it's time to do things different. Girlfriend, refuse to allow a deceptive self-image to continue robbing you of the true beauty residing on the inside of you! Allow God to peal away (pour out the old wine) the negative image. Feed your spirit on God's Word, which has the power to rebuild (pour new wine) a positive image. Then get out of your way! Become the female God has created you to be!

The Scripture Job 32:18-19 reads:

"For I am full of words, and the spirit within me compels me; inside I am like bottled up wine, like new wineskins ready to burst." (NIV)

When I finished writing this chapter, I happened to be scanning a women's magazine. I noticed the magazine printed a quote from an historic woman many of us, if not all of us should easily recognize.

After having read it, I thought to myself. What an appropriate way to end my book.

Farrell Ellis

"No one can make you feel inferior without your consent."

Eleanor Roosevelt

Scripture References

Scripture taken from the King James Bible; Cornerstone Bible Publishers™ Nashville, Tennessee, ©Copyright 1998

Scripture taken from Contemporary English Version (New Testament) Text: Copyright © 1995, American Bible Society Printed in the United States of America Eng. N. T. CEV 250-106335 ABS-5/98-50,000-50,000-W1

Scripture taken from THE MESSAGE. Copyright ©1993, 1994, 1995, 1996, 2000, 2001, 2002. Used by permission of NavPress Publishing Group."

Scripture taken from the HOLY BIBLE, NEW INTERNATIONAL VERSION 'NIV'. Copyright © 1973, 1978, 1984 by International Bible Society. Used by permission of International Bible Society.

Scripture taken from THE AMPLIFIED BIBLE, Old Testament copyright © 1865, 1987 by the Zondervan Corporation. The Amplified New Testament copyright © 1958, 1987 by The Lockman Foundation. Used by permission.

Author's Bio

Farrell Ellis resides in Wilmington, Delaware where she is the front-desk receptionist at a law firm. She has been an active member of Spirit Life Ministries International Church for over ten years participating in both the Hospitality and Ushers/Greeters ministries. In 2010, God gave her a vision for a women's conference. Farrell spoke publicly for the first time along with two other guest motivational speakers. She discovered a connection existed with her writing by inspiring readers through motivational speaking. Farrell held another women's conference in 2012. She took a leap of faith by stepping out on her own as the primary guest speaker.

Through God's Word, no matter what Farrell might envision, or dream, she has learned God is big enough to make the desires of her heart come to pass. Without question, she knows that God is able to do exceedingly above and beyond anything she could ever ask or think! Her debut book, *Go Beyond Your Dreams (Live Them!)* is certainly proof God is faithful to His Word.

For three years she repeatedly confessed Psalms 68:11 "The Lord gives the word [of power]; the women who bear and publish [the news] are a great host." (AMP) She not only confessed the words of that scripture, she allowed them to marinate within her heart until they became a living truth for her.

Farrell Ellis firmly believes that the Word of God residing within a saturated faith-filled heart, spoken out of one's own mouth has the power to produce visions and dreams into becoming realities!

To write or invite this great author for signings and motivational speaking engagements, please contact Farrell Ellis at: www.gbydfarrellellis.com

Go Beyond Your Dreams was written for women much like  myself, in search of whole, meaningful, and profitable lives. We're women with passionate visions and dreams for success. The Word of God tells us it's impossible to please God without faith. Too many of us will not pursue our God-given talents, visions or dreams. Go Beyond Your Dreams is meant to encourage women to begin incorporating faith into their daily lives. Real faith has the ability to manifest visions and dreams into our future. First we must start believing by faith with God, all things are possible! (Mark 9:23)

www.ingramcontent.com/pod-product-compliance
Lightning Source LLC
Chambersburg PA
CBHW051420290426
44109CB00016B/1375